LLEWELLYN'S 1995

MOON SIGN BOOK

& LUNAR PLANNING GUIDE

Copyright © 1994 Llewellyn Publications
All rights reserved.

Printed in the United States of America
Typography property of Llewellyn Worldwide, Ltd.
ISBN 1-56718-903-2

Edited by Cynthia Ahlquist
Cover design by Alexandra Lumen
Personal horoscopes by Gloria Star

Contributing Writers: Donna Cunningham, Verna Gates, Pat Esclavon Hardy, Barbara Koval, Gavin Kent McClung, Ralph Jordan Pestka, Kim Rogers Gallagher, Bruce Schofield, Nancy Soller, K.D. Spitzer, Patricia Telesco, Noel Tyl, Carly Wall

LLEWELLYN PUBLICATIONS
P.O. Box 64383-903
St. Paul, MN 55164-0383 U.S.A.

1995

DECEMBER 1994
S	M	T	W	T	F	S
				1	2	3
4	5	6	7	8	9	10
11	12	13	14	15	16	17
18	19	20	21	22	23	24
25	26	27	28	29	30	31

JANUARY 1995
S	M	T	W	T	F	S
1	2	3	4	5	6	7
8	9	10	11	12	13	14
15	16	17	18	19	20	21
22	23	24	25	26	27	28
29	30	31				

FEBRUARY 1995
S	M	T	W	T	F	S
			1	2	3	4
5	6	7	8	9	10	11
12	13	14	15	16	17	18
19	20	21	22	23	24	25
26	27	28				

MARCH 1995
S	M	T	W	T	F	S
			1	2	3	4
5	6	7	8	9	10	11
12	13	14	15	16	17	18
19	20	21	22	23	24	25
26	27	28	29	30	31	

APRIL 1995
S	M	T	W	T	F	S
						1
2	3	4	5	6	7	8
9	10	11	12	13	14	15
16	17	18	19	20	21	22
23	24	25	26	27	28	29
30						

MAY 1995
S	M	T	W	T	F	S
	1	2	3	4	5	6
7	8	9	10	11	12	13
14	15	16	17	18	19	20
21	22	23	24	25	26	27
28	29	30	31			

JUNE 1995
S	M	T	W	T	F	S
				1	2	3
4	5	6	7	8	9	10
11	12	13	14	15	16	17
18	19	20	21	22	23	24
25	26	27	28	29	30	

JULY 1995
S	M	T	W	T	F	S
						1
2	3	4	5	6	7	8
9	10	11	12	13	14	15
16	17	18	19	20	21	22
23	24	25	26	27	28	29
30	31					

AUGUST 1995
S	M	T	W	T	F	S
		1	2	3	4	5
6	7	8	9	10	11	12
13	14	15	16	17	18	19
20	21	22	23	24	25	26
27	28	29	30	31		

SEPTEMBER 1995
S	M	T	W	T	F	S
					1	2
3	4	5	6	7	8	9
10	11	12	13	14	15	16
17	18	19	20	21	22	23
24	25	26	27	28	29	30

OCTOBER 1995
S	M	T	W	T	F	S
1	2	3	4	5	6	7
8	9	10	11	12	13	14
15	16	17	18	19	20	21
22	23	24	25	26	27	28
29	30	31				

NOVEMBER 1995
S	M	T	W	T	F	S
			1	2	3	4
5	6	7	8	9	10	11
12	13	14	15	16	17	18
19	20	21	22	23	24	25
26	27	28	29	30		

DECEMBER 1995
S	M	T	W	T	F	S
					1	2
3	4	5	6	7	8	9
10	11	12	13	14	15	16
17	18	19	20	21	22	23
24	25	26	27	28	29	30
31						

JANUARY 1996
S	M	T	W	T	F	S
	1	2	3	4	5	6
7	8	9	10	11	12	13
14	15	16	17	18	19	20
21	22	23	24	25	26	27
28	29	30	31			

FEBRUARY 1996
S	M	T	W	T	F	S
				1	2	3
4	5	6	7	8	9	10
11	12	13	14	15	16	17
18	19	20	21	22	23	24
25	26	27	28	29		

CONTENTS

HOW TO USE YOUR
MOON SIGN BOOK

We get a number of letters and phone calls every year from readers asking the same types of questions. Most of these have to do with how to find certain information in the *Moon Sign Book* and how to use this information.

The best advice we can give is to read the entire introduction, in particular the section on how to use the tables. We provide examples, using the current Moon and Aspect Tables, so that you can follow along and easily figure out the best dates for all of your important activities.

The information in the remaining part of the book is divided into categories. If you want to find out when to cut your hair, look in the Health & Beauty section. Sections are listed in the Table of Contents for your convenience.

The Moon Tables do *not* take into account the Moon void of course. Just before the Moon enters a new sign it will have one last aspect to a planet. From that point until it enters the next sign, it is void. It is said that decisions made while the Moon is void never come to fruition. Sometimes purchases made during a Moon void turn out to be poorly made or a bad investment. If you want to avoid making your decisions during a void of course Moon, please refer to the "Moon Void of Course" section in this book. Many people do not pay attention to the voids, as it is virtually impossible to bypass all of them when making decisions.

Although we have included a list of retrograde planets in this year's *Moon Sign Book*, the Astro-Almanac does *not* take into account planetary retrogrades. For more information on these see Llewellyn's *Astrological Calendar*.

Note: All times given in the *Moon Sign Book* are set in *Eastern Standard Time*. You must adjust for your time zone and for daylight savings time.

THE PHASES & SIGNS
OF THE MOON

New Moon
Finalization, rest, hidden reorganizations, incipient beginnings or chaos, disorganization, confusion, regret, stagnation, covert revenge.

Full Moon
Fulfillment, culmination, completion, activity, social awareness or unfulfilled longing, unrest, fretfulness, sentimentality, overt revenge.

First Quarter
Germination, emergence, beginnings, outwardly directed activity.

Second Quarter
Growth, development, articulation of things which already exist.

Third Quarter
Maturity, fruition, assumption of full form of expression.

Fourth Quarter
Disintegration, drawing back for reorganization, rest, reflection.

Moon in Aries
Good for starting things, but lacking in staying power. Things occur rapidly, but also quickly pass.

Moon in Taurus
Things begun now last the longest and tend to increase in value. Things begun now become habitual and hard to alter.

Moon in Gemini
An inconsistent and fickle position for the Moon. Things begun now are easily moved by outside influences.

Moon in Cancer
Stimulates emotional rapport between people. Pinpoints need, supports growth and nurturance.

Moon in Leo
Draws emphasis to the self, to central ideas or institutions, away from connections with others and emotional needs.

Moon in Virgo
Favors accomplishment of details and commands from higher up while discouraging independent thinking and enterprise.

Moon in Libra
Increases self-awareness, favors self-examination and interaction with others but discourages spontaneous initiative.

Moon in Scorpio
Increases awareness of psychic power. Precipitates psychic crises and ends connections thoroughly.

Moon in Sagittarius
Encourages expansionary flights of the imagination and confidence in the flow of life.

Moon in Capricorn
Artificial, disciplined, controlled and institutional activities are favored. Develops strong structure.

Moon in Aquarius
Idealized conditions lead to potential emotional disappointment and disruption in the natural flow of life.

Moon in Pisces
Energy withdraws from the surface of life, hibernates within, secretly reorganizing and realigning for a new day.

NOT ALL COMMON ALMANACS
ARE THE SAME

For **astronomical** calculations the Moon's place in almanacs is given as being in the **constellation**. For **astrological** purposes the Moon's place is figured in the **zodiacal sign**, which is its true place in the zodiac, and nearly one sign (30 degrees) different from the astronomical constellation.

To illustrate: If the common almanac gives the Moon's place in Taurus (constellation) on a certain date, its true place in the zodiac is in Gemini (zodiacal sign). Thus, it is readily seen that those who use the common almanac may be planting seeds, or engaging in other endeavors, when they think the Moon is in a **fruitful sign**, while in reality it would be in one of the most **barren signs** in the zodiac.

Common almanacs are worthless to follow for planting. Some almanacs even make a bad matter worse by inserting at the head of their columns "Moon's Sign" when they mean "Moon's Constellation," and this has brought much unmerited discredit to the value of planting by the Moon. The constellations form a belt outside the zodiac, but do not conform with the signs in position or time.

The constellations are correct in astronomical but not in astrological calculations. Lack of knowledge about this fact incurred a great deal of criticism and skepticism regarding the Moon's influence in planting. To obtain desired results, planting must be done according to the Moon's place in the signs of the zodiac.

Therefore, using Llewellyn's *Moon Sign Book* for all of your planting and planning purposes is the best thing to do!

HOW TO USE THE MOON SIGN BOOK TABLES

Timing your activities is one of the most important things you can do to ensure success. In many Eastern countries, timing by the planets is so important that practically no event takes place without first setting up a chart for it. Weddings have occurred in the middle of the night because that was when the influences were the best. You may not want to take it that far, and you don't really need to set up a chart for each activity, but you can still make use of the influences of the Moon whenever possible. It's easy and it works!

In the *Moon Sign Book* you will find the information you need to plan just about any activity: weddings, fishing, buying a car or house, cutting your hair, traveling and more. Not all of the things you do will fall on favorable days, but we provide the guidelines you need to pick the best day out of the several from which you have to choose.

Let's run through some examples. Say you need to make an appointment to have your hair cut. You have thin hair and would like it to look thicker. Look in the Health & Beauty section under Hair Care. You see that you should cut hair during a Full Moon (marked FM in the Moon Tables or O under the Sun in the Lunar Aspectarian). You should, however, avoid the Moon in Virgo. We'll say that it is the month of June. Look up June in the Moon Tables. The Full Moon falls on June 11 at 11:04 PM. It is in the sign of Sagittarius, which is good for cutting hair. Since the Full Moon happens late in the evening, the next day would be just as good. The times are fairly flexible; you do not have to use the exact time of the Moon change.

That was easy. Let's move on to a more difficult example that uses the phase and sign of the Moon. You want to buy a house for a permanent home. Look in the Home & Family section under House. It says that you should buy a home when the Moon is in Taurus, Leo, Scorpio, or Aquarius (fixed signs). You need to get a loan, so you should look in the Business, Finance & Legal section under Loans. Here it says that the third and fourth quarters favor the borrower (you). You are going to buy the house in December. Look up December in the Moon Tables. The Moon is in the third quarter from December 7th through the 14th, and is in the fourth quarter from December 15 through the 31st. These dates are good for getting a loan. Now look at the signs. The Moon is in Leo (good) on the 11th, 12th, and 13th. It is in Scorpio (good) on the 17th (after

8:07 PM EST), 18th, and 19th. It is in Taurus and Aquarius (other good signs) during the first and second quarters—not good for getting a loan. So the best days are the 11th, 12th, 13th, 17th (after 8:07 PM EST), 18th, and 19th. Just match up the best signs and phases (quarters) to come up with the best dates.

With all activities, be sure to check the Favorable and Unfavorable Days for your Sun sign in the table adjoining the Lunar Aspectarian. If there is a choice between several dates, pick the one most favorable for you (marked F).

Now let's look at an example that uses signs, phases and aspects. You will find the aspects listed in the Lunar Aspectarian on the pages facing the Moon Tables. The letters listed under the planets stand for specific aspects: C=conjunction, X=sextile, Q=square, T=trine and O=opposition. You will be using the squares and oppositions more than the other aspects as these are considered negative.

Our example this time is fixing your car. We will use April as the sample month. Look in the Home & Family section under Automobile Repair. It says that the Moon should be in a fixed sign (Taurus, Leo, Scorpio, Aquarius) in the first or second quarter and well-aspected to the Sun. (Good aspects are sextiles and trines, marked X and T.) It also tells you to avoid negative aspects to Mars, Saturn, Uranus, Neptune and Pluto. (Negative aspects are squares and oppositions, marked Q and O.) Look in the Moon Tables under April. You will see that the Moon is in the first and second quarters from April 1st to the 15th. The dates that the Moon is in a fixed sign are the 2nd and 3rd (Taurus), and the 9th, 10th, and 11th (Leo). You can eliminate all the other dates.

Now look at the Lunar Aspectarian for April to find the aspects. April 2nd has an unfavorable aspect with Mars, which eliminates it immediately. April 3rd has no unfavorable aspects, but it does not have a positive aspect to the Sun. April 9th also has no favorable aspect to the Sun, and the 11th has an unfavorable aspect to Pluto. April 10th is the best choice because it has a trine (T) to the Sun and no unfavorable aspects to Mars, Jupiter, Saturn, Uranus, Neptune, or Pluto.

You have just gone through the entire process of choosing the best dates for a special event. With practice, you will be able to scan the information in the tables and do it very quickly. You will also begin to get a feel for what works best for you. Everyone has his or her own high and low cycles.

Gardening activities depend on many outside factors, weather being the most influential. Obviously, you can't go out and plant when there is still a foot of snow on the ground. You have to adjust to the conditions at hand. If the weather was bad or you were on vacation during the first quarter when it was best to plant, do it during the second quarter while the Moon is in a fruitful sign instead. If the Moon is not in a fruitful sign during the first or second quarter, choose a day when it is in a semi-fruitful sign. The best advice is to choose either the sign or phase that is *most* favorable when the two don't coincide.

To summarize, in order to make the most of your plans and activities, check with the *Moon Sign Book*. First, look up the activity in the corresponding section under the proper heading. Then, look for the information given in the tables (the Moon Tables, Lunar Aspectarian or Favorable and Unfavorable Days, or all three). Choose the best date according to the number of positive factors in effect. If most of the dates are favorable, then there is no problem choosing the one that will best fit your schedule. However, if there just don't seem to be any really good dates, pick the ones with the least number of negative influences. We guarantee that you will be very pleased with the results if you use nature's influences to your advantage.

For quick reference, use the Astro-Almanac. This is a general guide for planning certain events and activities.

HOW TO USE THE TABLES

First, read the preceding section on how to use your *Moon Sign Book*. You will be using the tables on the following pages in conjunction with the information given in the individual sections: Home & Family, Leisure & Recreation, Health & Beauty, Business, Finance & Legal, and Farm & Garden.

The Moon Tables include the date, sign the Moon is in, the element of that sign, the nature of the sign, the Moon's phase and the times that it changes sign or phase. The abbreviation FM signi-

fies Full Moon and NM signifies New Moon. The
times listed directly after the date are the times
when the Moon changes sign. The times listed after
the phase indicate the times when the Moon
changes phase. All times are listed in *Eastern Standard Time.* You need to adjust them according to
your own time zone. (Conversion tables have been
provided for your convenience.)

On the pages opposite the Moon Tables you
will find the Lunar Aspectarian and the Favorable
and Unfavorable Days. To use the Lunar Aspectarian, find the planet that the activity lists and run
down the column to the date desired. If you want
to find a favorable aspect (sextile or trine) to Mercury, run your finger down the column under Mercury until you find an X or T; positive or good
aspects are signified by these letters. Negative or
adverse aspects (square or opposition) are signified
by a Q or O. A conjunction, C, is sometimes good,
sometimes bad, depending on the activity or planets involved. The Lunar Aspectarian gives the
aspects of the Moon to the other planets.

The Favorable and Unfavorable Days table
lists all of the Sun signs. To find out if a day is positive for you, find your sign and then look down
the column. If it is marked F, it is very favorable. If
it is marked f, it is slightly favorable. U means very
unfavorable and u means slightly unfavorable.

KEY OF ABBREVIATIONS

X: sextile/positive
T: trine/positive
Q: square/negative
O: opposition/negative
C: conjunction/positive/negative/neutral

F: very favorable
f: slightly favorable
U: very unfavorable
u: slightly unfavorable

FM: Full Moon
NM: New Moon

To find out the exact times of the daily aspects, see Llewellyn's *1995 Daily Planetary Guide*. This will help you refine your timing even more.

LUNAR ACTIVITY GUIDE

ACTIVITY	SIGN	PHASE
Buy animals		New Moon, 1st
Baking	Aries, Cancer, Libra, Capricorn	1st or 2nd
Hair care: permanents, straightening, coloring	Aquarius	1st
Cut hair to stimulate growth	Cancer, Scorpio, Pisces	1st or 2nd
Cut hair for thickness	Any except Virgo	Full Moon
Cut hair to decrease growth	Gemini, Leo, Virgo	3rd or 4th

ACTIVITY	SIGN	PHASE
Start a diet to lose weight	Aries, Leo, Virgo, Sagittarius, Aquarius	3rd or 4th
Start a diet to gain weight	Cancer, Scorpio, Pisces	1st or 2nd
Buy clothes	Taurus, Libra	1st or 2nd
Buy antiques	Cancer, Scorpio, Capricorn	
Borrow money	Leo, Sagittarius, Aquarius, Pisces	3rd or 4th
Start a savings account	Taurus, Scorpio, Capricorn	1st or 2nd
Join a club	Gemini, Libra, Aquarius	
Give a party	Gemini, Leo, Libra, Aquarius	
Travel for pleasure	Gemini, Leo, Sagittarius, Aquarius	1st or 2nd
Begin a course of study	Gemini, Virgo, Sagittarius	1st or 2nd
Begin a new job	Taurus, Virgo, Capricorn	1st or 2nd
Canning	Cancer, Scorpio, Pisces	3rd or 4th

ACTIVITY	SIGN	PHASE
Make preserves and jellies	Taurus, Scorpio, Aquarius	3rd or 4th
Dry fruits and vegetables	Aries, Leo, Sagittarius	3rd
Remove teeth	Gemini, Virgo, Sagittarius, Capricorn, Pisces	1st or 2nd
Fill teeth	Taurus, Leo, Scorpio, Aquarius	3rd or 4th
Dressmaking, mending		1st or 2nd
Buy health foods	Virgo	
Buy medicine	Scorpio	
Buy permanent home	Taurus, Leo, Scorpio, Aquarius	
Buy property for speculation	Aries, Cancer, Libra, Capricorn	
Send mail	Gemini, Virgo, Sagittarius, Pisces	
Cut wood	Any except Cancer, Scorpio	3rd or 4th

ACTIVITY	SIGN	PHASE
Beauty treatments	Taurus, Cancer, Leo, Libra, Scorpio, Aquarius	1st or 2nd
Brewing	Cancer, Scorpio, Pisces	3rd or 4th
Start building	Taurus, Leo, Aquarius	3rd or 4th
Bulbs for seed	Cancer, Scorpio, Pisces	2nd or 3rd
Pour cement	Taurus, Leo, Aquarius	Full Moon
Plant cereals	Cancer, Scorpio, Pisces	1st or 2nd
Cultivate	Aries, Gemini, Leo, Virgo, Sagittarius, Aquarius	4th
Break habits	Gemini, Leo, Virgo	3rd or 4th
Fix your car	Taurus, Virgo	1st or 2nd
Weddings	Taurus, Cancer, Leo, Libra, Pisces	2nd
Move	Taurus, Leo, Scorpio, Aquarius	

Paint	Taurus, Leo, Scorpio, Aquarius	3rd or 4th
Train a pet	Taurus	3rd or 4th
Buy a car	Taurus, Leo, Scorpio, Aquarius	3rd or 4th
Collect debts	Aries, Cancer, Libra, Capricorn	3rd or 4th

MOONRISE

The New Moon always rises with the Sun in the east to start a new lunar month. The Sun blots out the visibility of the New Moon as it comes up, but it can be seen as a thin crescent setting in the west at sunset a day or two after its rise.

The waxing or increasing Moon is known and easily remembered as the "right-hand Moon." The curve of the right-hand index finger and thumb follows the curve of the increasing crescent. Similarly, the waning or decreasing Moon can be remembered as the "left-hand Moon."

To establish the time of moonrise for each day of the month, add fifty minutes for each day after the beginning of a phase or subtract that amount for each day from the beginning of a new phase.

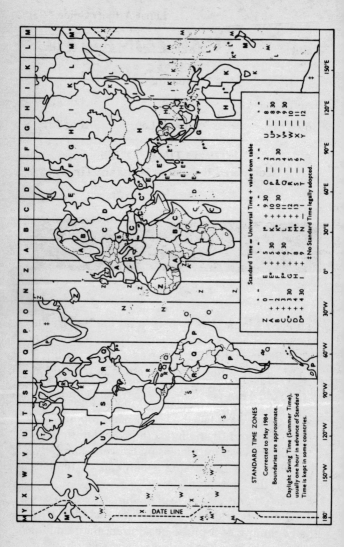

STANDARD TIME ZONES

Corrected to May 1984
Boundaries are approximate.

Daylight Saving Time (Summer Time),
usually one hour in advance of Standard
Time is kept in some countries.

Standard Time = Universal Time + value from table

A	+ 1	N	− 1
B	+ 2	O	− 2
C	+ 3	P	− 3
C*	+ 3 30	P*	− 3 30
D	+ 4	Q	− 4
D*	+ 4 30	R	− 5
E	+ 5	S	− 6
E*	+ 5 30	T	− 7
F	+ 6	U	− 8
F*	+ 6 30	U*	− 8 30
G	+ 7	V	− 9
H	+ 8	V*	− 9 30
I	+ 9	W	− 10
I*	+ 9 30	X	− 11
K	+ 10	Y	− 12
K*	+ 10 30		
L	+ 11		
M	+ 12		

‡ No Standard Time legally adopted.

TIME ZONE CONVERSIONS

WORLD TIME ZONES
(Compared to Eastern Standard Time)

(R) EST—Used
(S) CST—Subtract 1 hour
(T) MST—Subtract 2 hours
(U) PST—Subtract 3 hours
(V) Subtract 4 hours
(W) Subtract 5 hours
(X) Subtract 6 hours
(Y) Subtract 7 hours
(Q) Add 1 hour
(P) Add 2 hours
(O) Add 3 hours
(N) Add 4 hours
(Z) Add 5 hours

(A) Add 6 hours
(B) Add 7 hours
(C) Add 8 hours
(D) Add 9 hours
(E) Add 10 hours
(F) Add 11 hours
(G) Add 12 hours
(H) Add 13 hours
(I) Add 14 hours
(K) Add 15 hours
(L) Add 16 hours
(M) Add 17 hours

JANUARY MOON TABLE

DATE		MOON'S SIGN	ELEMENT	NATURE	MOON'S PHASE
1 Sun.		Capri.	Earth	Semi-fruit	1st 5:56 AM
2 Mon.	1:39 PM	Aquar.	Air	Barren	1st
3 Tue.		Aquar.	Air	Barren	1st
4 Wed.	4:49 PM	Pisces	Water	Fruitful	1st
5 Thu.		Pisces	Water	Fruitful	1st
6 Fri.	11:57 PM	Aries	Fire	Barren	1st
7 Sat.		Aries	Fire	Barren	1st
8 Sun.		Aries	Fire	Barren	2nd 10:46 AM
9 Mon.	10:58 AM	Taurus	Earth	Semi-fruit	2nd
10 Tue.		Taurus	Earth	Semi-fruit	2nd
11 Wed.	11:57PM	Gemini	Air	Barren	2nd
12 Thu.		Gemini	Air	Barren	2nd
13 Fri.		Gemini	Air	Barren	2nd
14 Sat.	12:20 PM	Cancer	Water	Fruitful	2nd
15 Sun.		Cancer	Water	Fruitful	2nd
16 Mon.	10:37 PM	Leo	Fire	Barren	FM 3:27 PM
17 Tue.		Leo	Fire	Barren	3rd
18 Wed.		Leo	Fire	Barren	3rd
19 Thu.	6:40 AM	Virgo	Earth	Barren	3rd
20 Fri.		Virgo	Earth	Barren	3rd

The SUN enters Aquarius at 8:00 am

DATE		MOON'S SIGN	ELEMENT	NATURE	MOON'S PHASE
21 Sat.	12:54 PM	Libra	Air	Semi-fruit	3rd
22 Sun.		Libra	Air	Semi-fruit	3rd
23 Mon.	5:33 PM	Scorpio	Water	Fruitful	4th 11:59 PM
24 Tue.		Scorpio	Water	Fruitful	4th
25 Wed.	8:37 PM	Sagit.	Fire	Barren	4th
26 Thu.		Sagit.	Fire	Barren	4th
27 Fri.	10:27 PM	Capri.	Earth	Semi-fruit	4th
28 Sat.		Capri.	Earth	Semi-fruit	4th
29 Sun.		Capri.	Earth	Semi-fruit	4th
30 Mon.	12:03 AM	Aquar.	Air	Barren	NM 5:48 PM
31 Tue.		Aquar.	Air	Barren	1st

Set in Eastern Standard Time

JANUARY

Lunar Aspectarian — Favorable and Unfavorable Days

	SUN	MERC.	VENUS	MARS	JUPITER	SATURN	URANUS	NEPTUNE	PLUTO	ARIES	TAURUS	GEMINI	CANCER	LEO	VIRGO	LIBRA	SCORPIO	SAGIT.	CAPRI.	AQUAR.	PISCES
1	C					X				u	f		U		f	u	f		F		f
2		C	X		X		C	C	X	u	f		U		f	u	f		F		f
3										f	u	f		U		f	u	f		F	
4			Q	O					Q	f	u	f		U		f	u	f		F	
5	X				Q	C					f	u	f		U		f	u	f		F
6			T				X	X	T		f	u	f		U		f	u	f		F
7		X		T						F		f	u	f		U		f	u	f	
8	Q							Q		F		f	u	f		U		f	u	f	
9			Q	T			Q			F		f	u	f		U		f	u	f	
10						X					F		f	u	f		U		f	u	f
11	T						T	T	O		F		f	u	f		U		f	u	f
12		T	O	Q	O	Q				f		F		f	u	f		U		f	u
13										f		F		f	u	f		U		f	u
14				X						f		F		f	u	f		U		f	u
15						T				u	f		F		f	u	f		U		f
16	O						O	O	T	u	f		F		f	u	f		U		f
17			T	T						f	u	f		F		f	u	f		U	
18		O								f	u	f		F		f	u	f		U	
19				C	Q				Q	f	u	f		F		f	u	f		U	
20			Q		O						f	u	f		F		f	u	f		U
21	T						T	T	X		f	u	f		F		f	u	f		U
22			X	X						U		f	u	f		F		f	u	f	
23	Q	T		X			Q	Q		U		f	u	f		F		f	u	f	
24						T					U		f	u	f		F		f	u	f
25		Q		Q			X	X	C		U		f	u	f		F		f	u	f
26	X					C	Q			f		U		f	u	f		F		f	u
27		X	C	T						f		U		f	u	f		F		f	u
28						X				u	f		U		f	u	f		F		f
29							C	C		u	f		U		f	u	f		F		f
30	C			X					X	u	f		U		f	u	f		F		f
31		C	X	O						f	u	f		U		f	u	f		F	

FEBRUARY MOON TABLE

DATE		MOON'S SIGN	ELEMENT	NATURE	MOON'S PHASE
1 Wed.	3:05 AM	Pisces	Water	Fruitful	1st
2 Thu.		Pisces	Water	Fruitful	1st
3 Fri.	9:12 AM	Aries	Fire	Barren	1st
4 Sat.		Aries	Fire	Barren	1st
5 Sun.	7:08 PM	Taurus	Earth	Semi-fruit	1st
6 Mon.		Taurus	Earth	Semi-fruit	1st
7 Tue.		Taurus	Earth	Semi-fruit	2nd 7:54 AM
8 Wed.	7:44 AM	Gemini	Air	Barren	2nd
9 Thu.		Gemini	Air	Barren	2nd
10 Fri.	8:17 PM	Cancer	Water	Fruitful	2nd
11 Sat.		Cancer	Water	Fruitful	2nd
12 Sun.		Cancer	Water	Fruitful	2nd
13 Mon.	6:32 AM	Leo	Fire	Barren	2nd
14 Tue.		Leo	Fire	Barren	2nd
15 Wed.	1:52 PM	Virgo	Earth	Barren	FM 7:16 AM
16 Thu.		Virgo	Earth	Barren	3rd
17 Fri.	7:01 PM	Libra	Air	Semi-fruit	3rd
18 Sat.		Libra	Air	Semi-fruit	3rd

The SUN enters Pisces at 10:11 pm

DATE		MOON'S SIGN	ELEMENT	NATURE	MOON'S PHASE
19 Sun.	10:55 PM	Scorpio	Water	Fruitful	3rd
20 Mon.		Scorpio	Water	Fruitful	3rd
21 Tue.		Scorpio	Water	Fruitful	3rd
22 Wed.	2:13 AM	Sagit.	Fire	Barren	4th 8:04 AM
23 Thu.		Sagit.	Fire	Barren	4th
24 Fri.	5:10 AM	Capri.	Earth	Semi-fruit	4th
25 Sat.		Capri.	Earth	Semi-fruit	4th
26 Sun.	8:14 AM	Aquar.	Air	Barren	4th
27 Mon.		Aquar.	Air	Barren	4th
28 Tue.	12:16 PM	Pisces	Water	Fruitful	4th

Set in Eastern Standard Time

FEBRUARY

Lunar Aspectarian Favorable and Unfavorable Days

	Sun	Merc.	Venus	Mars	Jupiter	Saturn	Uranus	Neptune	Pluto	Aries	Taurus	Gemini	Cancer	Leo	Virgo	Libra	Scorpio	Sagit.	Capri.	Aquar.	Pisces
1					Q	C			Q	f	u	f		U		f	u	f		F	
2								X			f	u	f		U		f	u	f		F
3			Q				X		T		f	u	f		U		f	u	f		F
4	X	X			T					F		f	u	f		U		f	u	f	
5			T	T				Q	Q	F		f	u	f		U		f	u	f	
6		Q				X					F		f	u	f		U		f	u	f
7	Q			Q				T			F		f	u	f		U		f	u	f
8							T		O		F		f	u	f		U		f	u	f
9		T			O	Q				f		F		f	u	f		U		f	u
10	T			X						f		F		f	u	f		U		f	u
11			O			T				u	f		F		f	u	f		U		f
12								O		u	f		F		f	u	f		U		f
13		O						O	T	u	f		F		f	u	f		U		f
14				C	T					f	u	f		F		f	u	f		U	
15	O								Q	f	u	f		F		f	u	f		U	
16			T		Q	O					f	u	f		F		f	u	f		U
17							T	T	X		f	u	f		F		f	u	f		U
18		T	Q		X					U		f	u	f		F		f	u	f	
19				X				Q	Q	U		f	u	f		F		f	u	f	
20	T	Q			T						U		f	u	f		F		f	u	f
21			X	Q			X	X			U		f	u	f		F		f	u	f
22	Q	X							C		U		f	u	f		F		f	u	f
23				T	C	Q				f		U		f	u	f		F		f	u
24	X									f		U		f	u	f		F		f	u
25			C			X		C		u	f		U		f	u	f		F		f
26							C		X	u	f		U		f	u	f		F		f
27		C		O	X					f	u	f		U		f	u	f		F	
28									Q	f	u	f		U		f	u	f		F	

MARCH MOON TABLE

DATE		MOON'S SIGN	ELEMENT	NATURE	MOON'S PHASE
1 Wed.		Pisces	Water	Fruitful	NM 6:48 AM
2 Thu.	6:30 PM	Aries	Fire	Barren	1st
3 Fri.		Aries	Fire	Barren	1st
4 Sat.		Aries	Fire	Barren	1st
5 Sun.	3:51 AM	Taurus	Earth	Semi-fruit	1st
6 Mon.		Taurus	Earth	Semi-fruit	1st
7 Tue.	3:56 PM	Gemini	Air	Barren	1st
8 Wed.		Gemini	Air	Barren	1st
9 Thu.		Gemini	Air	Barren	2nd 5:15 AM
10 Fri.	4:41 AM	Cancer	Water	Fruitful	2nd
11 Sat.		Cancer	Water	Fruitful	2nd
12 Sun.	3:29 PM	Leo	Fire	Barren	2nd
13 Mon.		Leo	Fire	Barren	2nd
14 Tue.	10:55 PM	Virgo	Earth	Barren	2nd
15 Wed.		Virgo	Earth	Barren	2nd
16 Thu.		Virgo	Earth	Barren	FM 8:26 PM
17 Fri.	3:18 AM	Libra	Air	Semi-fruit	3rd
18 Sat.		Libra	Air	Semi-fruit	3rd
19 Sun.	5:52 AM	Scorpio	Water	Fruitful	3rd
20 Mon.		Scorpio	Water	Fruitful	3rd

The SUN enters Aries at 9:14 pm

DATE		MOON'S SIGN	ELEMENT	NATURE	MOON'S PHASE
21 Tue.	7:57 AM	Sagit.	Fire	Barren	3rd
22 Wed.		Sagit.	Fire	Barren	3rd
23 Thu.	10:31 AM	Capri.	Earth	Semi-fruit	4th 3:10 PM
24 Fri.		Capri.	Earth	Semi-fruit	4th
25 Sat.	2:10 PM	Aquar.	Air	Barren	4th
26 Sun.		Aquar.	Air	Barren	4th
27 Mon.	7:18 PM	Pisces	Water	Fruitful	4th
28 Tue.		Pisces	Water	Fruitful	4th
29 Wed.		Pisces	Water	Fruitful	4th
30 Thu.	2:26 AM	Aries	Fire	Barren	NM 9:09 PM
31 Fri.		Aries	Fire	Barren	1st

Set in Eastern Standard Time

MARCH

Lunar Aspectarian · Favorable and Unfavorable Days

	SUN	MERC.	VENUS	MARS	JUPITER	SATURN	URANUS	NEPTUNE	PLUTO	ARIES	TAURUS	GEMINI	CANCER	LEO	VIRGO	LIBRA	SCORPIO	SAGIT.	CAPRI.	AQUAR.	PISCES
1	C				Q	C					f	u	f		U		f	u	f		F
2			X				X	X	T		f	u	f		U		f	u	f		F
3					T					F		f	u	f		U		f	u	f	
4		X		T				Q		F		f	u	f		U		f	u	f	
5			Q				Q			F		f	u	f		U		f	u	f	
6	X	Q			Q	X					F		f	u	f		U		f	u	f
7							T	T	O		F		f	u	f		U		f	u	f
8			T	X	O	Q				f		F		f	u	f		U		f	u
9	Q	T								f		F		f	u	f		U		f	u
10										f		F		f	u	f		U		f	u
11	T					T				u	f		F		f	u	f		U		f
12							O	O	T	u	f		F		f	u	f		U		f
13			O	C	T					f	u	f		F		f	u	f		U	
14		O							Q	f	u	f		F		f	u	f		U	
15											f	u	f		F		f	u	f		U
16	O				Q	O		T			f	u	f		F		f	u	f		U
17							T		X		f	u	f		F		f	u	f		U
18			T	X	X			Q		U		f	u	f		F		f	u	f	
19		T					Q			U		f	u	f		F		f	u	f	
20			Q	Q		T		X			U		f	u	f		F		f	u	f
21	T						X		C		U		f	u	f		F		f	u	f
22		Q		T	C	Q				f		U		f	u	f		F		f	u
23	Q		X							f		U		f	u	f		F		f	u
24		X				X				u	f		U		f	u	f		F		f
25	X						C	C	X	u	f		U		f	u	f		F		f
26				O	X					f	u	f		U		f	u	f		F	
27			C						Q	f	u	f		U		f	u	f		F	
28					Q						f	u	f		U		f	u	f		F
29		C				C		X			f	u	f		U		f	u	f		F
30	C						X		T		f	u	f		U		f	u	f		F
31				T	T					F		f	u	f		U		f	u	f	

31

APRIL MOON TABLE

DATE		MOON'S SIGN	ELEMENT	NATURE	MOON'S PHASE
1 Sat.	11:59 AM	Taurus	Earth	Semi-fruit	1st
2 Sun.		Taurus	Earth	Semi-fruit	1st
3 Mon.	11:50 PM	Gemini	Air	Barren	1st
4 Tue.		Gemini	Air	Barren	1st
5 Wed.		Gemini	Air	Barren	1st
6 Thu.	12:40 PM	Cancer	Water	Fruitful	1st
7 Fri.		Cancer	Water	Fruitful	1st
8 Sat.		Cancer	Water	Fruitful	2nd 12:35 AM
9 Sun.	12:16 AM	Leo	Fire	Barren	2nd
10 Mon.		Leo	Fire	Barren	2nd
11 Tue.	8:39 AM	Virgo	Earth	Barren	2nd
12 Wed.		Virgo	Earth	Barren	2nd
13 Thu.	1:20 PM	Libra	Air	Semi-fruit	2nd
14 Fri.		Libra	Air	Semi-fruit	2nd
15 Sat.	3:13 PM	Scorpio	Water	Fruitful	FM 7:08 AM
16 Sun.		Scorpio	Water	Fruitful	2nd
17 Mon.	3:52 PM	Sagit.	Fire	Barren	3rd
18 Tue.		Sagit.	Fire	Barren	3rd
19 Wed.	4:54 PM	Capri.	Earth	Semi-fruit	3rd
20 Thu.		Capri.	Earth	Semi-fruit	3rd

The SUN enters Taurus at 8:21 am

DATE		MOON'S SIGN	ELEMENT	NATURE	MOON'S PHASE
21 Fri.	7:38 PM	Aquar.	Air	Barren	4th 10:19 PM
22 Sat.		Aquar.	Air	Barren	4th
23 Sun.		Aquar.	Air	Barren	4th
24 Mon.	12:51 AM	Pisces	Water	Fruitful	4th
25 Tue.		Pisces	Water	Fruitful	4th
26 Wed.	8:42 AM	Aries	Fire	Barren	4th
27 Thu.		Aries	Fire	Barren	4th
28 Fri.	6:53 PM	Taurus	Earth	Semi-fruit	4th
29 Sat.		Taurus	Earth	Semi-fruit	NM 12:37 PM
30 Sun.		Taurus	Earth	Semi-fruit	4th

Set in Eastern Standard Time

APRIL

Lunar Aspectarian — Favorable and Unfavorable Days

Day	SUN	MERC.	VENUS	MARS	JUPITER	SATURN	URANUS	NEPTUNE	PLUTO	ARIES	TAURUS	GEMINI	CANCER	LEO	VIRGO	LIBRA	SCORPIO	SAGIT.	CAPRI.	AQUAR.	PISCES
1			X				Q	Q		F		f	u	f		U		f	u	f	
2				Q							F		f	u	f		U		f	u	f
3						X	T	T			F		f	u	f		U		f	u	f
4		X	Q						O	f		F		f	u	f		U		f	u
5	X			X		O	Q			f		F		f	u	f		U		f	u
6										f		F		f	u	f		U		f	u
7		Q	T							u	f		F		f	u	f		U		f
8	Q					T		O		u	f		F		f	u	f		U		f
9								O	T	u	f		F		f	u	f		U		f
10	T	T			C	T				f	u	f		F		f	u	f		U	
11									Q	f	u	f		F		f	u	f		U	
12			O			Q	O			f	u	f		F		f	u	f		U	
13							T	T	X	f	u	f		F		f	u	f		U	
14				X	X						f	u	f		F		f	u	f		U
15	O	O					Q	Q			f	u	f		F		f	u	f		U
16				Q		T					f	u	f		F		f	u	f		U
17			T				X	X	C		f	u	f		F		f	u	f		U
18					T	C				U		f	u	f		F		f	u	f	
19	T		Q			Q				U		f	u	f		F		f	u	f	
20		T								U		f	u	f		F		f	u	f	
21	Q		X			X	C	C	X	U		f	u	f		F		f	u	f	
22		Q			X						U		f	u	f		F		f	u	f
23				O							U		f	u	f		F		f	u	f
24	X								Q		U		f	u	f		F		f	u	f
25		X			Q	C					U		f	u	f		F		f	u	f
26			C				X	X	T		U		f	u	f		F		f	u	f
27				T	T					f		U		f	u	f		F		f	u
28							Q	Q		f		U		f	u	f		F		f	-
29	C									f		U		f	u	f		F		f	u
30				Q			X		T	f		U		f	u	f		F		f	u

33

MAY MOON TABLE

DATE		MOON'S SIGN	ELEMENT	NATURE	MOON'S PHASE
1 Mon.	6:53 AM	Gemini	Air	Barren	1st
2 Tue.		Gemini	Air	Barren	1st
3 Wed.	7:45 PM	Cancer	Water	Fruitful	1st
4 Thu.		Cancer	Water	Fruitful	1st
5 Fri.		Cancer	Water	Fruitful	1st
6 Sat.	7:55 AM	Leo	Fire	Barren	1st
7 Sun.		Leo	Fire	Barren	2nd 4:44 PM
8 Mon.	5:33 PM	Virgo	Earth	Barren	2nd
9 Tue.		Virgo	Earth	Barren	2nd
10 Wed.	11:30 PM	Libra	Air	Semi-fruit	2nd
11 Thu.		Libra	Air	Semi-fruit	2nd
12 Fri.		Libra	Air	Semi-fruit	2nd
13 Sat.	1:54 AM	Scorpio	Water	Fruitful	2nd
14 Sun.		Scorpio	Water	Fruitful	FM 3:49 PM
15 Mon.	1:59 AM	Sagit.	Fire	Barren	3rd
16 Tue.		Sagit.	Fire	Barren	3rd
17 Wed.	1:36 AM	Capri.	Earth	Semi-fruit	3rd
18 Thu.		Capri.	Earth	Semi-fruit	3rd
19 Fri.	2:40 AM	Aquar.	Air	Barren	3rd
20 Sat.		Aquar.	Air	Barren	3rd
21 Sun.	6:36 AM	Pisces	Water	Fruitful	4th 6:36 AM

The SUN enters Gemini at 7:34 am

DATE		MOON'S SIGN	ELEMENT	NATURE	MOON'S PHASE
22 Mon.		Pisces	Water	Fruitful	4th
23 Tue.	2:13 PM	Aries	Fire	Barren	4th
24 Wed.		Aries	Fire	Barren	4th.
25 Thu.		Aries	Fire	Barren	4th.
26 Fri.	12:46 AM	Taurus	Earth	Semi-fruit	4th
27 Sat.		Taurus	Earth	Semi-fruit	4th
28 Sun.	1:07 PM	Gemini	Air	Barren	4th
29 Mon.		Gemini	Air	Barren	NM 4:27 AM
30 Tue.		Gemini	Air	Barren	1st
31 Wed.	1:59 AM	Cancer	Water	Fruitful	1st

Set in Eastern Standard Time

MAY

Lunar Aspectarian   Favorable and Unfavorable Days

Day	SUN	MERC.	VENUS	MARS	JUPITER	SATURN	URANUS	NEPTUNE	PLUTO	ARIES	TAURUS	GEMINI	CANCER	LEO	VIRGO	LIBRA	SCORPIO	SAGIT.	CAPRI.	AQUAR.	PISCES
1		C					T		O		F		f	u	f		U		f	u	f
2			X		O					f		F		f	u	f		U		f	u
3				X		Q				f		F		f	u	f		U		f	u
4										u	f		F		f	u	f		U		f
5	X		Q			T		O		u	f		F		f	u	f		U		f
6		X						O	T	u	f		F		f	u	f		U		f
7	Q		T		T					f	u	f		F		f	u	f		U	
8						C			Q	f	u	f		F		f	u	f		U	
9		Q			Q						f	u	f		F		f	u	f		U
10	T					O		T	X		f	u	f		F		f	u	f		U
11		T			X		T			U		f	u	f		F		f	u	f	
12			O	X				Q		U		f	u	f		F		f	u	f	
13						Q				U		f	u	f		F		f	u	f	
14	O			Q	T			X			U		f	u	f		F		f	u	f
15						C	X		C		U		f	u	f		F		f	u	f
16		O		T	Q					f		U		f	u	f		F		f	u
17			T							f		U		f	u	f		F		f	u
18	T					X		C		u	f		U		f	u	f		F		f
19			Q	X		C		X		u	f		U		f	u	f		F		f
20		T								f	u	f		U		f	u	f		F	
21	Q		X	O					Q	f	u	f		U		f	u	f		F	
22		Q			Q						f	u	f		U		f	u	f		F
23	X					C	X	X	T		f	u	f		U		f	u	f		F
24					T					F		f	u	f		U		f	u	f	
25		X		T				Q		F		f	u	f		U		f	u	f	
26				T				Q		F		f	u	f		U		f	u	f	
27			C			X					F		f	u	f		U		f	u	f
28				Q			T	T	O		F		f	u	f		U		f	u	f
29	C	C			O					f		F		f	u	f		U		f	u
30						Q				f		F		f	u	f		U		f	u
31				X						f		F		f	u	f		U		f	u

JUNE MOON TABLE

DATE		MOON'S SIGN	ELEMENT	NATURE	MOON'S PHASE
1 Thu.		Cancer	Water	Fruitful	1st
2 Fri.	2:17 PM	Leo	Fire	Barren	1st
3 Sat.		Leo	Fire	Barren	1st
4 Sun.		Leo	Fire	Barren	1st
5 Mon.	12:47 AM	Virgo	Earth	Barren	1st
6 Tue.		Virgo	Earth	Barren	2nd 5:26 AM
7 Wed.	8:14 AM	Libra	Air	Semi-fruit	2nd
8 Thu.		Libra	Air	Semi-fruit	2nd
9 Fri.	12:04 PM	Scorpio	Water	Fruitful	2nd
10 Sat.		Scorpio	Water	Fruitful	2nd
11 Sun.	12:50 PM	Sagit.	Fire	Barren	2nd
12 Mon.		Sagit.	Fire	Barren	FM 11:04 PM
13 Tue.	12:05 PM	Capri.	Earth	Semi-fruit	3rd
14 Wed.		Capri.	Earth	Semi-fruit	3rd
15 Thu.	11:52 AM	Aquar.	Air	Barren	3rd
16 Fri.		Aquar.	Air	Barren	3rd
17 Sat.	2:13 PM	Pisces	Water	Fruitful	3rd
18 Sun.		Pisces	Water	Fruitful	3rd
19 Mon.	8:29 PM	Aries	Fire	Barren	4th 5:01 PM
20 Tue.		Aries	Fire	Barren	4th
21 Wed.		Aries	Fire	Barren	4th

The SUN enters Cancer at 3:34 pm

DATE		MOON'S SIGN	ELEMENT	NATURE	MOON'S PHASE
22 Thu.	6:35 AM	Taurus	Earth	Semi-fruit	4th
23 Fri.		Taurus	Earth	Semi-fruit	4th
24 Sat.	7:02 PM	Gemini	Air	Barren	4th
25 Sun.		Gemini	Air	Barren	4th
26 Mon.		Gemini	Air	Barren	4th
27 Tue.	7:57 AM	Cancer	Water	Fruitful	NM 7:51 PM
28 Wed.		Cancer	Water	Fruitful	1st
29 Thu.	8:02 PM	Leo	Fire	Barren	1st
30 Fri.		Leo	Fire	Barren	1st

Set in Eastern Standard Time

JUNE

Lunar Aspectarian — Favorable and Unfavorable Days

Day	SUN	MERC.	VENUS	MARS	JUPITER	SATURN	URANUS	NEPTUNE	PLUTO	ARIES	TAURUS	GEMINI	CANCER	LEO	VIRGO	LIBRA	SCORPIO	SAGIT.	CAPRI.	AQUAR.	PISCES
1			X							u		f	F		f	u	f		U		f
2						T	O	O	T	u		f	F		f	u	f		U		f
3	X	X			T					f	u		f	F	f	u		f		U	
4			Q						Q	f	u		f	F	f	u		f		U	
5				C	Q					f	u		f	F	f	u		f		U	
6	Q	Q				O		T			f	u		f	F	f		u	f		U
7			T					T	X		f	u		f	F	f		u	f		U
8	T	T			X					U		f	u		f	F		f	u	f	
9							Q	Q		U		f	u		f	F		f	u	f	
10				X							U		f	u		f	F		f	u	f
11			O			T	X	X	C		U		f	u		f	F		f	u	f
12	O	O			Q	C				f		U		f	u		f	F		f	u
13						Q				f		U		f	u		f	F		f	u
14					T					u	f		U		f	u		f	F		f
15			T			X	C	C	X	u	f		U		f	u		f	F		f
16		T			X					f	u	f		U	f	u			f	F	
17	T								Q	f	u	f		U	f	u			f	F	
18		Q	Q	O	Q						f	u	f		U		f	u		f	F
19	Q					C	X	X	T		f	u	f		U		f	u		f	F
20		X	X		T					F		f	u	f		U		f	u		f
21								Q		F		f	u	f		U		f	u		f
22	X					Q				F		f	u	f		U		f	u		f
23				T						f	F		f	u	f		U		f	u	
24						X	T	T	O	f	F		f	u	f		U		f	u	
25		C			O						f	F		f	u	f		U		f	u
26			C	Q		Q					f	F		f	u	f		U		f	u
27	C										f	F		f	u	f		U		f	u
28				X						u		f	F		f	u	f		U		f
29						T	O	O	T	u		f	F		f	u	f		U		f
30					T					f	u		f	F	f	u		f		U	

JULY MOON TABLE

DATE		MOON'S SIGN	ELEMENT	NATURE	MOON'S PHASE
1 Sat.		Leo	Fire	Barren	1st
2 Sun.	6:36 AM	Virgo	Earth	Barren	1st
3 Mon.		Virgo	Earth	Barren	1st
4 Tue.	2:56 PM	Libra	Air	Semi-fruit	1st
5 Wed.		Libra	Air	Semi-fruit	2nd 3:03 PM
6 Thu.	8:19 PM	Scorpio	Water	Fruitful	2nd
7 Fri.		Scorpio	Water	Fruitful	2nd
8 Sat.	10:38 PM	Sagit.	Fire	Barren	2nd
9 Sun.		Sagit.	Fire	Barren	2nd
10 Mon.	10:43 PM	Capri.	Earth	Semi-fruit	2nd
11 Tue.		Capri.	Earth	Semi-fruit	2nd
12 Wed.	10:21 PM	Aquar.	Air	Barren	FM 10:21 PM
13 Thu.		Aquar.	Air	Barren	3rd
14 Fri.	11:37 PM	Pisces	Water	Fruitful	3rd
15 Sat.		Pisces	Water	Fruitful	3rd
16 Sun.		Pisces	Water	Fruitful	3rd
17 Mon.	4:23 AM	Aries	Fire	Barren	3rd
18 Tue.		Aries	Fire	Barren	3rd
19 Wed.	1:21 PM	Taurus	Earth	Semi-fruit	4th 6:10 AM
20 Thu.		Taurus	Earth	Semi-fruit	4th
21 Fri.		Taurus	Earth	Semi-fruit	4th
22 Sat.	1:24 AM	Gemini	Air	Barren	4th
23 Sun.		Gemini	Air	Barren	4th
The SUN enters Leo at 2:30 am					
24 Mon.	2:17 PM	Cancer	Water	Fruitful	4th
25 Tue.		Cancer	Water	Fruitful	4th
26 Wed.		Cancer	Water	Fruitful	4th
27 Thu.	2:07 AM	Leo	Fire	Barren	NM 10:14 AM
28 Fri.		Leo	Fire	Barren	1st
29 Sat.	12:13 PM	Virgo	Earth	Barren	1st
30 Sun.		Virgo	Earth	Barren	1st.
31 Mon.	8:24 PM	Libra	Air	Semi-fruit	1st

Set in Eastern Standard Time

JULY

Lunar Aspectarian Favorable and Unfavorable Days

	SUN	MERC.	VENUS	MARS	JUPITER	SATURN	URANUS	NEPTUNE	PLUTO	ARIES	TAURUS	GEMINI	CANCER	LEO	VIRGO	LIBRA	SCORPIO	SAGIT.	CAPRI.	AQUAR.	PISCES
1		X	X							f	u	f		F		f	u	f		U	
2						Q			Q	f	u	f		F		f	u	f		U	
3	X	Q		C							f	u	f		F		f	u	f		U
4			Q			O	T	T	X		f	u	f		F		f	u	f		U
5	Q				X					U		f	u	f		F		f	u	f	
6			T				Q	Q		U		f	u	f		F		f	u	f	
7	T		T								U		f	u	f		F		f	u	f
8				X		T	X	X	C		U		f	u	f		F		f	u	f
9					C					f		U		f	u	f		F		f	u
10				Q		Q.				f		U		f	u	f		F		f	u
11		O	O							u	f		U		f	u	f		F		f
12	O			T		X	C	C	X	u	f		U		f	u	f		F		f
13					X					f	u	f		U		f	u	f		F	
14									Q	f	u	f		U		f	u	f		F	
15		T	T		Q						f	u	f		U		f	u	f		F
16	T			O		C		X			f	u	f		U		f	u	f		F
17				T			X		T		f	u	f		U		f	u	f		F
18		Q	Q							F		f	u	f		U		f	u	f	
19	Q							Q	Q	F		f	u	f		U		f	u	f	
20											F		f	u	f		U		f	u	f
21	X	X	X			X	T	T	O		F		f	u	f		U		f	u	f
22				T	O						F		f	u	f		U		f	u	f
23										f		F		f	u	f		U		f	u
24				Q		Q				f		F		f	u	f		U		f	u
25										u	f		F		f	u	f		U		f
26			C			T	O	O	T	u	f		F		f	u	f		U		f
27	C	C		X	T					u	f		F		f	u	f		U		f
28										f	u	f		F		f	u	f		U	
29						Q			Q	f	u	f		F		f	u	f		U	
30											f	u	f		F		f	u	f		U
31						O	T	T	X		f	u	f		F		f	u	f		U

39

AUGUST MOON TABLE

DATE	MOON'S SIGN	ELEMENT	NATURE	MOON'S PHASE
1 Tue.	Libra	Air	Semi-fruit	1st
2 Wed.	Libra	Air	Semi-fruit	1st
3 Thu. 2:29 AM	Scorpio	Water	Fruitful	2nd 10:16 PM
4 Fri.	Scorpio	Water	Fruitful	2nd
5 Sat. 6:14 AM	Sagit.	Fire	Barren	2nd
6 Sun.	Sagit.	Fire	Barren	2nd
7 Mon. 7:52 AM	Capri.	Earth	Semi-fruit	2nd
8 Tue.	Capri.	Earth	Semi-fruit	2nd
9 Wed. 8:28 AM	Aquar.	Air	Barren	2nd
10 Thu.	Aquar.	Air	Barren	FM 1:16 PM
11 Fri. 9:46 AM	Pisces	Water	Fruitful	3rd
12 Sun.	Pisces	Water	Fruitful	3rd
13 Sun. 1:41 PM	Aries	Fire	Barren	3rd
14 Mon.	Aries	Fire	Barren	3rd
15 Tue. 9:26 PM	Taurus	Earth	Semi-fruit	3rd
16 Wed.	Taurus	Earth	Semi-fruit	3rd
17 Thu.	Taurus	Earth	Semi-fruit	4th 10:05 PM
18 Fri. 8:40 AM	Gemini	Air	Barren	4th
19 Sat.	Gemini	Air	Barren	4th
20 Sun. 9:24 PM	Cancer	Water	Fruitful	4th
21 Mon.	Cancer	Water	Fruitful	4th
22 Tue.	Cancer	Water	Fruitful	4th
23 Wed. 9:13 AM	Leo	Fire	Barren	4th

The SUN enters Virgo at 9:35 am

DATE	MOON'S SIGN	ELEMENT	NATURE	MOON'S PHASE
24 Thu.	Leo	Fire	Barren	4th
25 Fri. 6:50 PM	Virgo	Earth	Barren	NM 11:31 PM
26 Sat.	Virgo	Earth	Barren	1st
27 Sun.	Virgo	Earth	Barren	1st
28 Mon. 2:15 AM	Libra	Air	Semi-fruit	1st
29 Tue.	Libra	Air	Semi-fruit	1st
30 Wed. 7:51 AM	Scorpio	Water	Fruitful	1st
31 Thu.	Scorpio	Water	Fruitful	1st

Set in Eastern Standard Time

AUGUST

Lunar Aspectarian   Favorable and Unfavorable Days

	SUN	MERC.	VENUS	MARS	JUPITER	SATURN	URANUS	NEPTUNE	PLUTO	ARIES	TAURUS	GEMINI	CANCER	LEO	VIRGO	LIBRA	SCORPIO	SAGIT.	CAPRI.	AQUAR.	PISCES
1	X	X	X	C	X					U		f	u	f		F		f	u	f	
2							Q	Q		U		f	u	f		F		f	u	f	
3	Q		Q							U		f	u	f		F		f	u	f	
4		Q				T		X			U		f	u	f		F			u	f
5			T	X	C		X		C		U		f	u	f		F			u	f
6	T	T			Q					f		U		f	u	f		F		f	u
7										f		U		f	u	f		F		f	u
8				Q			X		C	u	f		U		f	u	f		F		f
9				X			C		X	u	f		U		f	u	f		F		f
10	O		O	T						f	u	f		U		f	u	f		F	
11		O		Q					Q	f	u	f		U		f	u	f		F	
12											f	u	f		U		f	u	f		F
13						C	X	X	T		f	u	f		U		f	u	f		F
14				O	T					F		f	u	f		U		f	u	f	
15	T		T				Q	Q		F		f	u	f		U		f	u	f	
16		T									F		f	u	f		U		f	u	f
17	Q		Q			X		T			F		f	u	f		U		f	u	f
18				O		T			O		F		f	u	f		U		f	u	f
19		Q		T						f		F		f	u	f		U		f	u
20	X		X			Q				f		F		f	u	f		U		f	u
21										u	f		F		f	u	f		U		f
22		X		Q		T		O		u	f		F		f	u	f		U		f
23				T			O		T	u	f		F		f	u	f		U		f
24										f	u	f		F		f	u	f		U	
25	C		X						Q	f	u	f		F		f	u	f		U	
26			C	Q							f	u	f		F		f	u	f		U
27						O	T	T	X		f	u	f		F		f	u	f		U
28		C		X							f	u	f		F		f	u	f		U
29				C				Q		U		f	u	f		F		f	u	f	
30	X					Q				U		f	u	f		F		f	u	f	
31			X			T					U		f	u	f		F			u	f

SEPTEMBER MOON TABLE

DATE	MOON'S SIGN	ELEMENT	NATURE	MOON'S PHASE
1 Fri. 11:57 AM	Sagit.	Fire	Barren	1st
2 Sat.	Sagit.	Fire	Barren	2nd 4:03 AM
3 Sun. 2:45 PM	Capri.	Earth	Semi-fruit	2nd
4 Mon.	Capri.	Earth	Semi-fruit	2nd
5 Tue. 4:48 PM	Aquar.	Air	Barren	2nd
6 Wed.	Aquar.	Air	Barren	2nd
7 Thu. 7:09 PM	Pisces	Water	Fruitful	2nd
8 Fri.	Pisces	Water	Fruitful	FM 10:38 PM
9 Sat. 11:15 PM	Aries	Fire	Barren	3rd
10 Sun.	Aries	Fire	Barren	3rd
11 Mon.	Aries	Fire	Barren	3rd
12 Tue. 6:22 AM	Taurus	Earth	Semi-fruit	3rd
13 Wed.	Taurus	Earth	Semi-fruit	3rd
14 Thu. 4:48 PM	Gemini	Air	Barren	3rd
15 Fri.	Gemini	Air	Barren	3rd
16 Sat.	Gemini	Air	Barren	4th 4:09 PM
17 Sun. 5:16 AM	Cancer	Water	Fruitful	4th
18 Mon.	Cancer	Water	Fruitful	4th
19 Tue. 5:19 PM	Leo	Fire	Barren	4th
20 Wed.	Leo	Fire	Barren	4th
21 Thu.	Leo	Fire	Barren	4th
22 Fri. 3:01 AM	Virgo	Earth	Barren	4th
23 Sat.	Virgo	Earth	Barren	4th

The SUN enters Libra at 7:13 am

DATE	MOON'S SIGN	ELEMENT	NATURE	MOON'S PHASE
24 Sun. 9:50 AM	Libra	Air	Semi-fruit	NM 11:55 AM
25 Mon.	Libra	Air	Semi-fruit	1st
26 Tue. 2:20 PM	Scorpio	Water	Fruitful	1st
27 Wed.	Scorpio	Water	Fruitful	1st
28 Thu. 5:31 PM	Sagit.	Fire	Barren	1st
29 Fri.	Sagit.	Fire	Barren	1st
30 Sat. 8:11 PM	Capri.	Earth	Semi-fruit	1st

Set in Eastern Standard Time

SEPTEMBER

Lunar Aspectarian   Favorable and Unfavorable Days

	SUN	MERC.	VENUS	MARS	JUPITER	SATURN	URANUS	NEPTUNE	PLUTO	ARIES	TAURUS	GEMINI	CANCER	LEO	VIRGO	LIBRA	SCORPIO	SAGIT.	CAPRI.	AQUAR.	PISCES
1		X			C		X	X	C		U	f	u	f			F		f	u	f
2	Q		Q							f		U	f	u	f			F		f	u
3				X		Q				f		U	f	u	f			F		f	u
4	T	Q	T							u	f		U	f	u	f			F		f
5				Q		X	C	C	X	u	f		U	f	u	f			F		f
6		T			X					f	u	f		U	f	u	f			F	
7				T					Q	f	u	f		U	f	u	f			F	
8	O				Q						f	u	f		U	f	u	f			F
9	O					C	X	X	T		f	u	f		U	f	u	f			F
10					T					F		f	u	f		U	f	u	f		
11		O						Q		F		f	u	f		U	f	u	f		
12			O					Q		F		f	u	f		U	f	u	f		
13	T				X						F		f	u	f		U	f	u	f	
14			T				T	T	O		F		f	u	f		U	f	u	f	
15					O							F		f	u	f		U	f	u	f
16	Q	T				Q						F		f	u	f		U	f	u	f
17			Q	T								F		f	u	f		U	f	u	f
18		Q				T				f			F		f	u	f		U	f	u
19	X						O	O	T	f			F		f	u	f		U	f	u
20			X	Q	T					u	f			F		f	u	f		U	f
21		X							Q	u	f			F		f	u	f		U	f
22				X	Q					u	f			F		f	u	f		U	f
23						O		T		f	u	f			F		f	u	f		U
24	C							T	X	f	u	f			F		f	u	f		U
25		C	C		X					U	f	u	f			F		f	u	f	
26							Q	Q		U	f	u	f			F		f	u	f	
27			C								U	f	u	f			F		f	u	f
28						T	X	X	C		U	f	u	f			F		f	u	f
29	X	X	X		C					f		U	f	u	f			F		f	u
30						Q				f		U	f	u	f			F		f	u

43

OCTOBER MOON TABLE

DATE		MOON'S SIGN	ELEMENT	NATURE	MOON'S PHASE
1 Sun.		Capri.	Earth	Semi-fruit	2nd 9:36 AM
2 Mon.	11:00 PM	Aquar.	Air	Barren	2nd
3 Tue.		Aquar.	Air	Barren	2nd
4 Wed.		Aquar.	Air	Barren	2nd
5 Thu.	2:36 AM	Pisces	Water	Fruitful	2nd
6 Fri.		Pisces	Water	Fruitful	2nd
7 Sat.	7:42 AM	Aries	Fire	Barren	2nd
8 Sun.		Aries	Fire	Barren	3rd 10:52 AM
9 Mon.	3:05 PM	Taurus	Earth	Semi-fruit	3rd
10 Tue.		Taurus	Earth	Semi-fruit	3rd
11 Wed.		Taurus	Earth	Semi-fruit	3rd
12 Thu.	1:10 AM	Gemini	Air	Barren	3rd
13 Fri.		Gemini	Air	Barren	3rd
14 Sat.	1:20 PM	Cancer	Water	Fruitful	3rd
15 Sun		Cancer	Water	Fruitful	3rd
16 Mon.		Cancer	Water	Fruitful	4th 11:26 AM
17 Tue.	1:47 AM	Leo	Fire	Barren	4th
18 Wed.		Leo	Fire	Barren	4th
19 Thu.	12:12 PM	Virgo	Earth	Barren	4th
20 Fri.		Virgo	Earth	Barren	4th
21 Sat.	7:16 PM	Libra	Air	Semi-fruit	4th
22 Sun.		Libra	Air	Semi-fruit	4th
23 Mon.	11:07 PM	Scorpio	Water	Fruitful	NM 11:37 PM

The SUN enters Scorpio at 4:31 pm

DATE		MOON'S SIGN	ELEMENT	NATURE	MOON'S PHASE
24 Tue.	11:37 PM	Scorpio	Water	Fruitful	1st
25 Wed.		Scorpio	Water	Fruitful	1st
26 Thu.	12:57 AM	Sagit.	Fire	Barren	1st
27 Tue.		Sagit.	Fire	Barren	1st
28 Sat.	2:15 AM	Capri.	Earth	Semi-fruit	1st
29 Sun.		Capri.	Earth	Semi-fruit	1st
30 Mon.	4:24 AM	Aquar.	Air	Barren	2nd 4:17 PM
31 Tue.		Aquar.	Air	Barren	2nd

Set in Eastern Standard Time

OCTOBER

Lunar Aspectarian — Favorable and Unfavorable Days

	SUN	MERC.	VENUS	MARS	JUPITER	SATURN	URANUS	NEPTUNE	PLUTO	ARIES	TAURUS	GEMINI	CANCER	LEO	VIRGO	LIBRA	SCORPIO	SAGIT.	CAPRI.	AQUAR.	PISCES
1	Q	Q								u	f		U		f	u	f		F		f
2			Q	X		X	C	C	X	u	f		U		f	u	f		F		f
3	T				X					f	u	f		U		f	u	f		F	
4			T	Q						f	u	f		U		f	u	f		F	
5					Q				Q	f	u	f		U		f	u	f		F	
6				T		C		X			f	u	f		U		f	u	f		F
7		O					X		T		f	u	f		U		f	u	f		F
8	O				T					F		f	u	f		U		f	u	f	
9			O					Q	Q	F		f	u	f		U		f	u	f	
10											F		f	u	f		U		f	u	f
11				O		X	T	T	O		F		f	u	f		U		f	u	f
12		T									F		f	u	f		U		f	u	f
13	T				O	Q				f		F		f	u	f		U		f	u
14		Q								f		F		f	u	f		U		f	u
15			T							u	f		F		f	u	f		U		f
16	Q			T		T	O	O	T	u	f		F		f	u	f		U		f
17		X	Q							u	f		F		f	u	f		U		f
18					T					f	u	f		F		f	u	f		U	
19	X			Q					Q	f	u	f		F		f	u	f		U	
20			X		Q	O					f	u	f		F		f	u	f		U
21				X			T	T	X		f	u	f		F		f	u	f		U
22		C			X					U		f	u	f		F		f	u	f	
23	C							Q	Q	U		f	u	f		F		f	u	f	
24											U		f	u	f		F		f	u	f
25			C			T	X	X	C		U		f	u	f		F		f	u	f
26				C							U		f	u	f		F		f	u	f
27		X			C	Q				f		U		f	u	f		F		f	u
28	X									f		U		f	u	f		F		f	u
29		Q	X			X	C	C		u	f		U		f	u	f		F		f
30	Q			X					X	u	f		U		f	u	f		F		f
31		T			X					f	u	f		U		f	u	f		F	

45

NOVEMBER MOON TABLE

DATE		MOON'S SIGN	ELEMENT	NATURE	MOON'S PHASE
1 Wed.	8:18 AM	Pisce	Water	Fruitful	2nd
2 Thu.		Pisce	Water	Fruitful	2nd
3 Fri.	2:21 PM	Aries	Fire	Barren	2nd
4 Sat.		Aries	Fire	Barren	2nd
5 Sun.	10:35 PM	Taurus	Earth	Semi-fruit	2nd
6 Mon.		Taurus	Earth	Semi-fruit	2nd
7 Tue.		Taurus	Earth	Semi-fruit	FM 2:20 AM
8 Wed.	8:55 AM	Gemini	Air	Barren	3rd
9 Thu.		Gemini	Air	Barren	3rd
10 Fri.	8:57 PM	Cancer	Water	Fruitful	3rd
11 Sat.		Cancer	Water	Fruitful	3rd
12 Sun.		Cancer	Water	Fruitful	3rd
13 Mon.	9:38 AM	Leo	Fire	Barren	3rd
14 Tue.		Leo	Fire	Barren	3rd
15 Wed.	9:03 PM	Virgo	Earth	Barren	4th 6:41 AM
16 Thu.		Virgo	Earth	Barren	4th
17 Fri.		Virgo	Earth	Barren	4th
18 Sat.	5:18 AM	Libra	Air	Semi-fruit	4th
19 Sun.		Libra	Air	Semi-fruit	4th
20 Mon.	9:41 AM	Scorpio	Water	Fruitful	4th
21 Tue.		Scorpio	Water	Fruitful	4th
22 Wed.	10:57 AM	Sagit.	Fire	Barren	NM 10:43 AM

The SUN enters Sagittarius at 2:01 pm

DATE		MOON'S SIGN	ELEMENT	NATURE	MOON'S PHASE
23 Thu.		Sagit.	Fire	Barren	1st
24 Fri.	10:48 AM	Capri.	Earth	Semi-fruit	1st
25 Sat.		Capri.	Earth	Semi-fruit	1st
26 Sun.	11:15 AM	Aquar.	Air	Barren	1st
27 Mon.		Aquar.	Air	Barren	1st
28 Tue.	1:59 PM	Pisces	Water	Fruitful	1st
29 Wed.		Pisces	Water	Fruitful	2nd 1:28 AM
30 Thu.	7:51 PM	Aries	Fire	Barren	2nd

Set in Eastern Standard Time

NOVEMBER

Lunar Aspectarian | Favorable and Unfavorable Days

	SUN	MERC.	VENUS	MARS	JUPITER	SATURN	URANUS	NEPTUNE	PLUTO	ARIES	TAURUS	GEMINI	CANCER	LEO	VIRGO	LIBRA	SCORPIO	SAGIT.	CAPRI.	AQUAR.	PISCES
1			Q						Q	f	u	f		U		f	u	f		F	
2	T				Q	Q	C				f	u	f		U		f	u	f		F
3			T				X	X	T		f	u	f		U		f	u	f		F
4				T	T					F		f	u	f		U		f	u	f	
5							Q	Q		F		f	u	f		U		f	u	f	
6		O									F		f	u	f		U		f	u	f
7	O						X	T			F		f	u	f		U		f	u	f
8			O					T	O		F		f	u	f		U		f	u	f
9				O	O	Q				f		F		f	u	f		U		f	u
10										f		F		f	u	f		U		f	u
11		T								u	f		F		f	u	f		U		f
12	T					T		O		u	f		F		f	u	f		U		f
13							O		T	u	f		F		f	u	f		U		f
14		Q		T	T	T				f	u	f		F		f	u	f		U	
15	Q								Q	f	u	f		F		f	u	f		U	
16											f	u	f		F		f	u	f		U
17	X	X	Q	Q	Q	O		T			f	u	f		F		f	u	f		U
18							T		X		f	u	f		F		f	u	f		U
19			X	X	X			Q		U		f	u	f		F		f	u	f	
20							Q			U		f	u	f		F		f	u	f	
21						T				U		f	u	f		F		f	u	f	
22	C	C					X	X	C	U		f	u	f		F		f	u	f	
23					C	Q					U		f	u	f		F		f	u	f
24			C	C							U		f	u	f		F		f	u	f
25						X				f		U		f	u	f		F		f	u
26	X	X					C	C	X	f		U		f	u	f		F		f	u
27					X					u	f		U		f	u	f		F		f
28			X	X					Q	u	f		U		f	u	f		F		f
29	Q	Q				C				u	f		U		f	u	f		F		f
30				Q	Q		X	X	T	u	f		U		f	u	f		F		f

47

DECEMBER MOON TABLE

DATE	MOON'S SIGN	ELEMENT	NATURE	MOON'S PHASE
1 Fri.	Aries	Fire	Barren	2nd
2 Sat.	Aries	Fire	Barren	2nd
3 Sun. 4:40 AM	Taurus	Earth	Semi-fruit	2nd
4 Mon.	Taurus	Earth	Semi-fruit	2nd
5 Tue. 3:35 PM	Gemini	Air	Barren	2nd
6 Wed.	Gemini	Air	Barren	FM 8:28 PM
7 Thu.	Gemini	Air	Barren	3rd
8 Fri. 3:45 AM	Cancer	Water	Fruitful	3rd
9 Sat.	Cancer	Water	Fruitful	3rd
10 Sun. 4:25 PM	Leo	Fire	Barren	3rd
11 Mon.	Leo	Fire	Barren	3rd
12 Tue.	Leo	Fire	Barren	3rd
13 Wed. 4:27 AM	Virgo	Earth	Barren	3rd
14 Thu.	Virgo	Earth	Barren	3rd
15 Fri. 2:09 PM	Libra	Air	Semi-fruit	4th 12:32 AM
16 Sat.	Libra	Air	Semi-fruit	4th
17 Sun. 8:07 PM	Scorpio	Water	Fruitful	4th
18 Mon.	Scorpio	Water	Fruitful	4th
19 Tue. 10:13 PM	Sagit.	Fire	Barren	4th
20 Wed.	Sagit.	Fire	Barren	4th
21 Thu. 9:46 PM	Capri.	Earth	Semi-fruit	NM 9:22 PM
22 Fri.	Capri.	Earth	Semi-fruit	1st

The SUN enters Capricorn at 3:17 am

DATE	MOON'S SIGN	ELEMENT	NATURE	MOON'S PHASE
23 Sat. 8:52 PM	Aquar.	Air	Barren	1st
24 Sun.	Aquar.	Air	Barren	1st
25 Mon. 9:45 PM	Pisces	Water	Fruitful	1st
26 Tue.	Pisces	Water	Fruitful	1st
27 Wed.	Pisces	Water	Fruitful	1st
28 Thu. 2:06 AM	Aries	Fire	Barren	2nd 2:07 PM
29 Fri.	Aries	Fire	Barren	2nd
30 Sat. 10:22 AM	Taurus	Earth	Semi-fruit	2nd
31 Sun.	Taurus	Earth	Semi-fruit	2nd

Set in Eastern Standard Time

DECEMBER

Lunar Aspectarian   Favorable and Unfavorable Days

Day	SUN	MERC.	VENUS	MARS	JUPITER	SATURN	URANUS	NEPTUNE	PLUTO	ARIES	TAURUS	GEMINI	CANCER	LEO	VIRGO	LIBRA	SCORPIO	SAGIT.	CAPRI.	AQUAR.	PISCES
1	T	T	Q							F		f	u	f		U		f	u	f	
2						T		Q		F		f	u	f		U		f	u	f	
3			T	T			Q			F		f	u	f		U		f	u	f	
4						X					F		f	u	f		U		f	u	f
5							T	T	O		F		f	u	f		U		f	u	f
6	O									f		F		f	u	f		U		f	u
7		O			O	Q				f		F		f	u	f		U		f	u
8				O						f		F		f	u	f		U		f	u
9			O			T				u	f		F		f	u	f		U		f
10							O	O	T	u	f		F		f	u	f		U		f
11										f	u	f		F		f	u	f		U	
12	T					T				f	u	f		F		f	u	f		U	
13		T							Q	f	u	f		F		f	u	f		U	
14			T	T		O					f	u	f		F		f	u	f		U
15	Q				Q		T	T	X		f	u	f		F		f	u	f		U
16		Q		Q						U		f	u	f		F		f	u	f	
17	X		Q		X			Q	Q	U		f	u	f		F		f	u	f	
18		X		X							U		f	u	f		F		f	u	f
19			X			T	X	X			U		f	u	f		F		f	u	f
20									C	f		U		f	u	f		F		f	u
21	C				C	Q				f		U		f	u	f		F		f	u
22										u	f		U		f	u	f		F		f
23		C		C		X	C	C	X	u	f		U		f	u	f		F		f
24			C							f	u	f		U		f	u	f		F	
25						X				f	u	f		U		f	u	f		F	
26	X								Q		f	u	f		U		f	u	f		F
27		X		X	Q	C		X			f	u	f		U		f	u	f		F
28	Q		X				X		T		f	u	f		U		f	u	f		F
29				Q						F		f	u	f		U		f	u	f	
30		Q				T		Q	Q	F		f	u	f		U		f	u	f	
31	T		Q								F		f	u	f		U		f	u	f

ASTRO-ALMANAC

Llewellyn's unique Astro-Almanac is provided for quick reference. Because the dates indicated may not be the best for you personally, be sure to read the instructions starting with "How to Use the Moon Sign Book Tables," then go to the proper section of the book and read the detailed description provided for each activity.

For the most part, the dates given in the Astro-Almanac will correspond to the ones you can determine for yourself from the detailed instructions. But just as often, the dates given may not be favorable for your Sun sign or for your particular interests. *That's why it's important for you to learn how to use the entire process to come up with the most beneficial dates for you.*

The following pages are provided for easy reference for those of you who do not want detailed descriptions. The dates provided are determined from the sign and phase of the Moon and the aspects to the Moon. These are approximate dates only and do not take into account retrogrades or Moon voids. For more information, please see "Retrogrades" and "Moon Void of Course."

Please read the instructions on how to come up with the dates yourself. This is very important in some instances (such as planning surgery or making big purchases). You will find other lists of dates in the proper sections of the *Moon Sign Book*. We have special lists for Fishing and Hunting Dates, Gardening Dates, Dates for Destroying Plant and Animal Pests, and other types of activities. See the Table of Contents for a complete listing.

•JANUARY•

To advertise the sale of real estate or personal possessions: 26, 27

To advertise the start of a new venture: 12, 26, 27

To buy animals: 1, 2, 3, 7, 8, 30, 31

For neutering or spaying an animal: 1, 2, 3, 4, 11, 12, 13, 14, 15, 16, 17, 18, 19, 27, 28, 29, 30, 31

To dock or dehorn animals: 1, 2, 3, 4, 23, 24, 25, 26, 27, 28, 29, 30, 31

To train a pet: 10, 11

For a permanent wave: 10, 11, 17, 18, 19

To cut hair for thickness: 15

To cut hair to retard growth: 20, 21

To cut hair to stimulate growth: 5, 6, 15, 16

To apply for a job: 1, 2, 11, 21, 30,

To begin a new job: 1, 2, 10, 11, 30

To ask for a raise or promotion: 2, 6, 7, 22, 23, 27, 30

To entertain: 3, 4, 12, 13, 14, 17, 18, 19, 22, 23, 31

To join a club: 3, 4, 12, 13, 14, 22, 23, 31

For baking: 15, 16

For brewing: 15

To can fruits and vegetables: 16, 20, 21

To dry fruits and vegetables: 17, 18, 19, 26, 27

To make preserves and jellies: None

To buy a permanent home: None

To buy real estate for appreciation: 7, 22

To start new house construction: 10

To pour concrete: 1, 10, 15, 24, 28

To remodel a house: 10, 24, 25

To paint the house: 2, 6, 17, 22, 27, 31

To do roofing: None

To set fence posts: 1, 10, 15, 24, 28

To mow lawn to retard growth: 1, 17, 18, 19, 20, 21, 22, 23, 24, 25, 26, 27, 28, 29, 30

To cut timber: 1, 17, 18, 19, 20, 21, 22, 23, 26, 27, 28, 29, 30

To deal in legal matters: 2, 7, 17, 22, 26, 30
To sign contracts: 17, 31
To see the dentist: 10
To fill teeth: None
To extract teeth: 26, 27
To consult a physician: None
To buy medicine: 20, 21, 24, 25
To buy health foods: 20, 21
To start a diet to gain weight: 5, 6, 15, 16
To start a diet to lose weight: 17, 18, 19, 20, 21, 26, 27
To collect money: 1, 2, 7, 8, 9, 15, 16, 22, 23, 28, 29, 30
To start a savings account: 10, 11
To seek favors and/or credit: 5, 6, 17, 26, 27, 31
To begin a course of study: 12, 13, 14
To write letters: 5, 6, 12, 13, 14, 20, 21, 26, 27
To stop a bad habit: 21
For dressmaking and/or mending: 17, 22
To buy appliances: 2, 6, 11, 21, 25, 29
To buy antiques: 1, 2, 15, 16, 24, 25, 28, 29, 30
To buy cameras: 6, 11, 21, 25
To buy a car: 12, 27
To buy clothing: 10, 11, 22, 23
To purchase radios: 2, 6, 7, 11, 12, 21, 23, 25, 27, 29, 31
To buy televisions or computers: 2, 6, 11, 21, 25, 29
For a marriage ceremony: 1, 2, 5, 6, 7, 11, 17, 21, 22, 26, 27, 30, 31
To marry for happiness: 17, 22
To marry for longevity: None
To end a romance or file for divorce: 1, 16, 17, 18, 19, 20, 21, 22, 23, 24, 25, 26, 27, 28, 29, 30
To repair a car: 11
To sell real estate: 7, 15, 15
To sell personal possessions: 2, 6, 17, 22, 27, 31
For sporting activities: 7, 9, 17, 26, 27
For traveling: 12, 27

•FEBRUARY•

To advertise the sale of real estate or personal possessions: 22, 23

To advertise the start of a new venture: 9, 22, 23

To buy animals: 4, 5, 6, 7

For neutering or spaying an animal: 1, 8, 9, 10, 11, 12, 13, 14, 15, 24, 25, 26, 27, 28

To dock or dehorn animals: 1

To train a pet: 6, 7, 8

For a permanent wave: 6, 7, 8, 14, 15

To cut hair for thickness: 12, 13, 14, 15

To cut hair to retard growth: 16, 17

To cut hair to stimulate growth: 2, 3, 11, 12, 13

To apply for a job: None

To begin a new job: 6, 7, 8

To ask for a raise or promotion: 4, 5, 22, 25

To entertain: 1, 9, 10, 14, 15, 18, 19, 27, 28

To join a club: 1, 9, 10, 18, 19, 27, 28

For baking: 11, 12, 13

For brewing: None

To can fruits and vegetables: 16, 17

To dry fruits and vegetables: 15, 23, 24

To make preserves and jellies: 16

To buy a permanent home: 6, 7

To buy real estate for appreciation: 4, 5, 18

To start new house construction: 6

To pour concrete: 6, 11, 20, 25

To remodel a house: 6, 20, 22

To paint the house: 5, 16, 21, 25

To do roofing: 27, 28

To set fence posts: 6, 11, 20, 25

To mow lawn to retard growth: 15, 16, 17, 18, 19, 20, 21, 22, 23, 24, 25, 26, 27, 28

To cut timber: 15, 16, 17, 18, 19, 23, 24, 25, 26, 27, 28

To deal in legal matters: 4, 14, 18, 23, 27

To sign contracts: 14, 27
To see the dentist: 1, 6
To fill teeth: 27, 28
To extract teeth: 23, 24
To consult a physician: None
To buy medicine: 16, 17, 20, 21, 22
To buy health foods: 16, 17
To start a diet to gain weight: 2, 3, 11, 12, 13
To start a diet to lose weight: 15, 16, 17, 23, 24, 27, 28
To collect money: 4, 5, 11, 12, 13, 18, 19, 25, 26
To start a savings account: 6, 7, 8
To seek favors and/or credit: 14, 23, 24, 27
To begin a course of study: 9, 10
To write letters: 2, 3, 9, 10, 16, 17, 23, 24
To stop a bad habit: 17
For dressmaking and/or mending: None
To buy appliances: 3, 8, 17, 21, 26
To buy antiques: 11, 12, 13, 20, 21, 22, 25, 26
To buy cameras: 2, 7, 17, 21
To buy a car: 9
To buy clothing: 6, 7, 8, 18, 19
To purchase radios: 3, 4, 8, 9 17, 18, 21, 22, 26, 27
To buy televisions or computers: 3, 8, 17, 21, 26
For a marriage ceremony: 4, 5, 10, 14, 16, 18, 20, 21, 23, 24, 25, 27
To marry for happiness: 18
To marry for longevity: None
To end a romance or file for divorce: 15, 16, 17, 18, 19, 20, 21, 22, 23, 24, 25, 26, 27, 28
To repair a car: 8
To sell real estate: 4, 11
To sell personal possessions: 5, 16, 21, 25
For sporting activities: 4, 5, 14, 23
For traveling: 9

•MARCH•

To advertise the sale of real estate or personal possessions: 22

To advertise the start of a new venture: 9, 22

To buy animals: 3, 4, 5, 6, 7, 9, 31

For neutering or spaying an animal: 7, 8, 9, 10, 11, 12, 13, 14, 23, 24, 25, 26, 27

To dock or dehorn animals: 8, 9, 10, 11, 12, 13, 14, 15, 27

To train a pet: 6, 7

For a permanent wave: 6, 7, 13, 14

To cut hair for thickness: 13, 14

To cut hair to retard growth: 17

To cut hair to stimulate growth: 1, 2, 11, 12, 28, 29, 30

To apply for a job: 6, 25

To begin a new job: 6, 7, 15, 16

To ask for a raise or promotion: 2, 3, 4, 9, 18, 19, 23, 24, 27, 31

To entertain: 8, 9, 10, 13, 14, 18, 19, 26, 27

To join a club: 8, 9, 10, 18, 19, 26, 27

For baking: 11, 12

For brewing: 1, 28, 29, 30

To can fruits and vegetables: 16, 17

To dry fruits and vegetables: 22, 23

To make preserves and jellies: None

To buy a permanent home: 6, 7

To buy real estate for appreciation: 3, 18, 31

To start new house construction: 6

To pour concrete: 6, 11, 20, 24

To remodel a house: 6, 20, 21

To paint the house: 2, 8, 18, 23, 27

To do roofing: 26, 27

To set fence posts: 6, 11, 20, 24

To mow lawn to retard growth: 16, 17, 18, 19, 20, 21, 22, 23, 24, 25, 26, 27

To cut timber: 16, 17, 18, 19, 22, 23, 24, 25, 26, 27

To deal in legal matters: 3, 13, 18, 22, 26, 31
To sign contracts: 13, 26
To see the dentist: 6
To fill teeth: 26, 27
To extract teeth: 8, 9, 23
To consult a physician: 15, 16
To buy medicine: 15, 16, 17, 20, 21
To buy health foods: 15, 16, 17
To start a diet to gain weight: 1, 2, 11, 12, 30
To start a diet to lose weight: 16, 17, 22, 23, 26, 27
To collect money: 3, 4, 5, 11, 12, 18, 19, 24, 25, 31
To start a savings account: 6, 7
To seek favors and/or credit: 1, 2, 13, 22, 23, 26, 27, 30
To begin a course of study: 8, 9, 10, 15, 16
To write letters: 1, 2, 8, 9, 10, 15, 16, 17, 22, 23, 28, 29, 30
To stop a bad habit: 16
For dressmaking and/or mending: 18
To buy appliances: 2, 7, 16, 17, 21, 25, 30
To buy antiques: 11, 12, 20, 21, 24, 25
To buy cameras: 2, 7, 16, 20, 29
To buy a car: 9
To buy clothing: 6, 7, 18, 19
To purchase radios: 2, 4, 7, 9, 16, 17, 19, 21, 24, 25, 29, 30
To buy televisions or computers: 2, 7, 16, 17, 21, 25, 30
For a marriage ceremony: 1, 2, 3, 6, 8, 11, 13, 18, 21, 22, 23, 25, 26, 27, 30, 31
To marry for happiness: 11, 18
To marry for longevity: 6
To end a romance or file for divorce: 1, 16, 17, 18, 19, 20, 21, 22, 23, 24, 25, 26, 27, 28, 29, 30
To repair a car: 7
To sell real estate: 3, 11, 31
To sell personal possessions: 2, 8, 18, 23, 27
For sporting activities: 3, 4, 13, 22, 31
For traveling: 9

•APRIL•

To advertise the sale of real estate or personal possessions: 18

To advertise the start of a new venture: 4, 18

To buy animals: 1, 2, 3, 4, 6, 7, 8, 29, 30

For neuturing or spaying an animal: 3, 4, 5, 6, 7, 8, 9, 10, 11, 19, 20, 21, 22, 23, 24

To dock or dehorn animals: 4, 5, 6, 7, 8, 9, 10, 11

To train a pet: 2, 3, 29, 30

For a permanent wave: 2, 3, 10, 11, 29, 30

To cut hair for thickness: None

To cut hair to retard growth: 27, 28

To cut hair to stimulate growth: 7, 8, 9, 25, 26

To apply for a job: 29

To begin a new job: 2, 3, 12, 13, 29, 30

To ask for a raise or promotion: 1, 4, 7, 18, 20, 21, 22, 26, 27

To entertain: 4, 5, 6, 10, 11, 14, 15, 22, 23, 24

To join a club: 4, 5, 6, 14, 15, 22, 23, 24

For baking: 7, 8, 9

For brewing: 25, 26

To can fruits and vegetables: None

To dry fruits and vegetables: 18, 19, 27, 28

To make preserves and jellies: 7

To buy a permanent home: 2, 3, 7, 8, 29, 30

To buy real estate for appreciation: 1, 7, 14, 27

To start new house construction: 3, 30

To pour concrete: 3, 8, 16, 21, 30

To remodel a house: 3, 16, 17, 30

To paint the house: 1, 7, 17, 21, 26

To do roofing: 22, 23, 24, 29

To set fence posts: 3, 8, 16, 21, 30

To mow lawn to retard growth: 15, 16, 17, 18, 19, 20, 21, 22, 23, 24, 27, 28, 29

To cut timber: 15, 18, 19, 20, 21, 22, 23, 24, 27, 28, 29

To deal in legal matters: 10, 14, 18, 22, 27
To sign contracts: 10, 22
To see the dentist: 3, 30
To fill teeth: 22, 23, 24, 29
To extract teeth: 4, 5, 6
To consult a physician: 12, 13
To buy medicine: 12, 13, 16, 17
To buy health foods: 12, 13
To start a diet to gain weight: 7, 8, 9
To start a diet to lose weight: 18, 19, 22, 23, 24, 27, 28
To collect money: 1, 7, 8, 9, 14, 15, 20, 21, 27, 28
To start a savings account: 2, 3, 29, 30
To seek favors and/or credit: 10, 18, 19, 22, 24, 26
To begin a course of study: 4, 5, 6, 12, 13
To write letters: 4, 5, 6, 12, 13, 18, 19, 25, 26
To stop a bad habit: 13
For dressmaking and/or mending: None
To buy appliances: 3, 13, 17, 21, 26
To buy antiques: 7, 8, 9, 16, 17, 20, 21
To buy cameras: 3, 13, 17, 26, 30
To buy a car: 4
To buy clothing: 2, 3, 14, 15, 29, 30
To purchase radios: 3, 4, 10, 13, 17, 20, 21, 25, 26
To buy televisions or computers: 3, 13, 17, 21, 26
For a marriage ceremony: 1, 5, 7, 10, 14, 17, 18, 19, 21, 22, 24, 26, 27, 29
To marry for happiness: 7, 14, 29
To marry for longevity: 29
To end a romance or file for divorce: 15, 16, 17, 18, 19, 20, 21, 22, 23, 24, 25, 26, 27, 28, 29
To repair a car: 3
To sell real estate: 8, 27
To sell personal possessions: 1, 7, 17, 21, 26
For sporting activities: 10, 18, 27
For traveling: 4, 10

•MAY•

To advertise the sale of real estate or personal possessions: 15

To advertise the start of a new venture: 1, 15, 19

To buy animals: 1, 2, 4, 5, 6, 7, 29, 31

For neuturing or spaying an animal: 1, 2, 3, 4, 5, 6, 7, 8, 17, 18, 19, 20, 21, 28, 29, 30, 31

To dock or dehorn animals: 2, 3, 4, 5, 6, 7, 8, 9, 29, 30, 31

To train a pet: 1, 27, 28

For a permanent wave: 1, 7, 8, 27, 28

To cut hair for thickness: None

To cut hair to retard growth: 24, 25, 26, 29

To cut hair to stimulate growth: 4, 5, 6, 22, 23

To apply for a job: 10, 18, 19

To begin a new job: 1, 9, 10

To ask for a raise or promotion: 1, 2, 6, 7, 11, 19, 20, 24, 25, 27, 29

To entertain: 2, 3, 7, 8, 11, 12, 13, 20, 21, 29, 30, 31

To join a club: 2, 3, 11, 12, 13, 20, 21, 29, 30, 31

For baking: 4, 5, 6

For brewing: 22, 23

To can fruits and vegetables: None

To dry fruits and vegetables: 16, 17, 24, 25, 26, 29

To make preserves and jellies: 27

To buy a permanent home: 1, 4, 5, 6, 7

To buy real estate for appreciation: 11, 24

To start new house construction: 27

To pour concrete: 5, 14, 18, 27

To remodel a house: 14, 15, 27

To paint the house: 2, 7, 17, 21, 27

To do roofing: 20, 21, 27, 28

To set fence posts: 5, 14, 18, 27

To mow lawn to retard growth: 14, 15, 16, 17, 18, 19, 20, 21, 24, 25, 26, 27, 28, 29

To cut timber: 16, 17, 18, 19, 20, 21, 24, 25, 26, 27, 28, 29

To deal in legal matters: 7, 11, 19, 24
To sign contracts: 1, 7, 20
To see the dentist: 27
To fill teeth: 20, 21, 27, 28
To extract teeth: 2, 3, 29, 30, 31
To consult a physician: 9, 10
To buy medicine: 9, 10, 14, 15
To buy health foods: 9, 10
To start a diet to gain weight: 4, 5, 6
To start a diet to lose weight: 16, 17, 20, 21, 24, 25, 26
To collect money: 4, 5, 6, 11, 12, 13, 18, 19, 24, 25, 26
To start a savings account: 1, 27, 28
To seek favors and/or credit: 7, 17, 21, 23
To begin a course of study: 2, 3, 9, 10, 29, 30, 31
To write letters: 2, 3, 9, 10, 16, 17, 22, 23, 29, 30, 31
To stop a bad habit: 10
For dressmaking and/or mending: 7, 27
To buy appliances: 1, 11, 15, 19, 23, 28
To buy antiques: 4, 5, 6, 14, 15, 18, 19
To buy cameras: 10, 14, 23, 28
To buy a car: 29
To buy clothing: 1, 11, 12, 13, 27, 28
To purchase radios: 1, 6, 11, 15, 19, 20, 23, 25, 28, 29
To buy televisions or computers: 1, 11, 15, 19, 23, 28
For a marriage ceremony: 2, 5, 7, 10, 11, 15, 17, 18, 19, 21, 23, 24, 27, 29
To marry for happiness: 5, 7, 11, 27
To marry for longevity: None
To end a romance or file for divorce: 14, 15, 16, 17, 18, 19, 20, 21, 22, 23, 24, 25, 26, 27, 28, 29
To repair a car: 1, 28
To sell real estate: 5, 24
To sell personal possessions: 2, 7, 17, 21, 27
For sporting activities: 7, 16, 24, 25, 26
For traveling: 29

•JUNE•

To advertise the sale of real estate or personal possessions: 12

To advertise the start of a new venture: 12, 25

To buy animals: 1, 2, 3, 4, 5, 27, 28, 29, 30

For neutering or spaying an animal: 1, 2, 3, 4, 5, 13, 14, 15, 16, 17, 24, 25, 26, 27, 28, 29, 30

To dock or dehorn animals: 1, 2, 3, 4, 5, 6, 25, 26, 27, 28, 29, 30

To train a pet: 23, 24

For a permanent wave: 3, 4, 5, 23, 24, 30

To cut hair for thickness: None

To cut hair to retard growth: 20, 21, 22, 25, 26, 27

To cut hair to stimulate growth: 1, 2, 18, 19, 28, 29

To apply for a job: None

To begin a new job: 6, 7

To ask for a raise or promotion: 1, 3, 7, 8, 16, 20, 25, 30

To entertain: 3, 4, 5, 8, 9, 16, 17, 25, 26, 27, 30

To join a club: 8, 9, 16, 17, 25, 26, 27

For baking: 1, 2, 28, 29

For brewing: 19

To can fruits and vegetables: None

To dry fruits and vegetables: 12, 13, 20, 21, 22, 25, 26, 27

To make preserves and jellies: 1, 7

To buy a permanent home: 1, 2, 3, 4, 5, 28, 29, 30

To buy real estate for appreciation: 1, 8, 20

To start new house construction: 24

To pour concrete: 2, 11, 15, 24, 29

To remodel a house: 11, 24

To paint the house: 1, 7, 15, 20, 26

To do roofing: 16, 17, 23, 24

To set fence posts: 2, 11, 15, 24, 29

To mow lawn to retard growth: 12, 13, 14, 15, 16, 17, 20, 21, 22, 23, 24, 25, 26, 27

To cut timber: 12, 13, 14, 15, 16, 17, 20, 21, 22, 23, 24, 25, 26, 27

To deal in legal matters: 3, 8, 12, 16, 20, 30'
To sign contracts: 3, 16, 30
To see the dentist: 2, 4
To fill teeth: 16, 17, 23, 24
To extract teeth: 6, 25, 26, 27
To consult a physician: 6, 7
To buy medicine: 6, 7, 10, 11
To buy health foods: 6, 7
To start a diet to gain weight: 1, 2, 28, 29
To start a diet to lose weight: 12, 13, 16, 17, 20, 21, 22
To collect money: 1, 2, 8, 9, 14, 15, 20, 21, 22, 28, 29
To start a savings account: 23, 24
To seek favors and/or credit: 3, 12, 16, 17, 30
To begin a course of study: 6, 7, 12, 27
To write letters: 6, 7, 12, 13, 18, 19, 25, 26, 27
To stop a bad habit: 6
For dressmaking and/or mending: None
To buy appliances: 7, 11, 15, 19, 24
To buy antiques: 1, 2, 10, 11, 14, 15, 28, 29
To buy cameras: 6, 11, 19, 24
To buy a car: 25
To buy clothing: 8, 9, 23, 24
To purchase radios: 3, 7, 8, 11, 15, 16, 19, 20, 24, 25
To buy televisions or computers: 7, 11, 15, 19, 24
For a marriage ceremony: 1, 3, 7, 8, 15, 16, 17, 20, 22, 26, 27, 30
To marry for happiness: 1, 3, 8, 30
To marry for longevity: None
To end a romance or file for divorce: 12, 13, 14, 15, 16, 17, 18, 19, 20, 21, 22, 23, 24, 25, 26, 27
To repair a car: 24
To sell real estate: 2, 20, 29
To sell personal possessions: 1, 7, 15, 20, 26
For sporting activities: 3, 12, 20, 30
For traveling: 3, 25

•JULY•

To advertise the sale of real estate or personal possessions: 9

To advertise the start of a new venture: 9

To buy animals: 1, 2, 3, 5, 27, 28, 29, 30

For neutering or spaying an animal: 1, 2, 10, 11, 12, 13, 14, 22, 23, 24, 25, 26, 27, 28, 29

To dock or dehorn animals: 1, 2, 3, 23, 24, 25, 26, 27, 28, 29, 30, 31

To train a pet: 20, 21, 22

For a permanent wave: 1, 2, 20, 21, 22, 28, 29

To cut hair for thickness: None

To cut hair to retard growth: 18, 19, 23, 24

To cut hair to stimulate growth: 15, 16, 17, 25, 26, 27

To apply for a job: 3, 21

To begin a new job: 3, 4, 11, 12, 30, 31

To ask for a raise or promotion: 1, 5, 6, 7, 15, 17, 21, 26, 27

To entertain: 1, 2, 5, 6, 13, 14, 23, 24, 28, 29

To join a club: 5, 6, 13, 14, 23, 24

For baking: 25, 26, 27

For brewing: 25, 26, 27

To can fruits and vegetables: 25, 26, 27

To dry fruits and vegetables: 18, 19, 23, 24

To make preserves and jellies: 21, 26, 31

To buy a permanent home: 1, 2, 27, 28, 29

To buy real estate for appreciation: 5, 26, 27

To start new house construction: 21

To pour concrete: 8, 12, 21, 26

To remodel a house: 8, 21

To paint the house: 1, 7, 15, 21, 26, 31

To do roofing: 13, 14, 20, 21, 22

To set fence posts: 8, 12, 21, 26

To mow lawn to retard growth: 12, 13, 14, 18, 19, 20, 21, 22, 23, 24

To cut timber: 12, 13, 14, 18, 19, 20, 21, 22, 23, 24

To deal in legal matters: 5, 9, 13, 17, 27
To sign contracts: 1, 13, 21
To see the dentist: 21
To fill teeth: 13, 14, 20, 21, 22
To extract teeth: 3, 4, 23, 24, 30, 31
To consult a physician: 3, 4, 30, 31
To buy medicine: 3, 4, 7, 8, 30, 31
To buy health foods: 3, 4, 30, 31
To start a diet to gain weight: 27
To start a diet to lose weight: 13, 14, 18, 19
To collect money: 5, 6, 11, 12, 18, 19, 25, 26, 27
To start a savings account: 20, 21, 22
To seek favors and/or credit: 1, 9, 13, 15, 16, 17
To begin a course of study: 3, 4, 9, 10, 30, 31
To write letters: 3, 4, 9, 10, 15, 16, 17, 23, 24, 30, 31
To stop a bad habit: 4, 31
For dressmaking and/or mending: 1, 21
To buy appliances: 4, 8, 12, 17, 21, 31
To buy antiques: 7, 8, 11, 12, 25, 26, 27
To buy cameras: 4, 8, 16, 21, 31
To buy a car: None
To buy clothing: 5, 6, 20, 21, 22
To purchase radios: 1, 4, 6, 8, 12, 15, 17, 21, 27, 31
To buy televisions or computers: 4, 8, 12, 17, 21, 31
For a marriage ceremony: 1, 3, 5, 7, 9, 13, 15, 16, 17, 21, 26, 27, 31
To marry for happiness: 1, 5, 27
To marry for longevity: None
To end a romance or file for divorce: 12, 13, 14, 15, 16, 17, 18, 19, 20, 21, 22, 23, 24, 25, 26, 27
To repair a car: 21
To sell real estate: 26, 27
To sell personal possessions: 1, 7, 15, 21, 26, 31
For sporting activities: 9
For traveling: 1

•AUGUST•

To advertise the sale of real estate or personal possessions: 5, 6

To advertise the start of a new venture: 5, 6

To buy animals: 1, 2, 25, 26, 28, 29

For neutering or spaying an animal: 7, 8, 9, 10, 11, 18, 19, 20, 21, 22, 23, 24, 25

To dock or dehorn animals: 1, 2, 3, 11, 19, 20, 21, 22, 23, 24, 25, 26, 27, 28, 29, 30, 31

To train a pet: 16, 17, 18

For a permanent wave: 16, 17, 18, 24, 25

To cut hair for thickness: None

To cut hair to retard growth: 14, 15, 19, 20

To cut hair to stimulate growth: 12, 13, 21, 22, 23

To apply for a job: 9, 28

To begin a new job: 8, 9, 26, 27, 28

To ask for a raise or promotion: 5, 15, 16, 23, 26, 28, 31

To entertain: 1, 2, 3, 10, 11, 19, 20, 24, 25, 29, 30

To join a club: 1, 2, 3, 10, 11, 19, 20, 29, 30

For baking: 21, 22, 23

For brewing: 21, 22, 23

To can fruits and vegetables: 21, 22, 23

To dry fruits and vegetables: 14, 15, 19, 20, 24, 25

To make preserves and jellies: 26

To buy a permanent home: 25

To buy real estate for appreciation: 1, 14, 15, 23

To start new house construction: 17

To pour concrete: 4, 8, 17, 22, 31

To remodel a house: 4, 5, 17, 31

To paint the house: 1, 5, 15, 20, 26, 31

To do roofing: 10, 11, 16, 17, 18

To set fence posts: 4, 8, 17, 22, 31

To mow lawn to retard growth: 10, 11, 14, 15, 16, 17, 18, 19, 20, 24, 25

To cut timber: 10, 11, 14, 15, 16, 17, 18, 19, 20, 24, 25

To deal in legal matters: 1, 9, 14, 23, 28
To sign contracts: 16
To see the dentist: 17
To fill teeth: 10, 11, 16, 17, 18
To extract teeth: 19, 20, 26, 27, 28
To consult a physician: 26, 27, 28
To buy medicine: 4, 5, 26, 27, 28, 31
To buy health foods: 26, 27, 28
To start a diet to gain weight: None
To start a diet to lose weight: 10, 11, 14, 15, 24, 25
To collect money: 2, 3, 9, 15, 21, 23, 30
To start a savings account: 16, 17, 18
To seek favors and/or credit: 6, 25
To begin a course of study: 6, 7, 26, 27, 28
To write letters: 6, 7, 12, 13, 19, 20, 26, 27, 28
To stop a bad habit: 27
For dressmaking and/or mending: 1
To buy appliances: 5, 9, 13, 18, 27
To buy antiques: 4, 5, 8, 9, 21, 22, 23, 31
To buy cameras: 4, 13, 17, 27
To buy a car: 6
To buy clothing: 1, 2, 3, 16, 17, 18, 29, 30
To purchase radios: 1, 5, 6, 9, 13, 16, 18, 22, 27, 28
To buy televisions or computers: 5, 9, 13, 18, 27
For a marriage ceremony: 1, 5, 6, 9, 14, 15, 20, 23, 25, 26, 28, 30, 31
To marry for happiness: None
To marry for longevity: None
To end a romance or file for divorce: 10, 11, 12, 13, 14, 15, 16, 17, 18, 19, 20, 21, 22, 23, 24, 25
To repair a car: 18
To sell real estate: 14, 22, 23
To sell personal possessions: 1, 5, 15, 20, 26, 31
For sporting activities: 14, 25
For traveling: 6

•SEPTEMBER•

To advertise the sale of real estate or personal possessions: 1, 29

To advertise the start of a new venture: 1, 16, 29

To buy animals: 2, 24, 25, 29

For neutering or spaying an animal: 3, 4, 5, 6, 7, 14, 15, 16, 17, 18, 19, 20, 21, 22, 30

To dock or dehorn animals: 1, 17, 18, 19, 20, 21, 22, 23, 24, 25, 26, 27, 28, 29, 30

To train a pet: 13, 14

For a permanent wave: 13, 14, 20, 21, 22

To cut hair for thickness: None

To cut hair to retard growth: 10, 11, 12, 15, 16, 17, 23, 24

To cut hair to stimulate growth: 8, 9, 18, 19

To apply for a job: 4, 13, 24

To begin a new job: 4, 5, 24

To ask for a raise or promotion: 1, 4, 6, 14 , 21, 25, 29

To entertain: 6, 7, 15, 16, 17, 20, 21, 22, 25, 26

To join a club: 6, 7, 15, 16, 17, 25, 26

For baking: 18, 19

For brewing: 8, 18, 19

To can fruits and vegetables: 18, 19, 23, 24

To dry fruits and vegetables: 10, 11, 12, 15, 16, 17, 20, 21, 22

To make preserves and jellies: 14

To buy a permanent home: None

To buy real estate for appreciation: 10, 25

To start new house construction: 13

To pour concrete: 5, 13, 18, 28

To remodel a house: 1, 13, 28

To paint the house: 4, 14, 20, 25, 29

To do roofing: 13, 14

To set fence posts: 5, 13, 18, 28

To mow lawn to retard growth: 10, 11, 12, 13, 14, 15, 16, 17, 20, 21, 22, 23, 24

To cut timber: 10, 11, 12, 13, 14, 15, 16, 17, 20, 21, 22, 23, 24

To deal in legal matters: 6, 10, 20, 25, 29
To sign contracts: 6, 20, 21
To see the dentist: 13
To fill teeth: 13, 14
To extract teeth: 2, 16, 17, 23, 24, 29, 30
To consult a physician: 24
To buy medicine: 1, 23, 24, 27, 28
To buy health foods: 23, 24
To start a diet to gain weight: 8
To start a diet to lose weight: 10, 11, 12, 20, 21, 22, 23, 24
To collect money: 4, 10, 11, 18, 19, 25, 26
To start a savings account: 13, 14
To seek favors and/or credit: 6, 20, 29
To begin a course of study: 2, 3, 24, 29, 30
To write letters: 2, 3, 8, 9, 15, 16, 17, 23, 24, 29, 30
To stop a bad habit: 23
For dressmaking and/or mending: 14, 20, 25
To buy appliances: 1, 5, 9, 14, 24, 28
To buy antiques: 1, 4, 5, 18, 19, 27, 28
To buy cameras: 1, 9, 14, 23, 28
To buy a car: 16, 29
To buy clothing: 13, 14, 25, 26
To purchase radios: 1, 5, 6, 9, 14, 16, 21, 24, 25, 28, 29
To buy televisions or computers: 1, 5, 9, 14, 24, 28
For a marriage ceremony: 1, 4, 6, 10, 13, 14, 19, 20, 24, 25, 29
To marry for happiness: 13, 25
To marry for longevity: None
To end a romance or file for divorce: 8, 9, 10, 11, 12, 13, 14, 15, 16, 17, 18, 19, 20, 21, 22, 23, 24
To repair a car: 14
To sell real estate: 10, 18
To sell personal possessions: 4, 14, 20, 25, 29
For sporting activities: 3, 10, 20, 22, 29
For traveling: 16, 21, 29

•OCTOBER•

To advertise the sale of real estate or personal possessions: 27

To advertise the start of a new venture: 12, 27

To buy animals: 1, 28, 29, 30

For neutering or spaying an animal: 1, 2, 3, 4, 5, 12, 13, 14, 15, 16, 17, 18, 19, 28, 29, 30, 31

To dock or dehorn animals: 1, 16, 17, 18, 19, 20, 21, 22, 23, 24, 25, 26, 27, 28, 29, 30, 31

To train a pet: 10, 11, 12

For a permanent wave: 10, 11, 12, 18, 19

To cut hair for thickness: None

To cut hair to retard growth: 9, 13, 14, 20, 21

To cut hair to stimulate growth: 6, 7, 15, 16, 17

To apply for a job: None

To begin a new job: 1, 2, 29, 30

To ask for a raise or promotion: 3, 15, 17, 18, 22, 25, 29, 31

To entertain: 3, 4, 5, 13, 14, 18, 19, 22, 23, 31

To join a club: 3, 4, 5, 13, 14, 22, 23, 31

For baking: 15, 16, 17

For brewing: 16, 17

To can fruits and vegetables: 15, 16, 17, 20, 21

To dry fruits and vegetables: 8, 9, 13, 14, 18, 19

To make preserves and jellies: 15, 20

To buy a permanent home: None

To buy real estate for appreciation: 8, 15, 22

To start new house construction: 11

To pour concrete: 2, 11, 16, 25, 29

To remodel a house: 11, 25

To paint the house: 4, 15, 20, 25, 29

To do roofing: 10, 11, 12

To set fence posts: 2, 11, 16, 25, 29

To mow lawn to retard growth: 8, 9, 10, 11, 12, 13, 14, 18, 19, 20, 21, 22, 23

To cut timber: 8, 9, 10, 11, 12, 13, 14, 18, 19, 20, 21, 22, 23

To deal in legal matters: 3, 8, 18, 22, 27, 31

To sign contracts: 3, 12, 18, 31
To see the dentist: 11
To fill teeth: 10, 11, 12
To extract teeth: 20, 21, 27, 28
To consult a physician: None
To buy medicine: 20, 21, 24, 25, 26
To buy health foods: 20, 21
To start a diet to gain weight: 6, 7
To start a diet to lose weight: 8, 9, 18, 19, 20, 21
To collect money: 1, 2, 8, 9, 15, 16, 17, 22, 23, 29, 30
To start a savings account: 10, 11, 12
To seek favors and/or credit: 3, 4, 18, 19, 27, 28, 31
To begin a course of study: 27, 28
To write letters: 6, 7, 13, 14, 20, 21, 27, 28
To stop a bad habit: 21
For dressmaking and/or mending: None
To buy appliances: 2, 7, 11, 21, 25, 29
To buy antiques: 1, 2, 15, 16, 17, 24, 25, 26, 29, 30
To buy cameras: 6, 11, 21, 25
To buy a car: 27
To buy clothing: 10, 11, 12, 22, 23
To purchase radios: 2, 3, 7, 11, 12, 17, 21, 22, 25, 27, 29, 31
To buy televisions or computers: 2, 7, 11, 21, 25, 29
For a marriage ceremony: 3, 4, 13, 15, 18, 19, 20, 22, 23, 25,
    27, 28, 29, 31
To marry for happiness: 15, 18, 22
To marry for longevity: None
To end a romance or file for divorce: 8, 9, 10, 11, 12, 13,
    14, 15, 16, 17, 18, 19, 20, 21, 22, 23
To repair a car: 11
To sell real estate: 8, 16
To sell personal possessions: 4, 15, 20, 25, 29
For sporting activities: 8, 18, 27
For traveling: 27

•NOVEMBER•

To advertise the sale of real estate or personal possessions: 22, 23

To advertise the start of a new venture: 22, 23

To buy animals: 24, 25, 26, 27

Neuturing or spaying an animal: 1, 8, 9, 10, 11, 12, 13, 14, 15, 24, 25, 26, 27, 28

To dock or dehorn animals: 17, 18, 19, 20, 21, 22, 23, 24, 25, 26, 27, 28

To train a pet: 6, 7, 8

For a permanent wave: 6, 7, 8, 14, 15

To cut hair for thickness: 6, 7

To cut hair to retard growth: 9, 10, 16, 17, 18

To cut hair to stimulate growth: 2, 3, 11, 12, 13, 29, 30

To apply for a job: 17, 26

To begin a new job: 6, 7, 25, 26

To ask for a raise or promotion: 3, 11, 14, 19, 22, 26, 27, 28

To entertain: 1, 9, 10, 14, 15, 19, 20, 27, 28

To join a club: 1, 9, 10, 19, 20, 27, 28

For baking: 11, 12, 13

For brewing: None

To can fruits and vegetables: 11, 12, 13, 16, 17, 18

To dry fruits and vegetables: 9, 10, 14, 15

To make preserves and jellies: None

To buy a permanent home: None

To buy real estate for appreciation: 4, 19

To start new house construction: 7

To pour concrete: 7, 12, 21, 25

To remodel a house: 7, 21, 22

To paint the house: 3, 14, 19, 24, 28

To do roofing: 7, 8

To set fence posts: 7, 12, 21, 25

To mow lawn to retard growth: 7, 8, 9, 10, 14, 15, 16, 17, 18, 19, 20, 21, 22

To cut timber: 7, 8, 9, 10, 14, 15, 16, 17, 18, 19, 20

To deal in legal matters: 4, 14, 19, 23, 27
To sign contracts: 14, 27
To see the dentist: 7
To fill teeth: 7, 8
To extract teeth: 16, 17, 18, 23, 24
To consult a physician: None
To buy medicine: 16, 17, 18, 21, 22
To buy health foods: 16, 17, 18
To start a diet to gain weight: 2, 3, 29, 30
To start a diet to lose weight: 14, 15, 16, 17, 18
To collect money: 4, 5, 11, 12, 13, 19, 20, 25, 26
To start a savings account: 6, 7, 8
To seek favors and/or credit: 2, 3, 14, 23, 24, 27, 28
To begin a course of study: 23, 24
To write letters: 2, 3, 9, 10, 16, 17, 18, 23, 24, 29, 30
To stop a bad habit: 17
For dressmaking and/or mending: 14, 19
To buy appliances: 3, 8, 18, 22, 26, 30
To buy antiques: 11, 12, 13, 21, 22, 25, 26
To buy cameras: 3, 7, 17, 22, 30
To buy a car: None
To buy clothing: 6, 7, 8, 19, 20
To purchase radios: 3, 8, 11, 17, 18, 22, 26, 30
To buy televisions or computers: 3, 8, 18, 22, 26, 30
For marriage ceremony: 2, 3, 4, 12, 14, 17, 19, 22, 23, 24, 26, 27, 28
To marry for happiness: 12, 14, 19
To marry for longevity: None
To end a romance or file for divorce: 7, 8, 9, 10, 11, 12, 13, 14, 15, 16, 17, 18, 19, 20, 21, 22
To repair a car: 8
To sell real estate: 4, 12
To sell personal possessions: 3, 14, 19, 24, 28
For sporting activities: 4, 14, 23
For traveling: None

•DECEMBER•

To advertise the sale of real estate or personal possessions: 21

To advertise the start of a new venture: 21

To buy animals: 22, 23, 24

For neutering or spaying an animal: 5, 6, 7, 8, 9, 10, 11, 12, 13, 21, 22, 23, 24, 25

To dock or dehorn animals: 13, 14, 15, 16, 17, 18, 19, 20, 21, 22, 23, 24, 25

To train a pet: 4, 5

For a permanent wave: 4, 5, 11, 12, 13

To cut hair for thickness: None

To cut hair to retard growth: 7, 8, 14, 15

To cut hair to stimulate growth: 9, 10, 26, 27, 28

To apply for a job: None

To begin a new job: 4, 5, 22, 23

To ask for a raise or promotion: 1, 2, 12, 13, 17, 18, 19, 24, 25, 28, 30

To entertain: 6, 7, 8, 11, 12, 13, 16, 17, 24, 25

To join a club: 6, 7, 8, 16, 17, 24, 25

For baking: 9, 10

For brewing: None

To can fruits and vegetables: 9, 10, 14, 15

To dry fruits and vegetables: 6, 7, 8, 11, 12, 13, 20, 21

To make preserves and jellies: 14

To buy a permanent home: None

To buy real estate for appreciation: 2, 3, 17, 30

To start new house construction: 4

To pour concrete: 4, 9, 19, 23

To remodel a house: 4, 19, 20

To paint the house: 3, 14, 19, 24, 28

To do roofing: None

To set fence posts: 4, 9, 19, 23

To mow lawn to retard growth: 6, 7, 8, 11, 12, 13, 14, 15, 16, 17, 18, 19, 20, 21

To cut timber: 6, 7, 8, 11, 12, 13, 14, 15, 16, 17, 20, 21
To deal in legal matters: 2, 12, 17, 21, 25, 30
To sign contracts: 12, 13, 25
To see the dentist: 4
To fill teeth: None
To extract teeth: 15, 20, 21
To consult a physician: None
To buy medicine: 14, 15, 18, 19
To buy health foods: 14, 15
To start a diet to gain weight: 26, 27, 28
To start a diet to lose weight: 11, 12, 13, 14, 15, 20, 21
To collect money: 1, 2, 3, 9, 10, 17, 22, 30
To start a savings account: 4, 5
To seek favors and/or credit: 12, 21, 24, 25, 26, 28
To begin a course of study: 6, 21
To write letters: 6, 7, 8, 14, 15, 20, 21, 26, 27, 28
To stop a bad habit: 15
For dressmaking and/or mending: None
To buy appliances: 5, 15, 19, 23, 28
To buy antiques: 9, 10, 18, 19, 22, 23
To buy cameras: 5, 15, 19, 27
To buy clothing: 4, 5, 16, 17
To purchase radios: 1, 5, 13, 15, 18, 19, 23, 27, 28
To buy televisions or computers: 5, 15, 19, 23, 28
For a marriage ceremony: 1, 2, 3, 12, 14, 17, 19, 21, 24, 25, 26, 28, 30
To marry for happiness: 12
To marry for longevity: None
To end a romance or file for divorce: 6, 7, 8, 9, 10, 11, 12, 13, 14, 15, 16, 17, 18, 19, 20, 21
To repair a car: 5
To sell real estate: 2, 9, 30
To sell personal possessions: 3, 14, 19, 24, 28
For sporting activities: 2, 3, 12, 13, 21, 30
For traveling: 13

MOON VOID OF COURSE

Just before the Moon enters a new sign it will have one last aspect with one of the planets. Between that last major aspect and the entrance of the Moon into the next sign, it is said to be "void of course."

Decisions made while the Moon is void of course don't come to fruition in the way intended, and sometimes not at all. Decisions that are made during that time are usually later seen to be based on delusion, or an unrealistic presumption. When the Moon is void of course, try to carry on activities that previously had been planned.

Often purchases made during this time turn out to be poorly made, left unused, plagued with mechanical problems, or simply a bad investment.

It is nearly impossible in today's world to put off all decisions every time the Moon is void, but try to avoid this period for the most important ones. Or try to make the decision before the Moon is void, and then act on the decision at this time.

•JANUARY•

Last Aspect	Moon Enters New Sign
2 12:57 PM	2 Aquarius 1:39 PM
4 4:12 PM	4 Pisces 4:49 PM
6 11:24 PM	6 Aries 11:57 PM
9 2:50 AM	9 Taurus 10:58 AM
11 11:40 PM	11 Gemini 11:57 PM
12 7:01 PM	14 Cancer 12:20 PM
16 10:36 PM	16 Leo 10:37 PM
18 5:47 AM	19 Virgo 6:40 AM
21 6:58 AM	21 Libra 12:54 PM
23 5:07 PM	23 Scorpio 5:33 PM
25 7:12 PM	25 Sagittarius 8:37 PM
27 8:00 PM	27 Capricorn 10:27 PM
29 7:21 PM	30 Aquarius 12:03 AM
31 10:06 PM	1 Pisces 3:05 AM

•FEBRUARY•

Last Aspect	Moon Enters New Sign
3 6:21 AM	3 Aries 9:12 AM
5 2:18 PM	5 Taurus 7:08 PM
8 3:04 AM	8 Gemini 7:44 AM
10 7:23 AM	10 Cancer 8:17 PM
13 2:43 AM	13 Leo 6:32 AM
15 7:16 AM	15 Virgo 1:52 PM
17 3:55 PM	17 Libra 7:01 PM
19 8:04 PM	19 Scorpio 10:55 PM
21 11:34 PM	22 Sagittarius 2:13 AM
23 9:40 AM	24 Capricorn 5:10 AM
26 5:57 AM	26 Aquarius 8:14 AM
27 1:44 PM	28 Pisces 12:16 PM

•MARCH•

Last Aspect	Moon Enters New Sign
2 4:25 PM	2 Aries 6:30 PM
5 1:52 AM	5 Taurus 3:51 AM
7 2:07 PM	7 Gemini 3:56 PM
9 2:47 PM	10 Cancer 4:41 AM
12 2:10 PM	12 Leo 3:29 PM
13 7:22 PM	14 Virgo 10:55 PM
17 2:26 AM	17 Libra 3:18 AM
19 5:09 AM	19 Scorpio 5:52 AM
21 7:22 AM	21 Sagittarius 7:57AM
23 12:24 AM	23 Capricorn 10:31 AM
25 1:48 PM	25 Aquarius 2:10 PM
27 6:50 PM	27 Pisces 7:18 PM
30 2:19 AM	30 Aries 2:26 AM

•APRIL•

Last Aspect	Moon Enters New Sign
1 2:55 AM	1 Taurus 11:59 AM
3 2:31 PM	3 Gemini 11:50 PM
5 1:46 PM	6 Cancer 12:40 PM
8 3:24 PM	9 Leo 12:16 AM
10 3:11 PM	11 Virgo 8:39 AM
13 5:38 AM	13 Libra 1:20 PM
15 9:13 AM	15 Scorpio 3:13 PM
17 8:37 AM	17 Sagittarius 3:52 PM
19 3:47 PM	19 Capricorn 4:54 PM
21 7:36 PM	21 Aquarius 7:38 PM
24 12:43 AM	24 Pisces 12:51 AM
26 8:27 AM	26 Aries 8:42 AM
28 10:08 AM	28 Taurus 6:53 AM

•MAY•

Last Aspect	Moon Enters New Sign
1 6:23 AM	1 Gemini 6:53 AM
3 2:38 AM	3 Cancer 7:45 PM
6 7:09 AM	6 Leo 7:55 AM
8 4:43 PM	8 Virgo 5:33 PM
10 10:37 PM	10 Libra 11:30 PM
12 6:30 PM	13 Scorpio 1:54 AM
15 12:59 AM	15 Sagittarius 1:59 AM
16 7:36 PM	17 Capricorn 1:36 AM
19 1:26 AM	19 Aquarius 2:40 AM
21 6:36 AM	21 Pisces 6:40 AM
23 12:35 PM	23 Aries 2:13 PM
25 3:32 PM	26 Taurus 12:46 AM
28 11:06 AM	28 Gemini 1:07 PM
30 1:08 PM	31 Cancer 1:59 AM

•JUNE•

Last Aspect	Moon Enters New Sign
2 12:03 PM	2 Leo :217 PM
4 10:30 PM	5 Virgo 12:47 AM
7 5:59 AM	7 Libra 8:14 AM
9 12:02 PM	9 Scorpio 12:04 PM
11 12:44 PM	11 Sagittarius 12:50 PM
13 3:09 AM	13 Capricorn 12:05 PM
15 11:34 AM	15 Aquarius 11:52 AM
17 11:36 AM	17 Pisces 2:13 PM
19 7:53 PM	19 Aries 8:29 PM
22 5:48 AM	22 Taurus 6:35 AM
24 6:03 PM	24 Gemini 7:02 PM
26 9:11 PM	27 Cancer 7:57 AM
29 6:44 PM	29 Leo 8:02 PM

•JULY•

Last Aspect		Moon Enters New Sign		
2	3:06 AM	2	Virgo	6:36 AM
4	1:50 PM	4	Libra	2:56 PM
6	6:44 PM	6	Scorpio	8:19 PM
8	8:59 PM	8	Sagittarius	10:38 PM
10	2:22 PM	10	Capricorn	10:43 PM
12	8:29 PM	12	Aquarius	10:21 PM
14	8:12 PM	14	Pisces	11:37 PM
17	1:58 AM	17	Aries	4:24 AM
19	10:34 AM	19	Taurus	1:21 PM
21	11:12 PM	22	Gemini	1:24 AM
24	3:07 AM	24	Cancer	2:17 PM
26	10:44 PM	27	Leo	2:07 AM
29	8:06 AM	29	Virgo	12:13 PM
31	4:53 PM	31	Libra	8:24 PM

•AUGUST•

Last Aspect		Moon Enters New Sign		
2	10:57 PM	3	Scorpio	2:30 AM
5	2:43 AM	5	Sagittarius	6:14 AM
6	11:20 PM	7	Capricorn	7:52 AM
9	4:55 AM	9	Aquarius	8:28 AM
11	6:07 PM	11	Pisces	9:46 AM
13	9:48 AM	13	Aries	1:41 PM
15	4:42 PM	15	Taurus	9:26 PM
18	4:20 AM	18	Gemini	8:40 AM
20	4:05 PM	20	Cancer	9:24 PM
23	5:03 AM	23	Leo	9:13 AM
25	2:53 PM	25	Virgo	6:50 PM
28	12:07 AM	28	Libra	2:15 AM
30	2:42 AM	30	Scorpio	7:51 AM

•SEPTEMBER•

Last Aspect	Moon Enters New Sign
1 8:29 AM	1 Sagittarius 11:57 AM
3 10:44 AM	3 Capricorn 2:45 PM
5 3:12 PM	5 Aquarius 4:48 PM
7 3:52 PM	7 Pisces 7:09 PM
9 7:53 PM	9 Aries 11:15 PM
12 12:16 AM	12 Taurus 6:22 AM
14 1:13 PM	14 Gemini 4:48 PM
16 4:09 PM	17 Cancer 5:16 AM
19 1:59 PM	19 Leo 5:19 PM
21 11:57 PM	22 Virgo 3:01 AM
24 7:00 AM	24 Libra 9:50 AM
26 8:25 AM	26 Scorpio 2:20 PM
28 3:02 PM	28 Sagittarius 5:31 PM
30 3:34 AM	30 Capricorn 8:11 PM

•OCTOBER•

Last Aspect	Moon Enters New Sign
2 8:42 PM	2 Aquarius 11:00 PM
5 12:21 AM	5 Pisces 2:36 AM
7 5:30 AM	7 Aries 7:42 AM
9 1:49 PM	9 Taurus 3:05 PM
11 11:02 PM	12 Gemini 1:10 AM
13 5:20 PM	14 Cancer 1:20 PM
16 11:58 PM	17 Leo 1:47 AM
19 10:38 AM	19 Virgo 12:12 PM
21 5:56 PM	21 Libra 7:16 PM
23 5:28 PM	23 Scorpio 11:07 PM
25 11:58 PM	26 Sagittarius 12:57 AM
27 7:24 AM	28 Capricorn 2:15 AM
30 3:39 AM	30 Aquarius 4:24 AM

•NOVEMBER•

Last Aspect	Moon Enters New Sign
1 7:40 AM	1 Pisces 8:18 AM
3 1:51 PM	3 Aries 2:21 PM
5 4:42 PM	5 Taurus 10:35 PM
8 8:44 AM	8 Gemini 8:55 PM
9 9:01 PM	10 Cancer 8:57 PM
13 3:50 AM	13 Leo 9:38 AM
15 6:41 AM	15 Virgo 9:03 PM
18 12:23 AM	18 Libra 5:18 AM
20 5:14 AM	20 Scorpio 9:41 AM
22 10:43 AM	22 Sagittarius 10:57 AM
24 4:33 AM	24 Capricorn 10:48 AM
26 7:18 AM	26 Aquarius 11:15 AM
28 11:29 AM	28 Pisces 1:59 PM
30 3:45 PM	30 Aries 7:51 PM

•DECEMBER•

Last Aspect	Moon Enters New Sign
3 12:34 AM	3 Taurus 4:40 AM
5 11:36 AM	5 Gemini 3:35 PM
7 3:37 PM	8 Cancer 3:45 AM
10 12:50 PM	10 Leo 4:25 PM
12 6:51 PM	13 Virgo 4:27 AM
15 11:18 AM	15 Libra 2:09 PM
17 5:40 PM	17 Scorpio 8:07 PM
19 8:07 PM	19 Sagittarius 10:13 PM
21 9:22 PM	21 Capricorn 9:46 PM
23 7:08 PM	23 Aquarius 8:52 PM
25 6:35 PM	25 Pisces 9:45 PM
28 12:33 AM	28 Aries 2:06 AM
30 8:57 AM	30 Taurus 10:22 AM

RETROGRADES

When the planets cross the sky, they occasionally appear to move backward as seen from Earth. When a planet turns "backward" it is said to be *retrograde*. When it turns forward again it is said to go *direct*. The point at which the movement changes from one direction to another is called a *station*.

When a planet is retrograde its expression is delayed or out of kilter with the normal progression of events. Generally, it can be said that whatever is planned during this period will be delayed, but usually it will come to fruition when the retrograde is over. Of course, this only applies to activities ruled by the planet which is retrograde.

Although retrogrades of all the planets are of significance, those involving Mercury and Venus are particularly easy to follow and of personal use.

Mercury Retrograde

Mercury rules informal communications—reading, writing, speaking and short errands. Whenever Mercury goes retrograde, personal communications get fouled up or misunderstood more often. Letters get lost, more misspellings occur and so on. So the rule astrologers have developed is, *when Mercury is retrograde, avoid means of communication of an informal nature.*

Venus Retrograde

This is the planet of love, affection, friendship and marriage, so the retrograde is an unreliable time for these activities. Misunderstandings and alienations of an affectional nature are more common.

PLANETARY STATIONS FOR 1995
(Eastern Standard Time)

Planet	Begin		End	
Mars	01/02/95	4:14 PM	03/24/95	11:18 PM
Mercury	01/25/95	8:10 PM	02/15/95	11:59 PM
Pluto	03/03/95	5:19 PM	08/08/95	7:08 AM
Jupiter	04/01/95	6:19 AM	08/02/95	11:14 AM
Neptune	04/27/95	12:36 PM	10/04/95	7:14 PM
Uranus	05/04/95	10:45 PM	10/06/95	5:16 AM
Mercury	05/24/95	3:57 PM	06/17/95	1:51 PM
Saturn	07/06/95	2:03 AM	11/21/95	2:13 PM
Mercury	09/22/95	4:08 AM	10/13/95	7:42 PM

BEST DAYS FOR YOUR
SPECIAL PURPOSES

When you wish to choose a favorable day for something other than matters governed by your own ruling planet, read the following list and note the planet which rules the matter in question. Turn to the list of Favorable and Unfavorable Days in the Moon Tables section. Choose a date for the activity listed below that is both marked favorable (F or f) for your Sun sign and one that is marked with an X or T in the Lunar Aspectarian under the planet described. Never choose a date for any of these activities which is marked with an O or Q under Saturn, Mars or Uranus, as these are negative aspects. They tend to counteract good results.

The more good aspects in operation on the date you choose, the better the outlook for your affairs. *The better the day, the better the deed.* To recapitulate: Choose a date from the proper lists of dates marked X or T under the planet ruling the activity and also marked F or f in your own sign, but never a date marked O or Q in the Lunar Aspectarian to Mars, Saturn or Uranus.

Moon
For housecleaning or baking, putting up preserves, washing, using liquids or chemicals, for matters connected with babies or small children, and to deal with the public in general, choose the good aspects of the Moon.

Sun
To gain favors of persons of high rank, title or prominent social standing, or those in government office, to make a change or try for promotion, choose the good dates of the Sun.

Mercury
For writing or signing an important document, seeking news or information, shopping, studying, dealing with literary matters, choose the good dates of Mercury.

Venus
To give a successful party, ball or entertainment, to marry, for matters of courtship, art, beauty, adornment, to cultivate the friendship of a woman, choose the good dates of Venus.

Mars
For dealing with surgeons, dentists, hair stylists, assayers, contractors, mechanics, lumber workers,

police officers, army or navy personnel, choose the good dates of Mars.

Jupiter

To deal with physicians, educators, sportspeople, bankers, brokers, philanthropists, to collect money or make important changes, choose the good dates of Jupiter.

Saturn

For dealing with plumbers, excavators or miners, for starting a new building, leasing a house or dealing in land, choose the good dates of Saturn.

Uranus

For successful work on an invention, for dealing with inventors, metaphysicians, astrologers or new thought people, for new methods, or starting a journey, choose the good dates of Uranus.

Neptune

For affairs connected with the deep sea or liquids in general, for practicing psychometry or developing mediumship, photography, tobacco and drugs, choose the good dates of Neptune.

Pluto

For uncovering errors, overcoming habits, healing, fumigation, pasteurizing, pest control, also for matters related to the affairs of the dead, taxes, inheritance, etc., choose the good dates of Pluto.

TABLE OF TERMS REFERRING TO LUNAR QUARTERS (PHASES)

Sun-Moon Angle	Moon Sign Book Term	Common Terms	Division by:	
		2	4	8
0-90° after Conjunction	First Quarter	Increasing Waxing Light New	New Moon	New Moon / Crescent
90-180°	Second Quarter		First Quarter	First Quarter / Gibbous
180-270°	Third Quarter	Decreasing Waning Dark Old	Full Moon	Full Moon / Disseminating
270-360°	Fourth Quarter		Last Quarter	Last Quarter / Balsamic

Home & Family

★ Cooking & the Moon

HONEY MOON

Moon and June and honeymoon have rhymed in more than one love song, and that is because the June wedding has connections not only with Greco/Roman-Mediterranean traditions, but with the Anglo-Saxon as well. According to the lunar calendar of the ancient Anglo-Saxons, the month that followed the spectacular blossoming of flowers in May was called the Mead Moon. Mead is a sacred drink made of fermented honey, and many magickal properties have been attributed to it. After the abundance of pollen and nectar gathered by bees from the blossoms of May, beehives fairly overflowed with honey which could be gathered to make the sacred drink. And so the lunar month in June came to be known as the Mead Moon, or the Honey Moon.

—Excerpt from *Rites of Passage*
by Pauline Campanelli, illustrated by Dan Campanelli
(Llewellyn Publications, 1994)

HOME & FAMILY

Automobiles
Choose a favorable date for your Sun sign when the Moon is in a fixed sign (Taurus, Leo, Scorpio, Aquarius), well-aspected by the Sun (X or T) and not aspected by Mars and Saturn (the planets of accidents).

Automobile Repair
Repair work is more successful when begun with the Moon in a fixed sign (Taurus, Leo, Scorpio, Aquarius), and well-aspected to the Sun. First and second quarters are the best Moon phases. Avoid unfavorable aspects (Q or O) with Mars, Saturn, Uranus, Neptune or Pluto.

Baking
Baking should be done when the Moon is in a cardinal sign (Aries, Cancer, Libra, Capricorn). Bakers who have experimented with these rules say that

dough rises higher and bread is lighter during the increase of the Moon (first or second quarter).

Brewing
It is best to brew during the Full Moon and the fourth quarter. Plan to have the Moon in a water sign (Cancer, Scorpio, Pisces).

Building
Turning the first sod for the foundation of a home or laying the cornerstone for a public building marks the beginning of the building. Excavate, lay foundations, and pour cement when the Moon is full and in a fixed sign (Taurus, Leo, Aquarius). Saturn should be aspected, but not Mars, for Mars aspects may indicate accidents.

Canning
Can fruits and vegetables when the Moon is in either the third or fourth quarter, and when it is in one of the water signs (Cancer, Scorpio, Pisces). For preserves and jellies, use the same quarters but see that the Moon is in one of the fixed signs (Taurus, Scorpio, Aquarius).

Cement and Concrete
Pour cement for foundations and concrete for walks and pavements during the Full Moon. It is best, too, for the Moon to be in one of the fixed signs (Taurus, Leo, Aquarius).

Dressmaking
Design, cut, repair or make clothes during the first and second quarters on a day marked favorable for your Sun sign. Venus, Jupiter and Mercury should be aspected, but avoid Mars or Saturn aspects.

William Lily wrote in 1676, "make no new clothes, or first put them on when the Moon is in Scorpio or afflicted by Mars, for they will be apt to be torn and quickly worn out." (Also see *Buying Clothing* in the Business section.)

Fence Posts and Poles
Set posts or poles when the Moon is in the third or fourth quarter. The fixed signs (Taurus, Leo, Aquarius) are best for this.

House
If you desire a permanent home, buy when the Moon is in one of the fixed signs (Taurus, Leo, Scorpio, Aquarius). If you're buying for speculation and a quick turnover, be certain that the Moon is not in a fixed sign, but in one of the cardinal signs (Aries, Cancer, Libra, Capricorn).

House Furnishings
Follow the same rules for buying clothing, avoiding days when Mars is aspected. Days when Saturn is aspected make things wear longer and tend to a more conservative purchase. Saturn days are good for buying, and Jupiter days are good for selling.

Lost Articles
Search for lost articles during the first quarter and when your Sun sign is marked favorable. Also check to see that the planet ruling the lost item is trine, sextile or conjunct the Moon. The Moon governs household utensils, Mercury letters and books, and Venus clothing, jewelry and money.

Marriage
As a general rule, the best time for marriage to take place is during the increase of the Moon, just past the first quarter. Such marriages will bear a higher tendency towards optimism. Good signs for the Moon to be in are Taurus, Cancer, Leo, Libra and Pisces. The Moon in Taurus produces the most steadfast marriages, but if the partners later want to separate they may have a very difficult time. Avoid Aries, Gemini, Virgo, Scorpio and Aquarius. Make sure that the Moon is well-aspected (X or T), especially to Venus or Jupiter. Avoid aspects to Mars, Uranus or Pluto.

Moving into a House or Office
Make sure that Mars is not aspected to the Moon. Try to move on a day which is favorable to your Sun sign, or when the Moon is conjunct, sextile or trine the Sun.

Mowing the Lawn
Mow the lawn in the first or second quarter to increase growth. If you wish to retard growth, mow in the third or fourth quarter.

Painting
The best time to paint buildings is during the decrease of the Moon (third and fourth quarter).

If the weather is hot, do the painting while the Moon is in Taurus; if the weather is cold, paint while the Moon is in Leo. By painting in the fourth quarter, the wood is drier and the paint will penetrate; when painting around the New Moon the wood is damp and the paint is subject to scalding when hot weather hits it. It is not advisable to paint while the Moon is in a water sign if the temperature is below 70 degrees, as it is apt to creep, check or run.

Pets
Take home new pets when the date is favorable to your Sun sign, or the Moon is well-aspected by the Sun, Venus, Jupiter, Uranus or Neptune. Avoid days when the Moon is afflicted by the Sun, Mars, Saturn, Uranus, Neptune or Pluto.

When selecting a new pet it is good to have the Moon well-aspected by the planet which rules the animal. Cats are ruled by the Sun, dogs by Mercury, birds by Venus, horses by Jupiter, and fish by Neptune.

Train pets starting when the Moon is in Taurus. Neuter them in any sign but Virgo, Libra, Scorpio or Sagittarius. Avoid the week before and after the Full Moon. Declaw cats in the dark of the Moon. Avoid the week before and after the Full Moon and the sign of Pisces.

Predetermining Sex
Count from the last day of menstruation to the day next beginning, and divide the interval between the two dates into halves.

Pregnancy occurring in the first half produces females, but copulation should take place when the Moon is in a feminine sign.

Pregnancy occurring in the later half, up to within three days of the beginning of menstruation, produces males, but copulation should take place when the Moon is in a masculine sign. This three-day period to the end of the first half of the next period again produces females.

Romance
The same principles hold true for starting a relationship as for marriage. However, since there is less control over when a romance starts, it is sometimes necessary to study it after the fact. Romances begun under an increasing Moon are more likely to be permanent, or at least satisfying. Those started on the waning Moon will more readily transform the participants. The general tone of the relationship can be guessed from the sign the Moon is in. For instance, those begun when the Moon is in Capricorn will take greater effort to bring to a desirable conclusion, but may be very rewarding. Those begun when the Moon is in Aries may be impulsive and quick to burn out. Good aspects between the Moon and Venus are excellent influences. Avoid Mars, Uranus and Pluto aspects. Ending relationships is facilitated by a decreasing

Moon, particularly in the fourth quarter. This causes the least pain and attachment.

Sauerkraut
The best sauerkraut is made just after the Full Moon in a fruitful sign (Cancer, Scorpio, Pisces).

Shingling
Shingling should be done in the decrease of the Moon (third or fourth quarter) when it is in a fixed sign (Taurus, Leo, Scorpio, Aquarius). If shingles are laid during the New Moon, they have a tendency to curl at the edges.

Weaning Children
This should be done when the Moon is in Sagittarius, Capricorn, Aquarius or Pisces. The child should nurse the last time in a fruitful sign. Venus should then be trine, sextile or conjunct the Moon.

Wine and Drinks Other Than Beer
It is best to start when the Moon is in Pisces or Taurus. Good aspects (X or T) with Venus are favorable. Avoid aspects with Mars or Saturn.

COOKING & THE MOON

By Patricia Telesco

How often have you looked to the moonlit sky with admiration and wonder? Somehow this silver sphere encourages magical dreams and romance wherever it shines.

With this in mind, it is not surprising that the Moon is associated with the unconscious mind, the element of water, nurturing, intuitive nature and fertility. But what does this have to do with cooking? The answer to that question depends on a little creativity and thought.

Any food or beverage prepared when the Moon is shining can help to encourage inspirational energy in your life.

Many bits of superstition and folklore have been handed down to us regarding when is the best time to prepare certain foods. Here are a few examples for consideration in your own kitchen:

Beverages

It was thought prudent to brew when the Moon was waxing to full for proper fermentation to occur. Why not give mead making a try? Here is one easy recipe:

LUNAR MEAD

1-16 oz. bottle papaya juice (check health food stores)
12 medium apples, peeled and sliced
1-16 oz. bottle mineral water
2 cups fresh coconut, mashed, with juice
½ lemon, sliced
1½ pounds dark honey
1 teaspoon active yeast

Place the papaya juice, apples, mineral water and coconut in a large cooking pot on the first night of the Full Moon. Slowly warm these, adding the lemon and honey just as the water begins to boil. Skim any debris that rises from the honey off the top of the water while the mixture remains at a low rolling boil for about 15 minutes. Turn the heat off and cover. When the liquid is cool, remove the lemon slices and refrigerate until the next night.

Strain the liquid on the second night, removing as much of the apple as possible. Then warm the liquid slightly on the stove. Meanwhile, dissolve the yeast in ¼ cup warm water. When the beverage is lukewarm, add the yeast, stirring once, then cover the pot to sit until the next night. Do not refrigerate or you may kill the yeast.

Strain the entire mixture, using cheesecloth or other fine netting, into a *sterilized* gallon jug which can be loosely corked. You will notice that the liquid bubbles. This is a sign of proper fermentation. Leave the bottle covered loosely for about one month, then slowly tighten the cork. Mixture is ready to drink in about eight months. If you find that the mead is too sweet after eight months, try fermenting it longer.

Health Foods

To encourage continual health, stamina and vigor in your life, prepare healthy foods (chicken soup, orange juice, etc.) during a waxing to Full Moon.

To help rid yourself of maladies, shrink your sickness by cooking healthy foods during the waning Moon. If you can't do this during a waning Moon, consider the alternative of preparing the item just before dawn, when the moonlight is disappearing.

Lunar gourmets should take into consideration foods and herbs that are already spiritually aligned with the Moon. The following traditional affiliations came about from years of folklore, astrological associations, and old-fashioned observation.

ITEM	ASSOCIATION
Cabbage	good fortune
Coconut	purity, safety
Cucumber	beauty, sexuality
Lettuce	prosperity
Lemon	love, cleansing

ITEM	ASSOCIATION
Mesquite (use on barbecue)	well being, magic
Papaya	passion, love
Potato	grounding, healing
Turnip	protection, separation
Wintergreen	banishing, health

You might try eating a cabbage and lettuce salad when the Moon is full if you wish to encourage prosperity and luck in your life. To tone down a slightly overheated relationship, consume papaya mixed with coconut and honey during the waning Moon. To rid negative thought patterns from your life, drink a cup of wintergreen tea under a New Moon. The whole idea is to allow the emblematic nature of the Moon to embellish any type of food.

To take this concept one step further, you can enhance your culinary wizardry by considering the Moon sign as well as the phase. To illustrate, when you are concentrating on learning, don't just prepare a meal which includes celery or rosemary (for mental acuity). Prepare it during the waxing Moon of Aries or Libra to empower your effort. Here is a list of associations to consider. Remember to keep your intentions firmly in mind while you prepare and eat these foods.

Waxing Moon: Progress, development, fruitfulness, positive energy and improvements. **Examples:** Banana carrot cake, grape juice, peach pie or rice with bamboo shoots.

Waning Moon: Abatement, slowing, banishing negative energy. **Examples:** Garlic leek soup, mint tea, or sweet red pepper salad.

Blue Moon: The second Full Moon of a month; time for miracles! **Examples:** Pineapple-orange juice with a hint of allspice, huckleberry muffins, or fresh strawberries.

Moon in Aries: Purification, focus on personal arts or creative endeavors, removing obstacles. **Examples:** Chamomile tea with one bay leaf added, lemon pie, roast beef with shallots and horseradish.

Moon in Taurus: Resourcefulness, stubborn will, prosperity, perseverance. **Examples:** Green salad with alfalfa sprouts and slivered almonds, banana nut bread, tomato sauce, fresh celery.

Moon in Gemini: Leisure and transformation, overcoming bad habits, stabilizing drastically different energies. **Examples:** Olives and candied ginger, parsley, black beans and rice.

Moon in Cancer: Ingenuity and shrewdness. **Examples:** Sage and cheese quiche, peach ice cream, date cookies.

Moon in Leo: New proficiencies or characteristics, strength. **Examples:** Tea with a hint of saffron, mulberry wine, ginger ale, bread with a hint of nutmeg.

Moon in Virgo: Productivity, monetary improvements, success. **Examples:** Apple pie spiced with cinnamon and ginger, cucumber dill salad, minted peas, oatmeal, mustard sauces.

Moon in Libra: Symmetry, uncovering the hidden, development of insight, perception. **Examples:** Onion soup, spearmint tea, baked celery with thyme sauce.

Moon in Scorpio: Contemplation, analysis, fire. **Examples:** Caraway spiced rolls, rosemary herbed sauce, orange cashew pie, fish with lime juice.

Moon in Sagittarius: Groundwork, thrift and command of personal matters. Being on target. **Examples**: Fresh vegetable salad, all root foods like beets, onions, carrots; orange juice with a touch of cinnamon.

Moon in Capricorn: Evolution, support, focus on the secret self. **Examples:** Pot pies, turnovers and souffle, homemade tea or wine.

Moon in Aquarius: Sharing, rest, peaceful leisure. **Examples:** Anything with lemon or olives, lamb with mint sauce, creamy white foods like mashed potatoes.

Moon in Pisces: Abundance, flow, fertility and miracles. **Examples:** tomato rice soup, date or wheat breads, sunflower seeds, coconut cookies.

PERFUMES OF THE ZODIAC

Each sign of the zodiac rules a special category of perfume essences, in keeping with the symbolic nature of the sun's ruling planet, according to astrology.

Aries perfumes are all pungent, with overtones of bitterness, and are often described as "masculine."

Taurus rules sweet, flowery fragrances, especially those distilled from roses and other fragile blooms symbolic of romance.

Gemini's perfumes convey an airy, fresh-outdoors impression to the sense of smell.

Cancer pertains to all those perfumes derived from water flowers, such as the lotus, and in which ambergris is the base.

Leo's fragrances are stronger than average, and have a lasting, penetrating quality. The "anointing oil" of kings and priests was a Leo substance.

Virgo's perfumes are just the opposite, being gentle and "modest," such as those extracted from the lily-of-the-valley.

Libra rules over odors obtained from vine blossoms and climbing flowers.

Scorpio perfumes have musk as their base, and are "heavy" and "hypnotic" in effect.

Sagittarius has rule over the typical "Oriental" perfumes, with their exotic and "foreign" qualities.

Capricorn's fragrances are those taken from night-blooming flowers, such as the jasmine.

Aquarius rules highly pungent, spicy perfumes, such as are used in colognes and aftershave lotions.

Pisces essences are heavy and exotic like Scorpio's, and seem to have enchantment and captivation as their purpose.

Leisure & Recreation

★ Fishing & Hunting Dates
★ Moon Guide to Gambling

LEISURE & RECREATION

The best time to perform an activity is when its ruling planet is in favorable aspect to the Moon or when the Moon is in its ruling sign—that is, when its ruling planet is trine, sextile or conjunct the Moon (marked T, X or C in the Lunar Aspectarian or when its ruling sign is marked F in the Favorable and Unfavorable Days tables).

Animals and Hunting
Animals in general: Mercury, Jupiter, Virgo, Pisces
Animal training: Mercury, Virgo
Cats: Leo, Sun, Virgo, Venus
Dogs: Mercury, Virgo
Fish: Neptune, Pisces, Moon, Cancer
Birds: Mercury, Venus
Game animals: Sagittarius
Horses, trainers, riders: Jupiter, Sagittarius
Hunters: Jupiter, Sagittarius

Arts

Acting, actors: Neptune, Pisces, Sun, Leo
Art in general: Venus, Libra
Ballet: Neptune, Venus
Ceramics: Saturn
Crafts: Mercury, Venus
Dancing: Venus, Taurus, Neptune, Pisces
Drama: Venus, Neptune
Embroidery: Venus
Etching: Mars
Films, filmmaking: Neptune, Leo, Uranus, Aquarius
Literature: Mercury, Gemini
Music: Venus, Libra, Taurus, Neptune
Painting: Venus, Libra
Photography: Neptune, Pisces, Uranus, Aquarius
Printing: Mercury, Gemini
Theaters: Sun, Leo, Venus

Fishing

During the summer months the best time of the day for fishing is from sunrise to three hours after, and from about two hours before sunset until one hour after. In cooler months, the fish are not biting until the air is warm. At this time the best hours are from noon to 3 PM. Warm and cloudy days are good. The most favorable winds are from the south and southwest. Easterly winds are unfavorable. The best days of the month for fishing are those on which the Moon changes quarters, especially if the change occurs on a day when the Moon is in a watery sign (Cancer, Scorpio, Pisces). The best period in any month is the day after the Full Moon.

Friends
The need for friendship is greater when Uranus aspects the Moon, or the Moon is in Aquarius. Friendship prospers when Venus or Uranus is trine, sextile, or conjunct the Moon. The chance meeting of acquaintances and friends is facilitated by the Moon in Gemini.

Parties (Hosting or Attending)
The best time for parties is when the Moon is in Gemini, Leo, Libra, or Sagittarius with good aspects to Venus and Jupiter. There should be no aspects to Mars or Saturn.

Sports
Acrobatics: Mars, Aries
Archery: Jupiter, Sagittarius
Ball games in general: Venus
Baseball: Mars
Bicycling: Uranus, Mercury, Gemini
Boxing: Mars
Calisthenics: Mars, Neptune
Chess: Mercury, Mars
Competitive sports: Mars
Coordination: Mars
Deep-sea diving: Neptune, Pisces
Exercising: Sun
Football: Mars
Horse racing: Jupiter, Sagittarius
Jogging: Mercury, Gemini
Physical vitality: Sun
Polo: Uranus, Jupiter, Venus, Saturn

Racing (other than horse): Sun, Uranus
Ice skating: Neptune
Roller skating: Mercury
Sporting equipment: Jupiter, Sagittarius
Sports in general: Sun, Leo
Strategy: Saturn
Swimming: Neptune, Pisces, Moon, Cancer
Tennis: Mercury, Venus, Uranus, Mars
Wrestling: Mars

Travel
Air travel: Mercury, Sagittarius, Uranus
Automobile travel: Mercury, Gemini
Boating: Moon, Cancer, Neptune
Camping: Leo
Helicopters: Uranus
Hotels: Cancer, Venus
Journeys in general: Sun
Long journeys: Jupiter, Sagittarius
Motorcycle travel: Uranus, Aquarius
Parks: Sun, Leo
Picnics: Venus, Leo
Rail travel: Uranus, Mercury, Gemini
Restaurants: Moon, Cancer, Virgo, Jupiter
Short journeys: Mercury, Gemini
Vacations, holidays: Venus, Neptune

Long trips which threaten to exhaust the traveler are best begun when the Sun is well-aspected to the Moon and the date is favorable for the traveler. If traveling with others, good aspects from Venus are desirable. For enjoyment, aspects to Jupiter are preferable; for visiting, aspects to Mercury. To prevent accidents, avoid squares or oppositions to Mars, Saturn, Uranus or Pluto.

For air travel, choose a day when the Moon is in Gemini or Libra, and well-aspected by Mercury and/or Jupiter. Avoid adverse aspects of Mars, Saturn or Uranus.

Writing
Write for pleasure or publication when the Moon is in Gemini. Mercury should be direct. Favorable aspects to Mercury, Uranus and Neptune promote ingenuity.

Other Entertainments
Barbecues: Moon, Mars
Casinos: Venus, Sun, Jupiter
Festivals: Venus
Parades: Jupiter, Venus

FISHING AND HUNTING DATES

Jan. 4, 4:49 PM–Jan. 6, 11:57 PM
Jan. 14, 12:20 PM–Jan. 16, 10:37 PM
Jan. 23, 5:33 PM–Jan. 25, 8:37 PM
Feb. 1, 3:05 AM–Feb. 3, 9:12 AM
Feb. 10, 8:17 PM–Feb. 13, 6:32 AM
Feb. 19, 10:55 PM–Feb. 22, 2:13 AM
Feb. 28, 12:16 PM–Mar. 2, 6:30 PM
Mar. 10, 4:41 AM–Mar. 12, 3:29 PM
Mar. 19, 5:52 AM–Mar. 21, 7:57 AM
Mar. 27, 7:18 PM–Mar. 30, 2:26 AM
Apr. 6, 12:40 PM–Apr. 9, 12:16 AM
Apr. 15, 3:13 PM–Apr. 17, 3:52 PM
Apr. 24, 12:51 AM–Apr. 26, 8:42 AM
May 3, 7:45 PM–May 6, 7:55 AM
May 13, 1:54 AM–May 15, 1:59 AM
May 21, 6:40 AM–May 23, 2:13 PM
May 31, 1:59 AM–Jun. 2, 2:17 PM
Jun. 9, 12:04 PM–Jun. 11, 12:50 PM
Jun. 17, 2:13 PM–Jun. 19, 8:29 PM

Jun. 27, 7:57 AM–Jun. 29, 8:02 PM
Jul. 6, 8:19 PM–Jul. 8, 10:38 PM
Jul. 14, 11:37 PM–Jul. 17, 4:23 AM
Jul. 24, 2:17 PM–Jul. 27, 2:07 AM
Aug. 3, 2:29 AM–Aug. 5, 6:14 AM
Aug. 11, 9:46 AM–Aug. 13, 1:41 PM
Aug. 20, 9:24 PM–Aug. 23, 9:13 AM
Aug. 30, 7:51 AM–Sep. 1, 11:57 AM
Sep. 7, 7:09 PM–Sep. 9, 11:15 PM
Sep. 17, 5:16 AM–Sep. 19, 5:19 PM
Sep. 26, 2:20 PM–Sep. 28, 5:31 PM
Oct. 5, 2:36 AM–Oct. 7, 7:42 AM
Oct. 14, 1:20 PM–Oct. 17, 1:47 AM
Oct. 23, 11:07 PM–Oct. 26, 12:57 AM
Nov. 1, 8:18 AM–Nov. 3, 2:21 PM
Nov. 10, 8:57 PM–Nov. 13, 9:38 AM
Nov. 20, 9:41 AM–Nov. 22, 10:57 AM
Nov. 28, 1:59 PM–Nov. 30, 7:51 PM
Dec. 8, 3:45 AM–Dec. 10, 4:25 PM
Dec. 17, 8:07 PM–Dec. 19, 10:13 PM
Dec. 25, 9:45 PM–Dec. 28, 2:06 AM

MOON GUIDE TO GAMBLING

By Ralph Jordan Pestka

I have played tens of thousands of hours of poker. Sitting across the table from all types of players over the years, I have gained a great deal of insight into their approaches to gambling. Once I took up the serious study of astrology, I discovered it fit perfectly well with my efforts at poker. You see, poker is a people game. It is a gamble, but it is a gamble in which numerous individuals are pitted against each other in a continual decision-making process. As I studied astrology and continued to play poker, I asked acquaintances their birthdates. I soon learned to understand a great deal more about the nature of different gamblers according to the astrological influences imprinted on them at birth.

People reveal the core of their natures under the stress and challenge of winning and losing great sums of money. Any personal weaknesses will show, eventually, and indulgence or blind optimism will be revealed. Is there a calculating and crafty nature hiding behind those cards? It will be more obvious after ten or twenty hours of play.

Planets, Patterns, and Probabilities

Astrology and gambling have one thing in common. Both are concerned with the outcome of events. We can trace the roots of astrology and gambling far back into the pre-history of humanity. In our modern day we understand the principles underlying the laws of probability. In earlier times these laws were not formally understood, but rather were instincitively and intuitively perceived by some individuals. That is, some individuals could see that particular types of events showed patterns of repetition. Among these individuals were the first astrologers. Patterns of repetition, in essence, are what probability is all about, and probability is what astrology and gambling are all about.

In this article we will look at the particular patterns that relate to the transits of the Moon. These patterns weave in and out of an individual's life over the course of time, and relate to the aspect the transiting Moon makes to your natal Sun sign.

The Sun and the Moon are the great timekeepers; the Moon is considered the great "trigger." Its fast-moving aspects to the other planets are catalysts to many events. This is especially true regarding aspects the Moon makes to the Sun. The Sun rules Leo and the Fifth House, which rule risk, speculation, games of chance and gambling. The aspects the transiting Moon makes to your Sun sign reveal when more or less fortunate energies will surround you.

Gambling, Timing, and the Moon

You do not have to be an expert in the laws of probability to put them to use for your benefit and profit in gambling. You simply have to use your common sense.

You want the odds in your favor most of the time when you gamble. You can understand the laws of probability and what will occur over the long run, but must also understand that in the short run deviations will occur. This is where using the timing of astrology to win at gambling steps in. It means being in there and betting when the unusually fortunate deviations, the winning events, are more likely to occur for you. It also means standing on the sidelines and not betting when the losing events are more likely to occur for you.

The aspects the transiting Moon makes to your natal Sun will trigger more or less fortunate influences for you in your gambling. The following delineations for your Sun sign point out the general days on which to gamble, those days that are neutral and may go either way, and those days that may prove particularly trying or unfortunate. Gamble on your best days and be willing to bet more money. Do not bet on your less fortunate days, or restrict the amount you bet when things are less certain. By following the transiting Moon's aspects to your natal Sun sign you will be using one of the most basic and dependable astrological factors for timing and winning at gambling.

ARIES SUN SIGN
Moon Transiting In:

Aries—Can produce wins, but don't get egotistical and think you have a license to win.

Taurus—Winning is possible, but you may have the urge to splurge; control your spending.

Gemini—A neutral influence, but can stimulate your mind for numbers, memorization and problem-solving.

Cancer—Better hold back and save your money for a more fortunate day.

Leo—You could be fired up to gamble. Others are, too. Control your impulses and you can win. Lose control and you can lose big!

Virgo—Good for the professional gambler. The average gambler is better off holding back.

Libra—Competitive sports or games in which you directly compete can attract your betting dollars. Keep self-control. Avoid impulse or emotional betting and you could come out ahead.

Scorpio—You may borrow to gamble, go into debt, or gamble with the bill money. If you avoid these pitfalls you have a chance to win.

Sagittarius—Impulse and risk abound, so don't take any crazy chances. You could win, but control yourself.

Capricorn—Your wins may be small most of the time, but if you're going to hit the lottery, this could be the time.

Aquarius—You can win among friends or a friend can give you a winning tip. Surprises abound.

Pisces—If you're even in the mood to gamble, you may be uncertain, indecisive or distracted. Stay conservative if you are in the action.

TAURUS SUN SIGN
Moon Transiting In:

Taurus—If you risk your money now you will probably play the favorites. Look for the long shot that pays big. Your financial intuition is sharp.

Gemini—You can be fascinated by numbers games and by the numbers that have dollar signs in front of them. Keep your investment small and you may multiply your resources.

Cancer—Security concerns can dominate your thinking. Winning is possible, but if you start losing don't be stubborn; learn when to quit.

Leo—Others around you may be stimulated to gamble. Your own chances of winning are not that great. Bet small.

Virgo—Your best laid plans and systems can now be put to the test. Stay alert, analyze things, watch the details and you can come out ahead.

Libra—You spend best by studying, planning and organizing your gambling activities. Wait for a better period to put down your cash.

Scorpio—You may feel the challenge to hit it big. Sports and competitions you bet on or participate in are most likely to win you money.

Sagittarius—You have to spend it to make it, and bet it to win it, but if you borrow it you'll most likely lose it. You can win, but don't let your blind optimism cause you to gamble with more than you can afford.

Capricorn—You could be ready for some serious speculation. Depend on your experience and expertise in financial matters and you can find the winning bets.

Aquarius—Lotteries, sweepstakes and electronic gambling machines may be fortunate now. You may hit a big payoff that makes you famous among your friends.

Pisces—Your intuition is heightened, but make sure it's not just wishful thinking. Winning is possible. Don't loan money to gambling friends.

Aries—You are better off holding back now. Events may be too fast-breaking or too anxious and distracting for you to use your best judgment.

GEMINI SUN SIGN

Moon Transiting In:

Gemini—You naturally thrive on action and you can be ready to gamble big. Self-control is essential to end up in the winner's circle.

Cancer—Your better money-making instincts dominate now. Winning is possible. Memory serves you well.

Leo—You may get carried away by the gambling fever surrounding you. Lotteries, number games and casinos can hold winning opportunities, but don't risk it all.

Virgo—This transit favors detailed analysis, looking over forms, refining your systems. Don't bet yet; save your cash for a better transit.

Libra—Many opportunities for speculative gains. You can apply what you have learned and test your skills and systems.

Scorpio—Not a fortunate time. You may be better off reviewing wins and losses, refining your techniques and investigating new strategies.

Sagittarius—Sports and racing competitions can attract your attention. Winning is possible, but remain objective and reserved. Don't let optimism carry you away.

Capricorn—You may have visions of scoring big. There is money to be won, and you may get a piece of it now.

Aquarius—Friends could be a part of your gambling scene. You may think you finally have the perfect system; be cautious. Winning is possible, but don't lose more than you can afford.

Pisces—Draw on your sixth sense and gain the intuitive insights that lead to winning. Remain sensitive to your inner promptings.

Aries—Your mind may be too fast for your pocketbook. Winning is possible, but you had better set your budget before you begin to gamble.

Taurus—This period is better used for socializing, entertainment or relaxation. Wins may be small or you may risk more than you should.

CANCER SUN SIGN
Moon Transiting In:

Cancer—Security interests can dominate now. Winning is possible.

Leo—This can be fortunate. You will know how to get the most out of your gambling dollars.

Virgo—A neutral influence with a down tendency. You may be better off saving your money.

Libra—You are not likely to win big now, although you may win the door prize.

Scorpio—Your instincts and intuition are sharp for risky business. You can turn a small bet into a big payoff. Draw on your memory and remain sensitive to your psychic promptings.

Sagittarius—If you make a living through speculation, this transit could produce a tidy profit. The average gambler may be swept away by visions of riches and should be conservative.

Capricorn—You are inclined to bet on the favorites or stay conservative. You'd be smart to keep your bets small as wins can be meager.

Aquarius—Your brain may be working overtime, trying to figure out how to win big. Number games can be lucky. Do not lend money to gambling friends.

Pisces—A fortunate time. Stay in touch with your feelings. They can lead to a big win.

Aries—You may win in competition or sports. Maintain composure and self-control or you can gamble fast and lose.

Taurus—Sweepstakes and contests may be lucky. The lotteries may produce a winner. Remain conservative, as this is not your best time.

Gemini—You would do just as well to save your money under this transit. Distractions, indecision or anxieties can keep you from using your best judgment.

LEO SUN SIGN
Moon Transiting In:

Leo—Your time to shine! Good fortune will usually come your way, but don't think you can do no wrong or you can lose everything you've won.

Virgo—You are more pragmatic and perhaps even nervous about taking risks. Be particular about your bets.

Libra—You may gain by mixing social activities with your gambling. A neighbor or relative may prove a fortunate influence.

Scorpio—This is a less fortunate period. It may produce some wins, but you should remain conservative in the amount you risk.

Sagittarius—You may want to gamble, especially on sports or races. You can win big if you are smart, but don't let enthusiasm cause you to lose too much if you see that it's not your day.

Capricorn—You are probably better off tending to more serious business. Winning is not likely and you will hate yourself if you lose.

Aquarius—You think you have it all figured out, ready to battle the bookies or casinos, but it's not a very fortunate time. Keep your eyes on the competition.

Pisces—Winning is possible. Depend on your best financial instincts and intuition.

Aries—Sports, competitions and contests are strongly favored. Your tendency is to gamble too much, so keep your self-control.

Taurus—Get the most value from your betting dollar. Stick with your most dependable gambles. A big win from a small bet is possible.

Gemini—Picking numbers may prove surprisingly profitable. Lotteries, bingo and keno games give you a big chance on a small investment.

Cancer—Not very fortunate. You are better off renewing your inner resources in preparation for a new cycle of excitement and risk.

VIRGO SUN SIGN
Moon Transiting In:

Virgo—Luck through wagering in very particular and limited ways. Bet one horse out of ten races or buy only one lottery ticket.

Libra—Winning is possible, but you may be indecisive or influenced by others' opinions. Keep your risk small if you gamble.

Scorpio—Your skill with numbers and odds can serve you well. This may not produce a big win but it can be profitable.

Sagittarius—You are better off holding back. If you do gamble, keep it small.

Capricorn—Your instincts for finding the best bet will come, though winnings may be modest.

Aquarius—If you are numbers crazy this transit may be lucky. Others are better off studying forms and systems and saving their bets for another day.

Pisces—You are not at your best for picking the winners. Confusion or indecision can cost you.

Aries—Decisive and exacting application of your best gambling instincts may produce a big win on a small investment.

Taurus—This transit could produce winners. Take your time to find the best odds for your money.

Gemini—You should have at least one lottery ticket, as you can achieve public recognition for numbers games.

Cancer—Don't let feelings cloud your thinking or you may imagine you have the perfect system. Winning is possible, but bet conservatively.

Leo—You could get caught up in an urge to gamble. Lose control and you can lose big.

LIBRA SUN SIGN
Moon Transiting In:

Libra—Winning is possible if you keep your balance. Don't let the lure of luxury cause you to risk too much.

Scorpio—You may know just how to extract the cash. Your sense of values serves you well.

Sagittarius—Numbers games or racing events may be fortunate. Maintain your self-control. You could lose much if you are not lucky, and lose your winnings if you are too self-confident.

Capricorn—Forget this transit for winning. If you do win, it could be small, and a loss will leave you very sour.

Aquarius—A most fortunate transit. You can win in social settings, numbers games and electronic gambling.

Pisces—Not that fortunate. Relax and take care of yourself. Save your betting dollars for a better time.

Aries—Competition of every type can attract your bets. You can pick the winners. Stay in touch with your intuitive/psychic impulses.

Taurus—A lottery ticket may be a good idea. If you are destined to win a massive sum, this could be the time.

Gemini—Big numbers attract you. You understand the patterns behind numbers. You can win now, but don't risk more than you can afford.

Cancer—Winning is possible, but security matters may occupy your attention. Remain realistic, as your emotions could hinder smart betting.

Leo—Electronic games, lotteries and casinos could be profitable. A generally favorable transit.

Virgo—Get in touch with facts and real figures. You could be too confused, distracted or undecided to be right. Proceed cautiously.

SCORPIO SUN SIGN
Moon Transiting In:

Scorpio—Your desire for gain could be great. Draw on your deep insights and intuition.

Sagittarius—Maintain self-control and remain realistic and this can produce some wins.

Capricorn—Tends toward the down side. It may be better to wait, learn and plan.

Aquarius—Unusual or surprising events could surround your gambling and end up costing you money. Remain conservative.

Pisces—Your insight and intuition serve you well. Winning could be easy, almost like magic!

Aries—If you dig in and work at it you may come up a winner. Pace yourself and maintain your discipline or you may end up losing.

Taurus—Don't let feelings cause you to take a risk. Winning is possible, but this is not your best time.

Gemini—You have a chance to win if you use your head. You may tend to bet too often or stay in the action long after you have gotten ahead. Learn to quit when you are a winner.

Cancer—Your intuitive knowledge of gambling can make you a winner. Definitely one of your better periods.

Leo—You could strike it rich under this transit! If you are going to achieve fame for winning, this is when it could happen, but don't get carried away.

Virgo—Adept with numbers, you may want to play the lottery, bingo or keno. Not your most fortunate time, but it can produce some wins.

Libra—You could bet emotionally, be undecided or not get the best value for your dollar. You should probably wait for a more fortunate transit.

SAGITTARIUS SUN SIGN
Moon Transiting In:

Sagittarius—You can be ready for action and willing to gamble big. Maintain perspective and self-control and you can cash in a winner.

Capricorn—You could have one eye on your bank book and one on the racing form. Betting on favorites or being conservative would be wise.

Aquarius—Gambling among friends, neighbors or in social settings may prove favorable. Electronic and numbers games are possible winners.

Pisces—Subconscious desires for grandeur and great wealth may cloud your betting choices. Not your most fortunate transit. Bet small if at all.

Aries—You can put your natural instincts for gambling and risk to good use. Depend on intuition.

Taurus—If you work at it, this can produce some winners. Try to get a big payoff for a small investment. Not very fortunate, so be prudent.

Gemini—You may want to "show 'em" and prove you are a winner. Maintain your perspective and composure. Winning in competitive events is possible, but remain conservative.

Cancer—Don't let your feelings or sentiments cause you to bet more than you can afford. Winning is possible, but you should look for small bets that pay big.

Leo—You could be too willing to gamble; you'll lose big if you lose self-control. Depend on your experience and common sense.

Virgo—Numbers games may be lucky. Watch out for races, sports and competitions, as these could go against you.

Libra—Groups can be favorable. You can be good at picking the winners in competitions.

Scorpio—A time for caution. Your desire to gamble can overcome your best judgment and cause you to lose more than you can afford. It wouldn't hurt to wait.

CAPRICORN SUN SIGN
Moon Transiting In:

Capricorn—You are inclined to limit your bets. Bet on the favorites. Don't risk much money. Your gambling forte is your conservative and realistic approach.

Aquarius—Gambling among friends, in groups, or on electronic and numbers games can turn a profit.

Pisces—A dream or your intuition may lead you to pick winning numbers. This transit is a neutral influence so you should not risk a lot.

Aries—Emotion and impulse could get the best of you and cause losses.

Taurus—Your heightened sense of values can lead you to get good odds. Definitely one of your better times to risk your resources.

Gemini—Worry, indecision or mental irritations may get in the way of your winning. You should probably save your money for a more fortunate time.

Cancer—Cautions against emotional betting. Keep in touch with your intuition and competitive events could produce winners.

Leo—A strong transit for the urge to win big. Research or inside information could mean big gains. Maintain self-control.

Virgo—Pay attention to details, examine records, tables, charts. Possible wins.

Libra—You can pick between individuals or teams in competitions. Evaluate the important factors for winning.

Scorpio—You can profit among friends or by pooling money. Your mind is sharp for gambling with multiple numbers.

Sagittarius—This is not the time to get carried away by the gambling fever surrounding you. Control yourself and you can win. Blind faith could cost you.

AQUARIUS SUN SIGN
Moon Transiting In:

Aquarius—Gambling among friends, with groups or in social settings is favored now. Stay in tune to ingenious bets; they could surprise you.

Pisces—Subtle and intuitive insight can lead to winning, but don't risk everything.

Aries—Using your computer brain is a good idea, but guard against impulse betting.

Taurus—Tough to win under this transit. Winnings small and slow to come. Minimize risk.

Gemini—This transit could produce wins. Don't go off on a tangent, betting too much or too often. Control your betting with your mind and you can win.

Cancer—If you work with a gambling system, this is a good time to apply what you have learned. Remain sensitive to your intuitive impulses. Not your most fortunate time, but winning is possible.

Leo—You can place your gambling in perspective now. Casino gambling and gambling among friends or in groups could be productive. Remain reserved.

Virgo—Maintain your mental balance; don't risk more than you can afford to lose. Investigation and detailed digging could reveal winners.

Libra—A fortunate influence in general. Numbers games or competitions could bring winners. Remain in control, as you are more willing to risk a great deal.

Scorpio—Past research and experience can lead you to winners. Gains come through hard work, but the possibility for success is present.

Sagittarius—You can win big among friends, groups or in social settings. Lotteries and numbers games are also favored. Stay within a budget, as you are more inclined to risk too much.

Capricorn—If you have a hidden advantage you may be able to profit in speculation. Proceed with caution and you may show a small profit.

PISCES SUN SIGN
Moon Transiting In:

Pisces—Intuition is your guide. Remain sensitive to dreams, visions, larger concepts and you can find winners.

Aries—A willingness to risk your resources boldly. You can win, but don't let impulse masquerade as courage. Stay within a budget.

Taurus—A rather neutral influence. You may have intuitive insight into numbers. Modest wagering could be worth it.

Gemini—You may be too distracted, bet emotionally or rely too much on the opinions of others. You might want to skip it during this transit.

Cancer—Your psychic and intuitive insight could pay big dividends in risk and speculation. This is definitely the time to have a bet in.

Leo—A willingness to risk too much could cost you dearly. Others may be eager to gamble, but this may not be your time. Keep wages small if you do bet.

Health & Beauty

★ **Astro-Ecology**
★ **Diet & the Moon**
★ **The Perfect Gift**
★ **Soapmaking & the Moon**

HEALTH & BEAUTY

Beauty Care

For beauty treatments, skin care and massage, the Moon should be in Taurus, Cancer, Leo, Libra, Scorpio or Aquarius and sextile, trine or conjunct Venus and/or Jupiter.

Fingernails should be cut when the Moon is not in any aspect with Mercury or Jupiter. Saturn and Mars must not be marked Q or O because this makes the nails grow slowly or thin and weak. The Moon should be in Aries, Taurus, Cancer or Leo. For toenails, the Moon should not be in Gemini or Pisces. Corns are best cut when the Moon is in the third or fourth quarter.

Dental Work

Pick a day that is marked favorable for your Sun sign. Mars should be marked X, T or C and Saturn, Uranus and Jupiter should not be marked Q or O.

Teeth are best removed during the increase of the Moon in the first or second quarter in Gemini, Virgo, Sagittarius, Capricorn or Pisces. The day should be favorable for your lunar cycle, and Mars and Saturn should be marked C, T or X.

Fillings should be done when the Moon is in a fixed sign (Taurus, Leo, Scorpio, Aquarius) and decreasing in light. The same applies for having impressions made for plates.

Dieting

Weight gain occurs more readily when the Moon is in a water sign (Cancer, Scorpio, Pisces). Experience has shown that weight may be lost if a diet is started when the Moon is decreasing in light (third or fourth quarter) and when it is in Aries, Leo, Virgo, Sagittarius or Aquarius. The lunar cycle should be favorable on the day you wish to begin your diet.

Eyeglasses

Eyes should be tested and glasses fitted on a day marked favorable for your Sun sign and on a day which falls during your favorable lunar cycle. Mars should not be in aspect with the Moon. The same applies for any treatment of the eyes, which should also be started during the increase of the Moon (first or second quarter).

Habits

To end any habit, start on a day when the Moon is in the third or fourth quarter and in a barren sign.

Gemini, Leo or Virgo are the best times, while Aries and Capricorn are suitable, too. Make sure your lunar cycle is favorable. Avoid lunar aspects to Mars or Jupiter. Aspects to Neptune or Saturn are helpful. These rules apply to smoking and will produce a good start.

Hair Care

Haircuts are best when the Moon is in a mutable sign (Gemini, Sagittarius, Pisces) or earthy sign (Taurus, Capricorn), well-placed and aspected, but not in Virgo, which is barren. For faster growth, the Moon should be in a water sign (Cancer, Scorpio, Pisces). To make hair grow thicker, cut it when the Moon is full or in opposition to the Sun (marked O in the Lunar Aspectarian). However, if you want your hair to grow more slowly, the Moon should be in Gemini or Leo in the third or fourth quarter with Saturn square or opposite the Moon.

Permanents, straightening and hair coloring will take well if the Moon is in Aquarius and Venus is marked T or X. You should avoid doing your hair if Mars is marked Q or O, especially if heat is to be used. For permanents, a trine to Jupiter is helpful. The Moon also should be in the first quarter and at the same time check the lunar cycle for a favorable day in relation to your Sun sign.

Health

Diagnosis is more likely to be successful when the Moon is in a cardinal sign (Aries, Cancer, Libra, Capricorn), and less so when in a mutable sign.

Begin a program for recuperation or recovery when the Moon is in a cardinal or fixed sign and the day is favorable to your sign. Enter hospitals at these times. For surgery, see Surgical Procedures. Buy medicines when the Moon is in Scorpio if they are made from natural substances.

Surgical Procedures

The flow of blood appears to be related to the Moon's phases. *Time* magazine reported on 1,000 tonsillectomy case histories analyzed by Dr. Edson J. Andrews—only 18 percent of associated hemorrhaging occurred in the fourth and first quarters. Thus, an astrological rule: To reduce the hazard of hemorrhage after a surgical procedure, plan to have the surgery within one week before or after the Full Moon. Also select a date when the Moon is not in the sign governing the part of the body involved in the operation. The farther removed the Moon sign from the sign ruling the afflicted part of the body, the better for healing. There should be no lunar aspects to Mars, and favorable aspects to Venus and Jupiter should be present.

Cosmetic surgery should be done in the increase of the Moon, when the Moon is not in square or opposition to Mars. Avoid days when the Moon is square or opposite Saturn or the Sun.

ASTRO-ECOLOGY

By Pat Esclavon-Hardy

As we enter a new millennium, we stand between our past on this planet and a wondrous future—a future that is calling for our participation now! Will we make it to the 21st Century as a planet? Will our Earth be livable? It is very clear we have fallen out of balance with our Earth. Awareness is upon us to act on this delicate issue.

I saw a bumper sticker the other day that read, "One earth, one sky, one ocean, one solar system." Stop and think about this. These are the four elements—earth, air, water and fire! The basics of ecology; the basics of astrology. This is astro-ecology. I would define astro-ecology as the study of natural timing derived by planetary cycles (astro) with the science and study of the relationships between organisms and their environments (ecology). We are living one of the oldest teachings of our planetary heritage, astrology. We, as astrologers, have been taught to love the Earth. For centuries, farmers and Native Americans have used "astro-ecology" to raise crops, to hunt and fish in respect to natural timing and to preserve the balance of the ecosystem.

Another phrase, "Love our Mother," shows that we are all talking about "astro-ecology" in our daily lives. Look around you at today's mainstream words that reflect astrological principles. Astrologers have been looking for acceptance from the public in many ways, and if we view the principles of astrology in the contiguity of ecology, we see a more feasible understanding of astrology in our society.

Earth is home, and the solar system is our neighborhood. It is not separate; we are all related, and astrology reminds us that we live on a planet, that there are other planets, and we have a relationship with these other planets within our neighborhood, the solar system.

To bring the astrological perspective in view with the ecological, let us look at Moon signs. Since the Moon in astrology represents the nurturing, caring, and sensitive aspects of our personalities, people with different Moon signs choose to care for our planet's well-being in different ways. Moon signs provide a focus for learning about saving our planet.

The information below comes from various books and magazines on recycling and how we can save the earth.

Moon in Aries (fire element): You may want to take action by initiating a project against the burning of waste materials that could harm the environment. Bring awareness and demand action from the companies that sell disposable lighters or razor blades to come up with solutions for disposing and recycling their products. If you are interested in automobiles, you may want to get involved with the various recycling issues of old batteries, oil, tires, glass and parts.

FACT: Each year 1.7 billion disposable pens, 500 million disposable lighters and 2 billion disposable razors are trashed. Also, over 3 million automobiles are abandoned each year in the United States.

Moon in Taurus (earth element): You may want to become involved in fund raising for a local ecological project. Research food packaging. Maybe make preserves, jellies or can your own foods. Start a beautification program for land areas that have been neglected, bringing value to the area for those who live in the community.

FACT: Packaging accounts for $1 of every $11 spent for food. One-third of our garbage is packaging.

Moon in Gemini (air element): You may want to network with different Earth-saving groups and share ideas of how to find recycling resources such as books, magazines, pamphlets, lectures, seminars and workshops in your neighborhood, community, or county. Get the word out about different ways to recycle. Pass out informative material about earth friendliness and recycling at work, school, or in your neighborhood. Become energy conscious when purchasing machines and equipment.

FACT: The largest single component in landfills is newspaper. When replacing appliances, recycle discarded ones through salvage yards or charitable collection centers and shop for energy efficient replacements.

Moon in Cancer (water element): You may want to get involved in a community project involving fixing up an unsightly piece of land for a park or playground. Raise awareness about the recycling of fluids that are unfriendly to the earth. Recycling motor oil prevents soil and water contamination. Do fixups around the house to prevent wasted resources.

FACT: The smallest drip of a leaky faucet can waste over 50 gallons of water per day. Only 3 percent of the world's water is fresh water.

Moon in Leo (fire element): You may want to find a product you can market that is earth friendly and biodegradable. Look into outdoor equipment or teach hikers, bikers and campers to be earth friendly. Set up a recycling program for household cans, paper, glass, and plastics that gets the family involved. Reduce the flammable materials in children's clothing by researching alternatives. You may want to get involved in helping to reduce the number of violent toys available to children.

FACT: More than one billion trees are used annually to manufacture disposable diapers.

Moon in Virgo (earth element): Do you have a love for animals? Getting involved with your local humane society or with issues concerning animal testing may bring out your passion for animals. Another interest may be to grow herbs for medicinal purposes. Nature's remedies are the plants that have grown for centuries. With this in mind, you may research pesticides to awareness to the public about chemicals that are poisonous to our food supply, bodies, and land.

FACT: More than 200 million tons of pesticides are used annually in California alone.

Moon in Libra (air element): You may want to do a favor for someone who needs it, but who would never ask. You can volunteer to help a coworker for an hour at the office. This is truly volunteer, however; don't look for extra pay or paybacks. Find one occasion to give your time or resources to children, adults, the aged, or your favorite charity. Host a social event for earth awareness and recycling.

FACT: Using recycled paper products, buying items in recycled packaging and refusing products that are over-packaged reduces solid waste.

Moon in Scorpio (water element): You are an excellent candidate for researching something to its depth and getting the answer required to facilitate an ecological change in our society. Encourage people to start food and yard waste composts. On a larger scale, bring awareness to the public waste companies (i.e., garbage collectors) that solid waste transformation should be updated.

FACT: Currently, 80 percent of solid waste is being dumped in 6,000 landfills. Another 10 percent is recycled, and the remaining 10 percent is incinerated.

Moon in Sagittarius (fire element): You can assist schools, churches, and other groups in bringing recycling and earth-saving philosophies to their awareness. Gather facts and data that will prove your point as you give talks and distribute information that helps others to get involved.

FACT: Enough aluminum is discarded every three months to completely rebuild our nation's commercial air fleet. The shipping industry dumps more than 450,000 plastic containers into the sea every day.

Moon in Capricorn (earth element): You may want to study government and social programs that contribute to recycling and Earth-saving policies. Raise awareness about grants and special funds made available for beginning projects of this nature. Check with large corporations who are dedicated to recycling and earth friendliness, as there may be avenues you can follow to acquire what you need for the projects. On a personal level, you can reduce the amount of resource expenditures in your home and work environment. Turn down your hot water heater to save energy, and turn off lights when leaving a room.

FACT: Reducing your thermostat only one degree reduces your heating bill 2 percent. Energy Miser incandescent light bulbs save energy, while long-life bulbs use more energy than standard bulbs.

Moon in Aquarius (air element): You can help tremendously by writing to your senators, congress people and anyone in the political decision-making process to encourage earth saving techniques and projects for the public. Become better educated by reading about ways to be a better steward of our world. Talk to groups and organizations about recycling goals.

FACT: The average American family produces about 100 pounds of garbage per week. Plastic bags can be washed, reused, and when discarded they can be recycled.

Moon in Pisces (water element): You are encouraged to bring awareness as to the polluting of our rivers, streams, lakes and oceans. Learn what you can do to help keep our drinking water standards safe. You may want to contact Greenpeace about the killing of sea life, excess fishing in certain waters or garbage dumping into our waters.

FACT: An estimated 14 billion pounds of trash are dumped into the oceans every year. Hazardous waste materials are also part of this trash.

For more information about saving the planet, check your local library for these and other resources:

The Earth Works Group. *The Recycler's Handbook*. Berkeley, CA: The Earthworks Press, 1990.

The Earth Works Group. *50 Simple Things You Can Do To Save the Earth*. Berkeley, CA: The Earth Works Press, 1989.

Elkington, J. et al. *The Green Consumer*. New York, NY: Penguin Books, 1990.

MacEachern, Diane. *Save Our Planet*. New York, NY: Dell, 1990.

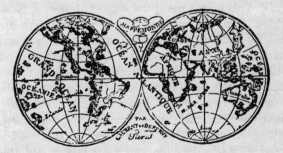

DIET & THE MOON

By Kim Rogers-Gallagher

When the Creator built humans, s/he made a minor mistake: we should never have been given free will *and* appetites. Oh, sure, it must have seemed innocent enough—how could anyone have known we'd be so bad at juggling what's good for us with what tastes good?

This brings me to the subject of dieting. Now, "diet" is a real four-letter word, but since it's distinctly "human" to overdo, overeat, and then wail about our waistlines, let's talk about it, and see if we can't make the procedure a little less painful.

Being a Sagittarian, one of the pioneers of the "more is always better" league, I understand particularly well the problem of trying to cut back on anything. As an astrologer, however, I'm qualified to offer a bit of advice that can really help; a few little tips designed to make "The D word" a lot less like suffering and a lot more like the right thing to do.

Since our bodies work so well with the rhythm of the Moon, the best way to start an astrological diet is to work with her tide, rather than against it. So let's look at how the Moon affects us as she passes through each sign, and try to come up with the best way to handle the subject of food—naturally.

ARIES: It's tough to say no to yourself, no matter what you want, when the Moon is in Aries. Aries is pure impulse—it just can't wait—and that's what our moods are like when the Moon is in Aries. However, since Aries is ruled by Mars, and since Mars is in charge of muscles, there is something constructive you can do after you finish the pastry. Exercise, exercise, exercise—use all that active red energy, and go workout. At the very least, you'll be burning off the calories you put in. At best, since Aries is the first sign, a natural starting point for all kinds of projects, you may have started something you'll want to continue—regardless of where the Moon is on your second visit to the gym.

TAURUS: When the Moon is in Taurus, folks set out to "spoil" each other with the very best. Like no other sign, Taurus truly appreciates what our planet has to offer. With all that good, solid earth energy circulating, it's awfully hard not to think about food, so don't fight it. Instead, take this two-day period and prepare food—all your food for the week. Cook your little heart out. Play galloping gourmet. Cook everything you can for the rest of the week—often, it's just being too hungry to wait for something nutritious that knocks many of us off our diets. Fast-food restaurants were built on that "quicker is better" philosophy. Now, everybody needs a treat now and then. Give yourself one now—but just one. Watch the cholesterol for the rest of the month, okay?

GEMINI: Gemini is ruled by the planet Mercury, the head of the department of communications. It's a mutable air sign, so it likes to move around— quickly. When the Moon is in Gemini, we like to move around, too, and variety truly becomes the spice of life. We suddenly get a taste for something new—for a change. Now is a good time to change your eating habits—the time of day you eat, for example, as well as the quantity and type of food. You're probably in the mood for a walk, too, and that's a great calorie-burner. You may be too busy to think much about food when the Moon is in Gemini. If you can slow down long enough to think about your appetite, however, now is the time to visit an outdoor cafe and participate in a distinctly Gem-inian activity: people-watching.

CANCER: Cancer is ruled by the Moon, and the Moon wrote the book on feelings. So when the Moon is here, we all get a dose of feelings, and find ourselves in the mood to take care of someone. Needless to say, during a Cancer Moon, you'll want to cook for somebody. So go ahead—cook warm, fuzzy foods, like soups, casseroles, and stews—the stuff Mom used to make. Then have your friends over for a family-style dinner. Since Cancer has a strong affiliation with dairy products, you might be tempted to overdo on creams and sauces, but try to contain yourself and save some calories for dessert. Cancer also rules round, fluid-filled containers, so pies and puddings should be on your menu, too. Cancer Moons are great times to fill your kitchen—and your whole house, in fact—with the smell of good home cooking.

LEO: When the Moon is in Leo, it's time for dinner theater. Don't forget that this dramatic, theatrical sign, long known as the sign of the performer, also loves to be entertained. Take yourself out to a supperclub when the Moon is here, and enjoy a show while you dine. If you can't find a dinner theater, any place where you can be treated like royalty will do it—the more elegant the better, of course, since Leo loves—and deserves—nothing more than the very best of everything. Dramatic foods are fun to have under this Moon, too. Flaming dishes are especially appropriate, since Leo is a fire sign. Restaurants where the food is prepared right in front of you, at table side, are perfect for a Leo Moon's mood.

VIRGO: Virgo is the sign that owns the health department, so under this Moon sign, good nutritional foods are the order of the day. Organic fruits and vegetables in particular are what you'll crave, and they're just wonderful for dieting. Lots of grain, like brans and wheats, are ultra-good for you, too. Raid your local health-food store and take home one of everything for when the Moon isn't in Virgo and you're digging through the cupboards in a frenzy looking for something to munch on. You can use this Moon to clean out your cupboards, too—toss out all the stuff you won't have any willpower to avoid when the Moon is in a fire sign. Regardless of what you choose to eat, make sure it's Virgoan pure—with no chemical additives of any kind.

LIBRA: Libra loves people, so when the Moon is in Libra, it's time to eat with someone. Elegant dinners for two are the best way to use the energies of this sociable air sign, who loves nothing better than light, pleasant conversation. Dinner parties are also perfect, as are any situations where you can nibble politely and mingle. If you're not in the mood for dining out, find yourself some foods that are "pretty"—pleasing to the eye, that is—and take someone special on a picnic. You can even brown-bag a lunch and spend the day in a museum. However you decide to use this two-day period, remember that Libra is the sign of balance. Try to keep your diet "balanced," too.

SCORPIO: Scorpio gets involved with everything to the point of obsession, and food is no exception. When the Moon is in this sign, ruled by Pluto—the head of the intensity department—no matter what you want, you want it bad. If you're going to take a chocolate cake home, hide in a closet and eat the whole thing, this is the time you'll choose to do it. Yes, obsessing on food is quite possible when the

Moon is here, but there are alternatives. Try using the intensity and power of Scorpio to take control—you can get obsessive about your diet, too. There's no sign stronger and more fixed—decisions made under Scorpio Moons are decisions that last. Decide now on an image you want to call your own.

SAGITTARIUS: When the Moon is in Sagittarius, the best thing you do for yourself is to learn this word: No. Practice it. Say it over and over again, in front of a mirror if you need to. Then try it when the cheesecake comes out. Good luck—because Sagittarius is not world-famous for willpower, moderation, or having "just a sliver" of anything. Sagittarius is an expert at overdoing. If one is good, two, then, must be better, and if two is good, well, how about the whole thing? Shouldn't that be just excellent? Sagittarius is ruled by Jupiter—the largest planet in the solar system. Jupiter is in charge of expansion, growth, excess and binging. Watch out for a tendency to overdo both food and drink, and feed the Sagittarius Moon another way—eat international foods. Just watch the mozzarella!

CAPRICORN: Here's another great Moon sign to start a diet. Capricorn is a cardinal Earth sign, ruled by Saturn, who virtually runs the department of self-discipline, willpower, and determination. Saturn knows how to get by on just the essentials—the bare minimum. He'd look a bit like Ichabod Crane, if you could draw him—a guy who was never known for being pudgy. For Capricorn, being frugal comes easily. That goes double for food. You can really cut back without a lot of agony when this Moon is here—and you might even want to stay cut back.

AQUARIUS: Aquarius is the most unconventional, erratic sign out there, the one that rebels most against the current status quo. As a result, our schedules change drastically when the Moon enters this sign, and whatever we've been doing for months is exactly what we won't want any part of now. That includes food. You'll be amazed at what you'll crave—and even more amazed at what you'll actually put into your mouth—under this eccentric air sign Moon. The oddest combinations will suddenly seem like great ideas—or you may just get fixed on one particular type of food for two and a half days. Whatever you serve yourself, no matter how odd, don't worry—as with all else, an Aquarian Moon doesn't last for long.

PISCES: Pisces is mutable water—it has no boundaries. When the Moon is in Pisces, our emotions don't have any boundaries, either. With nothing to separate us from the rest of what's out there, it's easy to feel everything that everyone else feels—like psychic sponges. Rather than getting depressed, now is a great time to help a diet along by drinking a lot of water. You won't be overly concerned about food, anyway—Pisces is ruled by Neptune, the queen of compassion, who isn't at all into the physical plane. The last thing in the world she's worried about is maintaining the physical body—she'd much rather find a way out. When the Moon is in this mutable water sign, don't fight it. Jump into a pool. Meditate, and drink your water.

To Diana

Lovely Goddess of the Bow!
Lovely Goddess of the arrows!
Of all hounds and of all hunting
Thou who wakest in starry heaven
When the sun is sunk in slumber
Thou with moon upon thy forehead,
Who the chase by night preferrest
Unto hunting in the daylight
With thy nymphs unto the music
Of the horn—thyself the huntress,
And most powerful: I pray thee
Think although but for an instant,
Upon us who pray unto thee!

—*Aradia*
C. C. Leland

THE PERFECT GIFT

By Donna Cunningham

Don't you feel great when you find the perfect present for a friend or loved one? There's nothing like that warm feeling of their astonishment and pleasure.

Knowing the birth charts of the special people in your life gives you a head start on buying something memorable. Several factors in the horoscope can alert you to their preferences in various areas of life. Knowing their Venus signs and aspects is helpful in choosing romantic offerings, because Venus shows how people express love—and what they need from others in order to feel loved. A Venus in Gemini person needs to have it in words, while a Venus in Capricorn person expects quality, even if you can only afford a single, perfect rose. A Sun-sign-based remembrance might be the best choice for the birthday—the solar return—because you want to boost the person's self-esteem by showing how special he or she is.

The Moon sign and important Moon aspects are clues to tokens that are comforting and comfortable, that warm the hearth and the heart. The Moon sign shows the conditions that people need for emotional fulfillment and security. It also reveals the particular domestic style that makes their house a home, so you can choose accordingly. Most Moon in Libra women, for instance, would cherish a Wedgewood dish, while some Moon in Aries people might use it for an ashtray.

You may be wondering how to find your loved ones' Moon signs, if you don't know them already. This information is available in the "How To Find Your Moon Sign" section of this book. Another resource for Moon sign data is my book, *Moon Signs*, which has tables in the back where you can easily look up everyone born between 1920 and 1999.

Types of gifts which would appeal to each Moon sign are listed below. Specific products aren't usually listed, since every season brings new offerings, but at least you'll know what department to browse. For the more astrologically-sophisticated reader, Moon aspects and house placements that are similar in their tastes and needs are also listed, in parentheses after the sign. (Not every aspect and house is mentioned, since not all the correspondences apply.) If these guidelines don't seem to hold true, there's a strong possibility that other planets are intervening—for instance, Cancer Moons born with Uranus also in Cancer would have more traits of Aquarian Moons, while the Moon in Leo people born while

Pluto was in Leo would be more like Moon in Scorpio people.

MOON IN ARIES (Moon/Mars aspects): Too many burnt pots later, you'll doubtlessly conclude they're not domestic. However, they would appreciate labor-saving devices, maid service, or being taken out to eat. Projects like bookshelves or closet space-makers can entertain them. Most of all, observe their latest interests and enthusiasms—the places they're far ahead of the pack—and get the state-of-the-art equipment for that. They'll appreciate the recognition of their leadership position as much as the gift itself.

MOON IN TAURUS: These people love their creature comforts like soft, loose clothing, delicious foods, fluffy blankets and linens. Cater to their senses, pamper their tastes—feed them well—and they will be happy. They might also like books or magazines about ways to save or invest money—or just plain cash. Many of them love plants and are gifted gardeners, so a flowering plant or tree would remind them of you for years to come.

MOON IN GEMINI (Moon/Mercury aspects, Moon in the 3rd House): Gemini Moons aren't generally very domestic, and their interests can be ephemeral, so you're not buying for eternity. Instead, satisfy their need for mental stimulation by endowing them with the latest fads in home items, the more shiny and modern the better. They like best-sellers or books about their current interests—not last month's! Their need to know can be filled by subscriptions to trendy magazines full of information on fascinating but diverse topics. If they have a home computer—and many of them do—they'd enjoy tinkering with new software.

MOON IN CANCER (Moon in the 4th house): The Moon in Cancer may very well outshine Sun in Cancer when it comes to domesticity. Thus, a gift for the home is often very welcome, especially nice cookware or bed linens. These people also love food, so catalogues with special delicacies sent by mail are a great place to shop. However, some of them overdo it and ultimately develop food sensitivities—or go on periodic diets—so check to see if they have any special dietary requirements. The cookbook collectors among them can always use a new and exotic volume—and they might even reward you with an invitation to a gourmet meal.

MOON IN LEO: Just as they can lavish generous attention on others on their special days, Moon in Leo people want, and almost need, to be the center of attention on their own special days. Make a fuss, let them be King or Queen for a day, and they will be happy as you assure them how very special they are to you. What you buy doesn't matter nearly as much as the flourish with which you present it—a birthday gram at the office, for instance, would be a dramatic demonstration of their importance. In jewelry, gold is always a good bet.

MOON IN VIRGO (Moon in the 6th house): These hard-working souls are happier with practical gifts than with frivolity. Many are true gourmet chefs and, in the kitchen or out, like to have the right tool for the right purpose—precision instruments, usually, to improve their craftsmanship. They have an interest—sometimes an obsession—where health and proper diet are concerned, so books or other items relating to good health are often welcome.

MOON IN LIBRA (Or, strong connections between the Moon and Venus): A beautiful home is almost a necessity to those with Moon in Libra, and many of them are gifted at decorating. (If your taste pales beside theirs, be merciful and don't give them something they'd die before they'd admit they hated!) Perhaps a gift certificate for some high-end gift shop or bath shop would be an inspired solution. Above all, they want to feel loved and appreciated, so flowers or some other romantic offering are never out of season—a love letter, French perfume, a misty sensitivity card, or even a poetry book.

MOON IN SCORPIO (Moon/Pluto aspects): These close-mouthed people may keep their needs and preferences quiet, but they're pleased if you play detective and figure out what they really want. What they *don't* want is to be surprised, so forget that surprise party. To intrigue their minds, try detective stories, steamy romances, mystical and occult books or supplies, or the latest self-help or psychology book. In clothing or equipment, brand names that reek of money are sure pleasers.

MOON IN SAGITTARIUS: These lively folks might enjoy sports equipment or tickets to games. They also love travel, so take them away for a weekend or even a day, or buy a travel book or subscription to a travel magazine. They are interested in philosophy and larger questions, like why the world is the way it is, so books, workshop tickets, or lectures may fascinate them. They also enjoy a good joke, so humorous gifts are more suited to them than almost any sign.

MOON IN CAPRICORN: As noted earlier, one perfect rose would be more appreciated than a bouquet of daisies. Quality and elegance of design are important to these people. Even if it means you can only remember them once a year, do it with style. Take them to a prestigious restaurant and make sure the gift box is from an elegant store. A welcome possibility are items related to the career or to success.

MOON IN AQUARIUS: Forget crockpots and knife sharpeners, and never give a Tupperware party in their honor. Instead find something truly avant garde or outrageous to do with them. Ask about their philosophical leanings or social causes and get the newest book or t-shirt related to it. They may be computer addicts or gadget collectors, and if so, something along that line would be your best clue.

MOON IN PISCES (Or strong aspects between the Moon and Neptune): These people are generally keenly sensitive to beauty and often love music, dance, or art. Thus, Pisces Moons may appreciate a recording of a favorite musical artist. Many of them also love fantasy and romance, so they might enjoy books or videotapes based on fairy tales, dreamy-eyed romance, or fantasy. Finally, spirituality can play a big role in their lives, so search through a metaphysical store for books, crystals, Tarot cards, or other items. Another happy thought would be a reading by a good psychic, astrologer or Tarot reader.

SOAPMAKING & THE MOON

By K. D. Spitzer

On a farm, soapmaking was traditionally a spring task, when the first breezes of spring would bring a primal and instinctive urge to open windows and clean the winter-soiled "nest." There is a rhythm and symmetry to farm tasks, each one dependent upon the successful completion of the one before.

In order to spring clean, you need soap, and before this century most people needed to make their own. In order to make soap, women cleaned the last of the ashes from the winter fires and added them to the ones they'd been saving, and thus began a process which would produce the lye needed to make the soap. At this time they would check over their meat stores so they could begin to render the fat they needed to make the soap.

On one of the last clear, crisp days of autumn before the first snowfall and during a dry, waning Moon, the hogs and cattle were slaughtered and dressed; some of the fats were rendered. What was not used to preserve the meat was saved for soap.

First a fire would be built outdoors, because rendering fat is a smelly business. Rendering means melting down chunks of fat. This is a slow process which requires careful tending of the fire as well as the pot. The little crisp pieces left after straining are called chit'lins or chitterlings. In some rural areas they are still a special taste treat.

The best animal fat for soapmaking comes from beef rather than pork. Hog fat or lard makes a very soft soap. The best fat of all comes from the kidney area, and is called leaf lard in pigs and suet in cattle. Suet makes the hardest soaps or candles.

The rendered fat made a somewhat harsh, but still perfectly acceptable soft soap for washing dishes, laundering and housecleaning. Poorer households would save cooking greases all winter. These fats required the additional step of being cleaned before use, and although the resulting soap was effective, it was a very poor quality. However, you cannot fault the economy, as eight pounds of grease will make six pounds of soap!

Lye is the magical ingredient in the alchemy that turns fat into soap. It was made by dripping rain water through hardwood ashes. Oak or maple were the preferred woods. Special barrels called ash hoppers were lined with straw and packed with the accumulated ashes. Rain water was poured into the hopper and allowed to drain through holes drilled in the bottom. Younger children would be assigned the task of keeping the ashes well-watered.

The strength of the resulting brew was tested with an egg. If an egg placed in the liquid immediately sank, the lye needed to run through the ashes again. If it floated and bobbed on the surface, the lye was too strong. The ideal was a slow, lazy descent of the egg to the bottom.

There have long been soapmakers' guilds; a very secretive bunch they were, too, so it is not surprising that Scorpio is not only one of their rulers, but one of the signs that best suits the soapmaking process. The best time to make soap is when the Moon is in any of the fixed signs (Aquarius, Taurus, Leo and Scorpio). Anyone who has tried making it should appreciate reliance on the Moon at this time, to aid in the alchemical process.

Soapmaking should also take place in a waning Moon, which in the spring means when the Moon is in Scorpio or Aquarius. The waning Moon presents dry conditions, which are best for this process.

The ingredients are available locally at the grocery, health food, or farm store. The process of making it is simple (and addictive!). You need a stainless steel kettle, a wooden spoon, glass measuring cups and glass or plastic molds.

To render beef suet, run the fat through a meat grinder or chop into small pieces in a food processor. Put in a stainless steel pot and place over low heat. When melted, pour through several layers of cheesecloth to strain out any pieces of meat. Clean, rendered fat can be frozen until needed.

Using a few drops of essential oils to scent your soaps can add another pleasurable dimension to the process. Just be sure and use the real thing. Colognes or perfumes will not work.

Mild Complexion Bar

> Petroleum jelly
> 4 cups coconut oil
> 1 cup clean, rendered beef fat
> 2 cups soft water, separated
> ½ cup lye flakes
> ⅓ cup Borax
> ½ cup boiling water
> few drops essential oil to scent

Grease molds with petroleum jelly. Melt oils and fats together and let cool. Boil one cup of the water and dissolve borax in it. Allow to cool. Dissolve lye in remaining water and set aside.

When lye and fat are lukewarm, pour lye into fat, stirring constantly. Continue to stir until mixture becomes thick and creamy. Add the Borax solution and any essential oils for scent. Continue to stir until thick. Pour into molds.

It may take up to 3 days to be firm enough to unmold. Let air dry for 3-4 weeks to cure and then wrap for later use. Makes about 7½ cups liquid before molding. Use half pure olive oil for a castile-like soap.

Vegetable Soap

> 2 cups coconut oil, olive oil, solid vegetable
> shortening or a combination of them
> ¾ cup cold soft water
> ¼ cup lye flakes

Grease molds with petroleum jelly. Melt oil and/or shortening until liquid, but do not allow it to become too hot. Dissolve lye in cold water. Stir into fat over low heat until thickened. It may take almost an hour for saponification (hydrolosis of fats), so stir often enough to keep it well-mixed. When thickened, pour into molds.

This soap will set very slowly because of the lack of animal fats, so don't be surprised if it requires a week to set up before unmolding. Also it will probably need at least 6 weeks to air dry and cure. This soft soap makes a very thin lather, but strict vegetarians will appreciate the fact that it is animal fat-free.

Sun-Moon Blend Concept Chart
(Excerpt from *Synthesis and Counseling in Astrology* by Noel Tyl)

☉	☽
♈ Energy to lead, to exert force.	♈ Need to be important, to be "Number One."
♉ Energy to build and maintain.	♉ Need to preserve security; to keep things as they are or are supposed to be.
♊ Energy to diversify, to communicate.	♊ Need to be bright, scintillating, informed, intense.
♋ Energy to create security.	♋ Need to be emotionally secure, especially in the family.
♌ Energy to be recognized.	♌ Need to be respected, loved, and honored.
♍ Energy to refine, to discriminate.	♍ Need to be correct, exact, insightful.
♎ Energy to please and gain appreciation.	♎ Need to be appreciated; to be fair, attractive, and popular.
♏ Energy to control by knowing; to plumb depths and reach top.	♏ Need to be in control; to be seen as deep, significant, reliable, self-sufficient, right.
♐ Energy for self-assertion, for what is right.	♐ Need to have one's opinions respected.
♑ Energy to organize, strategize, and deploy resources; ambition.	♑ Need to administrate progress, make things happen.
♒ Energy to innovate, to intellectualize, to all, with others.	♒ Need to be socially significant, unusual.
♓ Energy to feel and understand and sacrifice.	♓ Neeed to identify ideal, understand impressions, work with intangible.

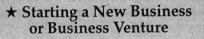

Business & Legal

★ Starting a New Business
  or Business Venture

★ Using the Moon for
  Business & Legal
  Decisions

STARTING A NEW BUSINESS OR BUSINESS VENTURE

When starting a new business or any type of new venture, check to make sure that the Moon is in the first or second quarter. You should also check the aspects of the Moon to the type of venture with which you are becoming involved. Look for positive aspects to the planet that rules the activity and avoid any dates marked Q or O, as you are sure to have trouble with the client or deal.

Activities and Occupations Ruled by the Sun
Advertising, executive positions, acting, finance, government, jewelry, law and public relations.

Activities and Occupations Ruled by Mercury
Accounting, brokerage, clerical, disc jockey, doctor, editor, inspector, librarian, linguist, medical technician, scientist, teacher, writer, publishing, communication and mass media.

Activities and Occupations Ruled by Venus
Architect, art and artist, beautician, dancer, designer, fashion and marketing, musician, poet, and chiropractor.

Activities and Occupations Ruled by Mars
Barber, butcher, carpenter, chemist, construction, dentist, metal worker, surgeon and the soldier.

Activities and Occupations Ruled by Jupiter
Counseling, horse training, judge, lawyer, legislator, minister, pharmacist, psychologist, public analyst, social clubs, research and self-improvement.

Activities and Occupations Ruled by Saturn
Agronomy, math, mining, plumbing, real estate, repairperson, printer, paper-making and working with older people.

Activities and Occupations Ruled by Uranus
Aeronautics, broadcasting, electrician, inventing, lecturing, radiology and computers.

Activities and Occupations Ruled by Neptune
Photography, investigator, institutions, shipping, pets, movies, wine merchant, health foods, resorts, travel by water and welfare.

Activities and Occupations Ruled by Pluto
Acrobatics, athletic manager, atomic energy, research, speculation, sports, stockbroker and any purely personal endeavors.

USING THE MOON FOR BUSINESS & LEGAL DECISIONS

By Bruce Scofield

A decision is an event. Like the birth of a person, it has its own horoscope and is a reflection of the astrological configurations in effect at the time. Sometimes we reach decisions without much thought; sometimes only after agonizing mental exercise. More importantly, sometimes our decisions turn out to be good ones, and sometimes they don't. A close look at what the Moon is doing at the time we reach a decision will say a lot about how things will unfold in the future.

There are several important bits of lunar information that should be considered when evaluating a decision and its potential. One is whether or not the Moon was void of course when the decision was made. If it was, the chances of later events going off in unforeseen directions is high. A few months ago I was setting up a schedule for our local astrological association. Out of the blue, a speaker called up and asked if he could be on our January program. It was an open slot so I scheduled the event, but I commented to him that the Moon was void of course as we made this decision, and nobody could know what would actually happen. I made him agree that if there were any weather-related problems, we didn't have to pay him his fee. Well, the weather turned bad and the snow came down, but our speaker decided to come anyway. The bus he arrived on was late and the building in which we were to have his lecture closed because of the weather. With some scrambling on the telephone, we got a few people out to one of our member's apartments and had an interesting, intimate meeting with our speaker. In fact, it was so successful that we did the same thing the next night. He got his pay and we got our speaker—but it didn't turn out as expected. This is the key to understanding the void of course Moon—you can't control what will unfold.

Using lunar aspects is another way of evaluating a decision and its repercussions. When the Moon is making sextiles and trines to the planets, the decision is probably a fairly solid one. If it is making hard aspects, the decision may meet with some resistance, or it will need to be changed. It doesn't matter so much what the planet is in this regard, just the aspect. Further, the last aspect the Moon makes while in a sign (this is the aspect made just before it goes void of course) will often describe the final outcome of the decision. It's best to avoid making major long-range decisions or choices during a time that the Moon will end its transit through the sign with a nasty square to Saturn or Mars. While this information is not available from this book, you can find everything you need in *Llewellyn's Daily Planetary Guide*.

A third consideration is the lunar cycle itself. Lore about the sequence of New Moon, first quarter, Full Moon and third quarter goes back to ancient times. The old rules were that one should start most things, make most decisions and move forward as the Moon was moving from New to Full. The period from Full to New was more favorable for activities and decisions that were concerned with processing or digesting information, or with matters that were generally hidden or obscure in some way. Another point is that events and decisions should not be initiated on the day of the quarters (where there is too much stress), or right on the New Moon (premature) or Full Moon (too late). If you follow the news every day you'll see these patterns unfold in front of you.

The sign that the Moon is in has its place in our methods also. When the Moon is in a Fire sign (Aries, Leo and Sagittarius), events and decisions tend to be propelled forward by enthusiasm and spirit. When it is in an Earth sign (Taurus, Virgo and Capricorn), practical matters impinge on the decision, and you will need to pay attention to details to keep the process moving along. With the Air signs (Gemini, Libra and Aquarius), there will be much dialogue about the matter and accurate communications will be necessary every step of the way. The Water signs (Cancer, Scorpio and Pisces) influence decisions in subtle ways by making them more responsive and reactive to outside influences. From another angle, decisions made under the Cardinal signs (Aries, Cancer, Libra and Capricorn) tend to move quickly toward fulfillment. Those made under Fixed signs (Taurus, Leo, Scorpio and Aquarius) tend to resist change and endure all sorts of obstacles. Mutable signs (Gemini, Virgo, Sagittarius and Pisces) facilitate adaptation and adjustment, and are very good with projects that need to keep changing.

Beyond making the decision, there is the implementation of actions that take the decision forward. This is the world of electional astrology, the branch of astrology that deals with the selection of a favorable time to do things. Using the above guidelines, you should be able to find a day, even a time, to act on your decisions—one that will produce a predictable flow of events that brings you to your goal. In one sense, this is using natural cycles to get what we want. In another sense, it's bending our will to the astrological influences around us. All of life, both body and mind, flows with the constantly changing fields of force spelled out by the positions of the planets, the Sun, and, our closest cosmic neighbor, the Moon.

ALTERNATIVE CONCEPTS
FOR THE SIGNS OF THE ZODIAC

Aries	♈	The Initiator
Taurus	♉	The Maintainer
Gemini	♊	The Questioner
Cancer	♋	The Nurturer
Leo	♌	The Loyalist
Virgo	♍	The Modifier
Libra	♎	The Judge
Scorpio	♏	The Catalyst
Sagittarius	♐	The Adventurer
Capricorn	♑	The Pragmatist
Aquarius	♒	The Reformer
Pisces	♓	The Visionary

Farm & Garden

★ Gardening by the Moon
★ Gardening Dates
★ Dates to Destroy Weeds
★ Other Garden-Related
   Activities
★ Phase/Sign Rulership
   Planting Guide
★ Companion Planting
★ Breeding Animals &
   Setting Eggs
★ Creating a Moon Garden

GARDENING BY THE MOON

Today, we still find those who reject the notion of Moon gardening—the usual non-believer is not the scientist, but the city dweller who has never had any real contact with nature and no conscious experience of natural rhythms.

Cato wrote that "fig, apple, olive, and pear trees, as well as vines, should be planted in the dark of the Moon in the afternoon, when there is no south wind blowing."

Camille Flammarian, the French astronomer, also testifies to Moon planting. "Cucumbers increase at Full Moon, as well as radishes, turnips, leeks, lilies, horseradish, saffron; onions, on the contrary, are much larger and better nourished during the decline and old age of the Moon than at its increase, during its youth and fullness, which is the reason the Egyptians abstained from onions, on account of their antipathy to the Moon. Herbs gathered while the Moon increases are of great efficiency. If the vines are trimmed at night when the Moon is in the sign of the Lion, Sagittarius, the Scorpion, or the Bull, it will save them from field-rats, moles, snails, flies, and other animals."

Dr. Clark Timmins is one of the few modern scientists to have conducted tests in Moon planting. The following is a summary of some of his experiments:

- Beets: When sown with the Moon in Scorpio, the germination rate was 71%; when sown in Sagittarius, the germination rate was 58%.
- Scotch marigold: When sown with the Moon in Cancer, the germination rate was 90%; when sown in Leo, the germination rate was 32%.
- Carrots: When sown with the Moon in Scorpio, the germination rate was 64%; when sown in Sagittarius, the germination rate was 47%.
- Tomatoes: When sown with the Moon in Cancer, the germination rate was 90%; when sown in Leo, the germination rate was 58%.

Two things should be emphasized. First, remember that this is only a summary of the results of the experiments; the experiments themselves were conducted in a scientific manner to eliminate any variation in soil, temperature, moisture, etc., so that only the Moon's sign used in planting varied. Second, note that these astonishing results were obtained without regard to the phase of the Moon— the other factor we use in Moon planting, and which presumably would have increased the differential in germination rates.

Further experiments by Dr. Timmins involved transplanting Cancer and Leo-planted tomato seedlings while the Moon was increasing and in Cancer. The result was 100% survival. When the transplanting was done with the Moon decreasing and in Sagittarius, there was 0% survival.

The results of Dr. Timmins' tests show that the Cancer-planted tomatoes had first blossoms 12 days earlier than those planted under Leo; the Cancer-planted tomatoes had an average height of 20 inches at the same age when the Leo plants were only 15 inches high; the first ripe tomatoes were gathered from the Cancer plantings 11 days ahead of the Leo plantings; and finally, a count of the hanging fruit and comparison of size and weight shows an advantage to the Cancer plants over the Leo plants of 45%.

Dr. Timmins also observed that there have been similar tests that did not indicate results favorable to the Moon planting theory. As a scientist, he asked why one set of experiments indicated a positive verification of Moon planting, and others did not. He checked these other tests and found that the experimenters had not followed the *geocentric* system for determining the Moon sign positions, but the *heliocentric*. When the times used in these other tests were converted to the geocentric system, the dates chosen often were found to be in barren rather than fertile signs. Without going into the technical explanations, it is sufficient to point out that geocentric and heliocentric positions often vary by as much as four days. This is a large enough differential to place the Moon in Cancer, for example, in the heliocentric system, and at the same time in Leo by the geocentric system.

Most almanacs and calendars show the Moon's signs heliocentrically—and thus incorrectly for Moon planting—while the *Moon Sign Book* is calculated correctly for planting purposes, using the geocentric system.

Some readers are also confused because the *Moon Sign Book* talks of first, second, third and fourth quarters, while some almanacs refer to these same divisions as New Moon, first quarter, Full Moon and last quarter. Thus, the almanac says first quarter when the *Moon Sign Book* says second quarter. (Refer to the introductory material in this book for more information.)

There is nothing complicated about using astrology in agriculture and horticulture in order to increase both pleasure and profit, but there is one very important rule that is often neglected—use common sense! Of course this is one rule that should be remembered in every activity we undertake, but in the case of gardening and farming by the Moon it is not always possible to use the best dates for planting or harvesting, and we must select the next best and just try to do the best we can.

This brings up the matter of the other factors to consider in your gardening work. The dates we give as best for a certain activity apply to the entire country (with slight time correction), but in your section of the country you may be buried under three feet of snow on a date we say is a good day to plant your flowers. So we have factors of weather, season, temperature and moisture variations, soil conditions, your own available time and opportunity, and so forth. And don't forget the matter of the "green thumb." Some astrologers like to think it is all a matter of science, but gardening is also an art. In art you develop an instinctive identification with your work so that you influence it with your feelings and visualization of what you want to accomplish.

The *Moon Sign Book* gives you the place of the Moon for every day of the year so that you can select the best times once you have become familiar with the rules and practices of lunar agriculture. We try to give you specific, easy-to-follow directions so that you can get right down to work.

We give you the best dates for planting, and also for various related activities, including cultivation, fertilizing, harvesting, irrigation, and getting rid of weeds and pests. But we cannot just tell you when it's good to plant at the time. Many of these rules were learned by observation and experience, but as our body of experience grew, we could see various patterns emerging which allowed us to make judgments about new things. Then we tested the new possible applications and learned still more. That's what you should do, too. After you have worked with lunar agriculture for a while and have gained a working background of knowledge, you will probably begin to try new things—and we hope you will share your experiments and findings with us. That's how the science grows.

Here's an example of what we mean. Years

ago, Llewellyn George suggested that we try to combine our bits of knowledge about what to expect in planting under each of the Moon signs in order to benefit with several such lunar factors in one plant. From this came our rule for developing "thoroughbred seed." To develop thoroughbred seed, save the seed for three successive years from plants grown by the correct Moon sign and phase. You can plant in the first quarter phase and in the sign of Cancer for fruitfulness; the second year, plant seeds from the first year plants in Libra for beauty; and in the third year, plant the seeds from the second year plants in Taurus to produce hardiness. In a similar manner you can combine the fruitfulness of Cancer, the good root growth of Pisces, and the sturdiness and good vine growth of Scorpio. And don't forget the characteristics of Capricorn: hardy like Taurus, but drier and perhaps more resistant to drought and disease.

Unlike common almanacs, we consider both the Moon's phase and the Moon's sign in making our calculations for the proper timing of our work within nature's rhythm. It is perhaps a little easier to understand this if we remind you that we are all living in the center of a vast electromagnetic field that is the Earth and its environment in space. Everything that occurs within this electromagnetic field has an effect on everything else within the same field, but since we are living on the Earth we must relate these happenings and effects to our own health and happiness. The Moon and the Sun are the most important and dynamic of the rhythmically changing factors affecting the life of the Earth, and it is their relative positions to the Earth that we project for each day of the coming year.

Many people claim that not only do they achieve larger crops gardening by the Moon, but that their fruits and vegetables are much tastier and more healthful.

A number of organic gardeners have also become lunar gardeners using the natural growing methods within the natural rhythm of life forces that we experience through the relative movements of the Sun and Moon.

We provide a few basic rules and then give you month-by-month and day-by-day guidance for your farming and gardening work. You will be able to choose the best dates to meet your own needs and opportunities.

PLANTING BY THE MOON'S PHASES

During the increasing light (from New Moon to Full Moon), plant annuals that produce their yield above the ground. (An annual is a plant that completes its entire life cycle within one growing season and has to be seeded anew each year.)

During the decreasing light (from Full Moon to New Moon), plant biennials, perennials, bulb and root plants. (Biennials include crops that are planted one season to winter over and produce crops the next, such as winter wheat. Perennials and bulb and root plants include all plants that grow from the same root year after year.)

A simple, though less accurate, rule is to plant crops that produce above the ground during the increase of the Moon, and to plant crops that produce below the ground during the decrease of the Moon. This is the source of the old adage, "Plant potatoes during the dark of the Moon."

Llewellyn George went a step further and divided the lunar month into quarters. He called the first two from New Moon to Full Moon the first and second quarters, and the last two from Full Moon to New Moon the third and fourth quarters. Using these divisions, we can increase our accuracy in timing our efforts to coincide with natural forces.

First Quarter (Increasing)
Plant annuals producing their yield above the ground, which are generally of the leafy kind that produce their seed outside the fruit. Examples are asparagus, broccoli, Brussels sprouts, cabbage, cauliflower, celery, cress, endive, kohlrabi, lettuce, parsley, spinach, etc. Cucumbers are an exception, as they do best in the first quarter rather than the second, even though the seeds are inside the fruit. Also in the first quarter, plant cereals and grains.

Second Quarter (Increasing)
Plant annuals producing their yield above the ground, which are generally of the viney kind that produce their seed inside the fruit. Examples include beans, eggplant, melons, peas, peppers, pumpkins, squash, tomatoes, etc. These are not

hard and fast divisions. If you can't plant during the first quarter, plant during the second, and vice versa. There are many plants that seem to do equally well planted in either quarter, such as watermelon, garlic, hay, and cereals and grains.

Third Quarter (Decreasing)
Plant biennials, perennials, and bulb and root plants. Also plant trees, shrubs, berries, beets, carrots, onions, parsnips, peanuts, potatoes, radishes, rhubarb, rutabagas, strawberries, turnips, winter wheat, grapes, etc.

Fourth Quarter (Decreasing)
This is the best time to cultivate, turn sod, pull weeds and destroy pests of all kinds, especially when the Moon is in the barren signs of Aries, Leo, Virgo, Gemini, Aquarius and Sagittarius.

PLANTING BY THE MOON'S SIGNS

The phases and signs of the Moon are combined in the dates we give you for various activities. However, we want to give you some general rules in relation to each of the signs so that you can make various individual decisions as the occasion may require. In each of the 12 zodiacal signs, the Moon reflects the special characteristics associated with the sign, and your activities should be coordinated to benefit from this natural cycle.

Moon in Aries
Barren and dry, fiery and masculine. Used for destroying noxious growths, weeds, pests, etc., and for cultivating.

Moon in Taurus
Productive and moist, earthy and feminine. Used for planting many crops, particularly potatoes and root crops, and when hardiness is important. Also used for lettuce, cabbage, and similar leafy vegetables.

Moon in Gemini
Barren and dry, airy and masculine. Used for destroying noxious growths, weeds and pests, and for cultivation.

Moon in Cancer
Very fruitful and moist, watery and feminine. This is the most productive sign, used extensively for planting and irrigation.

Moon in Leo
Barren and dry, fiery and masculine. This is the most barren sign, used only for killing weeds and other noxious growths, and for cultivation.

Moon in Virgo
Barren and moist, earthy and feminine. Considered good for cultivation and destroying weeds and pests.

Moon in Libra
Semi-fruitful and moist, airy and masculine. Used for planting many crops and producing good pulp growth and roots. A very good sign for flowers and vines. Also used for seeding hay, corn fodder, etc.

Moon in Scorpio
Very fruitful and moist, watery and feminine. Nearly as productive as Cancer; used for the same purposes. Especially good for vine growth and sturdiness.

Moon in Sagittarius
Barren and dry, fiery and masculine. Used for planting onions, seeding hay and for cultivation.

Moon in Capricorn
Productive and dry, earthy and feminine. Used for planting potatoes, tubers, etc.

Moon in Aquarius
Barren and dry, airy and masculine. Used for cultivation and destroying noxious growths, weeds and pests.

Moon in Pisces
Very fruitful and moist, watery and feminine. Used along with Cancer and Scorpio, especially good for root growth.

GARDENING DATES

Jan. 1, 12:00 AM-
Jan. 1, 5:56 AM
Capricorn, 4th qtr.

Plant potatoes and tubers.
Prune.

Jan. 1, 5:56 AM-
Jan. 2, 1:39 PM
Capricorn, 1st qtr.

Graft or bud plants. Trim
to increase growth.

Jan. 4, 4:49 PM-
Jan. 6, 11:57 PM
Pisces, 1st qtr.

Plant annuals, grains. Irri-
gate. Fertilize (chemical).
Trim to increase growth.
Graft or bud plants.

Jan. 9, 10:58 AM-
Jan. 11, 11:57 PM
Taurus, 2nd qtr.

Plant annuals for hardi-
ness. Trim to increase
growth.

Jan. 14, 12:20 PM-
Jan. 16, 3:27 PM
Cancer, 2nd qtr.

Plant annuals, grains. Irri-
gate. Fertilize (chemical).
Trim to increase growth.
Graft or bud plants.

Jan. 16, 3:27 PM- Jan. 16, 10:37 PM Cancer, 3rd qtr.	Plant biennials, perennials, bulbs and roots. Irrigate. Fertilize (organic). Prune.
Jan. 16, 10:37 PM- Jan. 19, 6:40 AM Leo, 3rd qtr.	Cultivate. Destroy weeds and pests. Harvest fruits and root crops. Trim to retard growth.
Jan. 19, 6:40 AM- Jan. 21, 12:54 PM Virgo, 3rd qtr.	Cultivate, especially medicinal plants. Destroy weeds and pests. Trim to retard growth.
Jan. 23, 5:33 PM- Jan. 23, 11:59 PM Scorpio, 3rd qtr.	Plant biennials, perennials, bulbs and roots. Irrigate. Fertilize (organic). Prune.
Jan. 23, 11:59 PM- Jan. 25, 8:37 PM Scorpio, 4th qtr.	Plant biennials, perennials, bulbs and roots. Irrigate. Fertilize (organic). Prune.
Jan. 25, 8:37 PM- Jan. 27, 10:27 PM Sagittarius, 4th qtr.	Cultivate. Destroy weeds and pests. Harvest fruits and root crops. Trim to retard growth.
Jan. 27, 10:27 pm- Jan. 30, 12:03 AM Capricorn, 4th qtr.	Plant potatoes and tubers. Prune.
Jan. 30, 12:03 AM- Jan. 30, 5:48 PM Aquarius, 4th qtr.	Cultivate. Destroy weeds and pests. Harvest fruits and root crops. Trim to retard growth.

Feb. 1, 3:05 AM- Feb. 3, 9:12 AM Pisces, 1st qtr.	Plant annuals, grains. Irrigate. Fertilize (chemical). Trim to increase growth. Graft or bud plants.
Feb. 5, 7:08 PM- Feb. 7, 7:54 AM Taurus, 1st qtr.	Plant annuals for hardiness. Trim to increase growth.
Feb. 7, 7:54 AM- Feb. 8, 7:44 AM Taurus, 2nd qtr.	Plant annuals for hardiness. Trim to increase growth.
Feb. 10, 8:17 PM- Feb. 13, 6:32 AM Cancer, 2nd qtr.	Plant annuals, grains. Irrigate. Fertilize (chemical). Trim to increase growth. Graft or bud plants.
Feb. 15, 7:16 AM- Feb. 15, 1:52 PM Leo, 3rd qtr.	Cultivate. Destroy weeds and pests. Harvest fruits and root crops. Trim to retard growth.
Feb. 15, 1:52 PM- Feb. 17, 7:01 PM Virgo, 3rd qtr.	Cultivate, especially medicinal plants. Destroy weeds and pests. Trim to retard growth.
Feb. 19, 10:55 PM- Feb. 22, 2:13 AM Scorpio, 3rd qtr.	Plant biennials, perennials, bulbs and roots. Irrigate. Fertilize (organic). Prune.
Feb. 22, 2:13 AM- Feb. 22, 8:04 AM Sagittarius, 3rd qtr.	Cultivate. Destroy weeds and pests. Harvest fruits and root crops. Trim to retard growth.

Feb. 22, 8:04 AM- Feb. 24, 5:10 AM Sagittarius, 4th qtr.	Cultivate. Destroy weeds and pests. Harvest fruits and root crops Trim to retard growth.
Feb. 24, 5:10 AM- Feb. 26, 8:14 AM Capricorn, 4th qtr.	Plant potatoes and tubers. Prune.
Feb. 26, 8:14 AM- Feb. 28, 12:16 PM Aquarius, 4th qtr.	Cultivate. Destroy weeds nd pests. Harvest fruits and root crops. Trim to retard growth.
Feb. 28, 12:16 PM- Mar. 1, 6:48 AM Pisces, 4th qtr.	Plant biennials, perennials, bulbs and roots. Irrigate. Fertilize (organic). Prune.
Mar. 1, 6:48 AM- Mar. 2, 6:30 PM Pisces, 1st qtr.	Plant annuals, grains. Irrigate. Fertilize (chemical). Trim to increase growth. Graft or bud plants.
Mar. 5, 3:51 AM- Mar. 7, 3:56 PM Taurus, 1st qtr.	Plant annuals for hardiness. Trim to increase growth.
Mar. 10, 4:41 AM- Mar. 12, 3:29 PM Cancer, 2nd qtr.	Plant annuals, grains. Irrigate. Fertilize (chemical). Trim to increase growth. Graft or bud plants.
Mar. 16, 8:26 PM- Mar. 17, 3:18 AM Virgo, 3rd qtr.	Cultivate, especially medicinal plants. Destroy weeds and pests. Trim to retard growth.

Mar. 19, 5:52 AM– Mar. 21, 7:57 AM Scorpio, 3rd qtr.	Plant biennials, perennials, bulbs and roots. Irrigate. Fertilize (organic). Prune.
Mar. 21, 7:57 AM– Mar. 23, 10:31 AM Sagittarius, 3rd qtr.	Cultivate. Destroy weeds and pests. Harvest fruits and root crops. Trim to retard growth.
Mar. 23, 10:31 AM– Mar. 23, 3:10 PM Capricorn, 3rd qtr.	Plant potatoes and tubers. Prune.
Mar. 23, 3:10 PM– Mar. 25, 2:10 PM Capricorn, 4th qtr.	Plant potatoes and tubers. Prune.
Mar. 25, 2:10 PM– Mar. 27, 7:18 PM Aquarius, 4th qtr.	Cultivate. Destroy weeds and pests. Harvest fruits and root crops. Trim to retard growth.
Mar. 27, 7:18 PM– Mar. 30, 2:26 AM Pisces, 4th qtr.	Plant biennials, perennials bulbs and roots. Irrigate. Fertilize (organic). Prune.
Mar. 30, 2:26 AM– Mar. 30, 9:09 PM Aries, 4th qtr.	Cultivate. Destroy weeds and pests. Harvest fruits and root crops. Trim to retard growth.
Apr. 1, 11:59 AM– Apr. 3, 11:50 PM Taurus, 1st qtr.	Plant annuals for hardiness. Trim to increase growth.

Apr. 6, 12:40 PM– Apr. 8, 12:35 AM Cancer, 1st qtr.	Plant annuals, grains. Irrigate. Fertilize (chemical). Trim to increase growth. Graft or bud plants.
Apr. 8, 12:35 AM– Apr. 9, 12:16 AM Cancer, 2nd qtr	Plant annuals, grains. Irrigate. Fertilize (chemical). Trim to increase growth. Graft or bud plants.
Apr. 13, 1:20 PM– Apr. 15, 7:08 AM Libra, 2nd qtr.	Plant annuals for fragrance and beauty. Trim to increase growth.
Apr. 15, 3:13 PM– Apr. 17, 3:52 PM Scorpio, 3rd qtr.	Plant biennials, perennials, bulbs and roots. Irrigate. Fertilize (organic). Prune.
Apr. 17, 3:52 PM– Apr. 19, 4:54 PM Sagittarius, 3rd qtr.	Cultivate. Destroy weeds and pests. Harvest fruits and root crops. Trim to retard growth.
Apr. 19, 4:54 PM– Apr. 21, 7:38 PM Capricorn, 3rd qtr.	Plant potatoes and tubers. Prune.
Apr. 21, 7:38 PM– Apr. 21, 10:19 PM Aquarius, 3rd qtr.	Cultivate. Destroy weeds and pests. Harvest fruits and root crops. Trim to retard growth.
Apr. 21, 10:19 PM– Apr. 24, 12:51 AM Aquarius, 4th qtr.	Cultivate. Destroy weeds and pests. Harvest fruits and root crops. Trim to retard growth.

Apr. 24, 12:51 AM- Apr. 26, 8:42 AM Pisces, 4th qtr.	Plant biennials, perennials, bulbs and roots. Irrigate. Fertilize (organic). Prune.
Apr. 26, 8:42 AM- Apr. 28, 6:53 PM Aries, 4th qtr.	Cultivate. Destroy weeds and pests. Harvest fruits and root crops. Trim to retard growth.
Apr. 28, 6:53 PM- Apr. 29, 12:37 PM Taurus, 4th qtr.	Plant potatoes and tubers. Prune.
Apr. 29, 12:37 PM- May 1, 6:53 AM Taurus, 1st qtr.	Plant annuals for hardiness. Trim to increase growth.
May 3, 7:45 PM- May 6, 7:55 AM Cancer, 1st qtr.	Plant annuals, grains. Irrigate. Fertilize (chemical). Trim to increase growth. Graft or bud plants.
May 10, 11:30 PM- May 13, 1:54 AM Libra, 2nd qtr.	Plant annuals for fragrance and beauty. Trim to increase growth.
May 13, 1:54 AM- May 14, 3:49 PM Scorpio, 2nd qtr.	Plant annuals, grains. Irrigate. Fertilize (chemical). Trim to increase growth. Graft or bud plants.
May 14, 3:49 PM- May 15, 1:59 AM Scorpio, 3rd qtr.	Plant biennials, perennials, bulbs and roots. Irrigate. Fertilize (organic). Prune.

May 15, 1:59 AM– May 17, 1:36 AM Sagittarius, 3rd qtr.	Cultivate. Destroy weeds and pests. Harvest fruits and root crops. Trim to retard growth.
May 17, 1:36 AM– May 19, 2:40 AM Capricorn, 3rd qtr.	Plant potatoes and tubers. Prune.
May 19, 2:40 AM– May 21, 6:36 AM Aquarius, 3rd qtr.	Cultivate. Destroy weeds and pests. Harvest fruits and root crops. Trim to retard growth.
May 21, 6:36 AM– May 21, 6:40 AM Aquarius, 4th qtr.	Cultivate. Destroy weeds and pests. Harvest fruits and root crops. Trim to retard growth.
May 21, 6:40 AM– May 23, 2:13 PM Pisces, 4th qtr.	Plant biennials, perennials, bulbs and roots. Irrigate. Fertilize (organic). Prune.
May 23, 2:13 PM– May 26, 12:46 AM Aries, 4th qtr.	Cultivate. Destroy weeds and pests. Harvest fruits and root crops. Trim to retard growth.
May 26, 12:46 AM– May 28, 1:07 PM Taurus, 4th qtr.	Plant potatoes and tubers. Prune.
May 28, 1:07 PM May 29, 4:27 AM Gemini, 4th qtr.	Cultivate. Destroy weeds and pests. Harvest fruits and root crops. Trim to retard growth.

May 31, 1:59 AM- June 2, 2:17 PM Cancer, 1st qtr.	Plant annuals, grains. Irrigate. Fertilize (chemical). Trim to increase growth. Graft or bud plants.
June 7, 8:14 AM- June 9, 12:04 PM Libra, 2nd qtr.	Plant annuals for fragrance and beauty. Trim to increase growth.
June 9, 12:04 PM- June 11, 12:50 PM Scorpio, 2nd qtr.	Plant annuals, grains. Irrigate. Fertilize (chemical). Trim to increase growth. Graft or bud plants.
June 12, 11:04 PM- June 13, 12:05 PM Sagittarius, 3rd qtr.	Cultivate. Destroy weeds and pests. Harvest fruits and root crops. Trim to retard growth.
June 13, 12:05 PM- June 15, 11:52 AM Capricorn, 3rd qtr.	Plant potatoes and tubers. Prune.
June 15, 11:52 AM- June 17, 2:13 PM Aquarius, 3rd qtr.	Cultivate. Destroy weeds and pests. Harvest fruits and root crops. Trim to retard growth.
June 17, 2:13 PM- June 19, 5:01 PM Pisces, 3rd qtr.	Plant biennials, perennials, bulbs and roots. Irrigate. Fertilize (organic). Prune.
June 19, 5:01 PM- June 19, 8:29 PM Pisces, 4th qtr.	Plant biennials, perennials, bulbs and roots. Irrigate. Fertilize (organic). Prune.

June 19, 8:29 PM– June 22, 6:35 AM Aries, 4th qtr.	Cultivate. Destroy weeds and pests. Harvest fruits and root crops. Trim to retard growth.
June 22, 6:35 AM– June 24, 7:02 PM Taurus, 4th qtr.	Plant potatoes and tubers. Prune.
June 24, 7:02 PM– June 27, 7:57 AM Gemini, 4th qtr.	Cultivate. Destroy weeds and pests. Harvest fruits and root crops. Trim to retard growth.
June 27, 7:57 AM– June 27, 7:51 PM Cancer, 4th qtr.	Plant biennials, perennials, bulbs and roots. Irrigate. Fertilize (organic). Prune.
June 27, 7:51 PM– June 29, 8:02 PM Cancer, 1st qtr.	Plant annuals, grains. Irrigate. Fertilize (chemical). Trim to increase growth. Graft or bud plants.
July 4, 2:56 PM– July 5, 3:03 PM Libra, 1st qtr.	Plant annuals for fragrance and beauty. Trim to increase growth.
July 5, 3:03 PM– July 6, 8:19 PM Libra, 2nd qtr.	Plant annuals for fragrance and beauty. Trim to increase growth.
July 6, 8:19 PM– July 8, 10:38 PM Scorpio, 2nd qtr.	Plant annuals, grains. Irrigate. Fertilize (chemical). Trim to increase growth. Graft or bud plants.

July 10, 10:43 PM– July 12, 5:49 AM Capricorn, 2nd qtr.	Graft or bud plants. Trim to increase growth.
July 12, 5:49 AM– July 12, 10:21 PM Capricorn, 3rd qtr.	Plant potatoes and tubers. Prune.
July 12, 10:21 PM– July 14, 11:37 PM Aquarius, 3rd qtr.	Cultivate. Destroy weeds and pests. Harvest fruits and root crops. Trim to retard growth.
July 14, 11:37 PM– July 17, 4:23 AM Pisces, 3rd qtr.	Plant biennials, perennials, bulbs and roots. Irrigate. Fertilize (organic). Prune.
July 17, 4:23 AM– July 19, 6:10 AM Aries, 3rd qtr.	Cultivate. Destroy weeds and pests. Harvest fruits and root crops. Trim to retard growth.
July 19, 6:10 AM– July 19, 1:21 PM Aries, 4th qtr.	Cultivate. Destroy weeds and pests. Harvest fruits and root crops. Trim to retard growth.
July 19, 1:21 PM– July 22, 1:24 AM Taurus, 4th qtr.	Plant potatoes and tubers. Prune.
July 22, 1:24 AM– July 24, 2:17 PM Gemini, 4th qtr.	Cultivate. Destroy weeds and pests. Harvest fruits and root crops. Trim to retard growth.
July 24, 2:17 PM– July 27, 2:07 AM	Plant biennials, perennials, bulbs and roots. Irri-

Cancer, 4th qtr.	gate. Fertilize (organic). Prune.
July 27, 2:07 AM- July 27, 10:14 AM Leo, 4th qtr.	Cultivate. Destroy weeds and pests. Harvest fruits and root crops. Trim to retard growth.
July 31, 8:24 PM- Aug. 3, 2:29 AM Libra, 1st qtr.	Plant annuals for fragrance and beauty. Trim to increase growth.
Aug. 3, 2:29 AM- Aug 3, 10:16 PM Scorpio, 1st qtr.	Plant annuals, grains. Irrigate. Fertilize (chemical). Trim to increase growth. Graft or bud plants.
Aug. 3, 10:16 PM - Aug. 5, 6:14 AM Scorpio, 2nd qtr.	Plant annuals, grains. Irrigate. Fertilize (chemical). Trim to increase growth. Graft or bud plants.
Aug. 7, 7:52 AM- Aug. 9, 8:28 AM Capricorn, 2nd qtr.	Graft or bud plants. Trim to increase growth.
Aug. 10, 1:16 PM- Aug. 11, 9:46 AM Aquarius, 3rd qtr.	Cultivate. Destroy weeds and pests. Harvest fruits and root crops. Trim to retard growth.
Aug. 11, 9:46 AM- Aug. 13, 1:41 PM Pisces, 3rd qtr.	Plant biennials, perennials, bulbs and roots. Irrigate. Fertilize (organic). Prune.

Aug. 13, 1:41 PM- Aug. 15, 9:26 PM Aries, 3rd qtr.	Cultivate. Destroy weeds and pests. Harvest fruits and root crops. Trim to retard growth.
Aug. 15, 9:26 PM- Aug. 17, 10:05 PM Taurus, 3rd qtr.	Plant potatoes and tubers. Prune.
Aug. 17, 10:05 PM- Aug. 18, 8:40 AM Taurus, 4th qtr.	Plant potatoes and tubers. Prune.
Aug. 18, 8:40 AM- Aug. 20, 9:24 PM Gemini, 4th qtr.	Cultivate. Destroy weeds and pests. Harvest fruits and root crops. Trim to retard growth.
Aug. 20, 9:24 PM- Aug. 23, 9:13 AM Cancer, 4th qtr.	Plant biennials, perennials, bulbs and roots. Irrigate. Fertilize (organic). Prune.
Aug. 23, 9:13 AM- Aug. 25, 6:50 PM Leo, 4th qtr.	Cultivate. Destroy weeds and pests. Harvest fruits and root crops. Trim to retard growth.
Aug. 25, 6:50 PM- Aug. 25, 11:31 PM Virgo, 4th qtr.	Cultivate, especially medicinal plants. Destroy weeds and pests. Trim to retard growth.
Aug. 28, 2:15 AM- Aug. 30, 7:51 AM Libra, 1st qtr.	Plant annuals for fragrance and beauty. Trim to increase growth.
Aug. 30, 7:51 AM- Sept. 1, 11:57 AM	Plant annuals, grains. Irrigate. Fertilize (chemical).

Scorpio, 1st qtr.	Trim to increase growth. Graft or bud plants.
Sept. 3, 2:45 PM– Sept. 5, 4:48 PM Capricorn, 2nd qtr.	Graft or bud plants. Trim to increase growth.
Sept. 7, 7:09 PM– Sept. 8, 10:38 PM Pisces, 2nd qtr.	Plant annuals, grains. Irrigate. Fertilize (chemical). Trim to increase growth. Graft or bud plants.
Sept. 8, 10:38 PM– Sept. 9, 11:15 PM Pisces, 3rd qtr.	Plant biennials, perennials, bulbs and roots. Irrigate. Fertilize (organic). Prune.
Sept. 9, 11:15 PM– Sept. 12, 6:22 AM Aries, 3rd qtr.	Cultivate. Destroy weeds and pests. Harvest fruits and root crops. Trim to retard growth.
Sept. 12, 6:22 AM– Sept. 14, 4:48 PM Taurus, 3rd qtr.	Plant potatoes and tubers. Prune.
Sept. 14, 4:48 PM– Sept. 16, 4:09 PM Gemini, 3rd qtr.	Cultivate. Destroy weeds and pests. Harvest fruits and root crops. Trim to retard growth.
Sept. 16, 4:09 PM– Sept. 17, 5:16 AM Gemini, 4th qtr.	Cultivate. Destroy weeds and pests. Harvest fruits and root crops. Trim to retard growth.

Sept. 17, 5:16 AM- Sept. 19, 5:19 PM Cancer, 4th qtr.	Plant biennials, perennials, bulbs and roots. Irrigate. Fertilize (organic). Prune.
Sept. 19, 5:19 PM- Sept. 22, 3:01 AM Leo, 4th qtr.	Cultivate. Destroy weeds and pests. Harvest fruits and root crops. Trim to retard growth.
Sept. 22, 3:01 AM- Sept. 24, 9:50 AM Virgo, 4th qtr.	Cultivate, especially medicinal plants. Destroy weeds and pests. Trim to retard growth.
Sept. 24, 11:55 AM- Sept. 26, 2:20 PM Libra, 1st qtr.	Plant annuals for fragrance and beauty. Trim to increase growth.
Sept. 26, 2:20 PM- Sept. 28, 5:31 PM Scorpio, 1st qtr.	Plant annuals, grains. Irrigate. Fertilize (chemical). Trim to increase growth. Graft or bud plants.
Sept. 30, 8:11 PM- Oct. 1, 9:36 AM Capricorn, 1st qtr.	Graft or bud plants. Trim to increase growth.
Oct. 1, 9:36 AM- Oct. 2, 11:00 PM Capricorn, 2nd qtr.	Graft or bud plants. Trim to increase growth.
Oct. 5, 2:36 AM- Oct. 7, 7:42 AM Pisces, 2nd qtr.	Plant annuals, grains. Irrigate. Fertilize (chemical). Trim to increase growth. Graft or bud plants.
Oct. 7, 10:52 AM- Oct. 9, 3:05 PM	Cultivate. Destroy weeds and pests. Harvest fruits

Aries, 3rd qtr.	and root crops. Trim to retard growth.
Oct. 9, 3:05 PM- Oct. 12, 1:10 AM Taurus, 3rd qtr.	Plant potatoes and tubers. Prune.
Oct. 12, 1:10 AM- Oct. 14, 1:20 PM Gemini, 3rd qtr.	Cultivate. Destroy weeds and pests. Harvest fruits and root crops. Trim to retard growth.
Oct. 14, 1:20 PM- Oct. 16, 11:26 AM Cancer, 3rd qtr.	Plant biennials, perennials, bulbs and roots. Irrigate. Fertilize (organic). Prune.
Oct. 16, 11:26 AM- Oct. 17, 1:47 AM Cancer, 4th qtr.	Plant biennials, perennials, bulbs and roots. Irrigate. Fertilize (organic). Prune.
Oct. 17, 1:47 AM- Oct. 19, 12:12 PM Leo, 4th qtr.	Cultivate. Destroy weeds and pests. Harvest fruits and root crops. Trim to retard growth.
Oct. 19, 12:12 PM- Oct. 21, 7:16 PM Virgo, 4th qtr.	Cultivate, especially medicinal plants. Destroy weeds and pests. Trim to retard growth.
Oct. 23, 11:07 PM- Oct. 23, 11:37 PM Scorpio, 4th qtr.	Plant biennials, perennials, bulbs and roots. Irrigate. Fertilize (organic). Prune.
Oct. 23, 11:37 PM- Oct. 26, 12:57 AM	Plant annuals, grains. Irrigate. Fertilize (chemical).

Scorpio, 1st qtr.	Trim to increase growth. Graft or bud plants.
Oct. 28, 2:15 AM- Oct. 30, 4:24 AM Capricorn, 1st qtr.	Graft or bud plants. Trim to increase growth.
Nov. 1, 8:18 AM- Nov. 3, 2:21 PM Pisces, 2nd qtr.	Plant annuals, grains. Irrigate. Fertilize (chemical). Trim to increase growth. Graft or bud plants.
Nov. 5, 10:35 PM- Nov. 7, 2:20 AM Taurus, 2nd qtr.	Plant annuals for hardiness. Trim to increase growth.
Nov. 7, 2:20 AM- Nov. 8, 8:55 AM Taurus, 3rd qtr.	Plant potatoes and tubers. Prune.
Nov. 8, 8:55 AM- Nov. 10, 8:57 PM Gemini, 3rd qtr.	Cultivate. Destroy weeds and pests. Harvest fruits and root crops. Trim to retard growth.
Nov. 10, 8:57 PM- Nov. 13, 9:38 AM Cancer, 3rd qtr.	Plant biennials, perennials, bulbs and roots. Irrigate. Fertilize (organic). Prune.
Nov. 13, 9:38 AM- Nov. 15, 6:41 AM Leo, 3rd qtr.	Cultivate. Destroy weeds and pests. Harvest fruits and root crops. Trim to retard growth.
Nov. 15, 6:41 AM- Nov. 15, 9:03 PM Leo, 4th qtr.	Cultivate. Destroy weeds and pests. Harvest fruits and root crops. Trim to retard growth.

Nov. 15, 9:03 PM– Nov. 18, 5:18 AM Virgo, 4th qtr.	Cultivate, especially medicinal plants. Destroy weeds and pests. Trim to retard growth.
Nov. 20, 9:41 AM– Nov. 22, 10:43 AM Scorpio, 4th qtr.	Plant biennials, perennials, bulbs and roots. Irrigate. Fertilize (organic). Prune.
Nov. 22, 10:43 AM– Nov. 22, 10:57 AM Scorpio, 1st qtr.	Plant annuals, grains. Irrigate. Fertilize (chemical). Trim to increase growth. Graft or bud plants.
Nov. 24, 10:48 AM– Nov. 26, 11:15 AM Capricorn, 1st qtr.	Graft or bud plants. Trim to increase growth.
Nov. 28, 1:59 PM– Nov. 29, 1:28 AM Pisces, 1st qtr.	Plant annuals, grains. Irrigate. Fertilize (chemical). Trim to increase growth. Graft or bud plants.
Nov. 29, 1:28 AM– Nov. 30, 7:51 PM Pisces, 2nd qtr.	Plant annuals, grains. Irrigate. Fertilize (chemical). Trim to increase growth. Graft or bud plants.
Dec. 3, 4:40 AM– Dec. 5, 3:35 PM Taurus, 2nd qtr.	Plant annuals for hardiness. Trim to increase growth.
Dec. 6, 8:28 PM– Dec. 8, 3:45 AM Gemini, 3rd qtr.	Cultivate. Destroy weeds and pests. Harvest fruits and root crops. Trim to retard growth.

Dec. 8 3:45 AM- Dec. 10 4:25 PM Cancer, 3rd qtr.	Plant biennials, perennials, bulbs and roots. Irrigate. Fertilize (organic). Prune.
Dec. 10 4:25 PM- Dec. 13 4:27 AM Leo, 3rd qtr.	Cultivate. Destroy weeds and pests. Harvest fruits and root crops. Trim to retard growth.
Dec. 13 4:27 AM- Dec. 15 12:32 AM Virgo, 3rd qtr.	Cultivate, especially medicinal plants. Destroy weeds and pests. Trim to retard growth.
Dec. 15, 12:32 AM- Dec. 15 2:09 PM Virgo, 4th qtr.	Cultivate, especially medicinal plants. Destroy weeds and pests. Trim to retard growth.
Dec. 17, 8:07 PM- Dec. 19 10:13 PM Scorpio, 4th qtr.	Plant biennials, perennials, bulbs and roots. Irrigate. Fertilize (organic). Prune.
Dec. 19, 10:13 PM- Dec. 21 9:22 PM Sagittarius, 4th qtr.	Cultivate. Destroy weeds and pests. Harvest fruits and root crops. Trim to retard growth.
Dec. 21, 9:46 PM- Dec. 23 8:52 PM Capricorn, 1st qtr.	Graft or bud plants. Trim to increase growth.
Dec. 25, 9:45 PM- Dec. 28 2:06 AM Pisces, 1st qtr.	Plant annuals, grains. Irrigate. Fertilize (chemical). Trim to increase growth. Graft or bud plants.

DATES TO DESTROY
WEEDS AND PESTS

The Moon's sign and phase indicate the best dates to eliminate weeds, pests, insects, etc. Following are dates for 1995 when this will be most effective.

Jan. 16, 10:37 PM—Jan. 19, 6:40 AM (Leo 3rd qtr.)
Jan. 19, 6:40 AM—Jan 21, 12:54 PM (Vir. 3rd qtr.)
Jan. 25, 8:37 PM—Jan 27, 10:27 PM (Sag. 4th qtr.)
Jan. 30, 12:03 AM—Jan. 30, 5:35 PM (Aqu. 4th qtr.)
Feb. 15, 7:16 AM—Feb. 15, 1:52 PM (Leo 3rd qtr.)
Feb. 15, 1:52 PM—Feb. 17, 7:01 PM (Vir. 3rd qtr.)
Feb. 22, 2:13 AM—Feb. 24, 5:12 AM (Sag. 4th qtr.)
Feb. 26, 8:14 AM—Feb. 28, 12:16 PM (Aqu. 4th qtr.)
Mar. 16, 8:26 PM—Mar. 17, 3:18 AM (Vir. 3rd qtr.)
Mar. 21, 7:57 AM—Mar. 23, 10:31 AM (Sag. 3rd qtr.)
Mar. 25, 2:10 PM—Mar. 27, 7:18 PM (Aqu. 4th qtr.)
Mar. 30, 2:26 AM—Mar. 30, 9:09 PM (Ari. 4th qtr.)
Apr. 17, 3:52 PM—Apr. 19, 4:54 PM (Sag. 3rd qtr.)
Apr. 22, 7:38 PM—Apr. 24, 12:51 AM (Aqu. 3rd, 4th qtr.)
Apr. 26, 8:42 AM—Apr. 28, 6:53 PM (Ari. 4th qtr.)

May 15, 1:59 AM—May 17, 1:36 AM (Sag. 3rd qtr.)
May 19, 2:40 AM—May 21, 6:40 AM (Aqu. 3rd, 4th qtr.)
May 23, 2:13 PM—May 26, 12:46 AM (Ari. 4th qtr.)
May 28, 1:07 PM—May 29, 4:27 AM (Gem. 4th qtr.)
Jun. 12, 11:04 PM—Jun. 13, 12:05 PM (Sag. 3rd qtr.)
Jun. 15, 11:52 AM—Jun. 17, 2:13 PM (Aqu. 3rd qtr.)
Jun. 19, 8:29 PM—Jun. 22, 6:35 AM (Ari. 4th qtr.)
Jun. 24, 7:02 PM—Jun. 27, 7:57 AM (Gem. 4th qtr.)
Jul. 12, 10:21 PM—Jul. 14, 11:37 PM (Aqu. 3rd qtr.)
Jul. 17, 4:23 AM—Jul. 19, 1:21 PM (Ari. 3rd, 4th qtr.)
Jul. 22, 1:24 AM—Jul. 24, 2:17 PM (Gem. 4th qtr.)
Jul. 27, 2:07 AM—Jul. 27, 10:14 AM (Leo 4th qtr.)
Aug. 10, 1:16 PM—Aug. 11, 9:46 AM (Aqu. 3rd qtr.)
Aug. 13, 1:41 PM—Aug. 15, 9:26 PM (Ari. 3rd qtr.)
Aug. 18, 8:40 AM—Aug. 20, 9:24 PM (Gem. 4th qtr.)
Aug. 23, 9:13 AM—Aug. 25, 6:50 PM (Leo 4th qtr.)
Aug. 25, 6:50 PM—Aug. 25, 11:31 PM (Vir. 4th qtr.)
Sep. 9, 11:15 PM—Sep. 12, 6:22 AM (Ari. 3rd qtr.)
Sep. 14, 4:48 PM—Sep. 17, 5:16 AM (Gem. 3rd, 4th qtr.)
Sep. 19, 5:19 PM—Sep. 22, 3:01 AM (Leo 4th qtr.)
Sep. 22, 3:01 AM—Sep. 24, 9:50 AM (Vir. 4th qtr.)
Oct. 8, 10:52 AM—Oct. 9, 3:05 PM (Ari. 3rd qtr.)
Oct. 12, 1:10 AM—Oct. 14, 1:20 PM (Gem. 3rd qtr.)
Oct. 17, 1:47 AM—Oct. 19, 12:12 PM (Leo 4th qtr.)
Oct. 19, 12:12 PM—Oct. 21, 7:16 PM (Vir. 4th qtr.)
Nov. 8, 8:55 AM—Nov. 10, 8:57 PM (Gem. 3rd qtr.)
Nov. 13, 9:38 AM—Nov. 15, 9:03 PM (Leo 3rd, 4th qtr.)
Nov. 15, 9:03 PM—Nov. 18, 5:18 AM (Vir. 4th qtr.)
Dec. 6, 8:28 PM—Dec. 8, 3:45 AM (Gem. 3rd qtr.)
Dec. 10, 4:25 PM—Dec. 13, 4:27 AM (Leo 3rd qtr.)
Dec. 13, 4:27 AM—Dec. 15, 2:09 PM (Vir. 3rd, 4th qtr.)
Dec. 19, 10:13 PM—Dec. 21, 9:22 PM (Sag. 4th qtr.)

OTHER GARDEN-RELATED ACTIVITIES

Animal Husbandry
Animals are easiest to handle when the Moon is in Taurus, Cancer, Libra or Pisces. Avoid the Full Moon. Buy animals during the first quarter. Castrate animals in any sign except Leo, Scorpio or Sagittarius. Avoid the Full Moon. Slaughter for food in the first three days after the Full Moon in any sign except Leo.

Composting
Start compost when the Moon is in the fourth quarter in a water sign, especially Scorpio.

Cultivating
Cultivate when the Moon is in a barren sign and waning, ideally the fourth quarter in Aries, Gemini, Leo, Virgo or Aquarius.

Cutting Timber
Cut timber during the third and fourth quarters while the Moon is not in a water sign. This will diminish the rotting.

Drying Crops
Dry crops in the third quarter when the Moon is in a fire sign.

Fertilizing
Fertilize when the Moon is in a fruitful sign (Cancer, Scorpio, Pisces). Organic fertilizers are best used when the Moon is in the third or fourth quarter. Chemical fertilizers are best used in the first or second quarter.

Grafting
Graft during Capricorn, Cancer or Scorpio while the Moon is in the first or second quarter.

Harvesting
Harvest root crops when the Moon is in a dry sign (Aries, Leo, Sagittarius, Gemini, Aquarius) and in the third or fourth quarter. Harvest root crops intended for seed during the Full Moon. Harvest grain which will be stored just after the Full Moon, avoiding the water signs (Cancer, Scorpio, Pisces). Fire signs are best for cutting down on water content. Harvest fruits in the third and fourth quarters in the dry signs.

Irrigation
Irrigate when the Moon is in a water sign.

Mowing the Lawn
Mow in the first and second quarters to increase growth and lushness, in the third and fourth quarters to decrease growth.

Picking Mushrooms
Gather mushrooms at the Full Moon.

Pruning
Prune during the third and fourth quarters in Scorpio to retard growth and to promote better fruit, and in Capricorn to promote better healing.

Spraying
Destroy pests and weeds during the fourth quarter when the Moon is in a barren sign.

Transplanting
Transplant when the Moon is increasing and preferably in Cancer, Scorpio or Pisces.

A GUIDE TO PLANTING USING PHASE & SIGN RULERSHIPS

PLANT	PHASE	SIGN
Annuals	1st or 2nd	
Apple trees	1st or 2nd	Cancer, Pisces, Taurus
Artichokes	1st	Cancer, Pisces, Virgo
Asparagus	1st	Cancer, Scorpio, Pisces
Asters	1st or 2nd	Virgo, Libra
Barley	1st or 2nd	Cancer, Pisces, Libra, Capricorn Virgo
Beans (bush & pole)	2nd	Cancer, Taurus Pisces, Libra,
Beans (kidney, white & navy)	1st or 2nd	Cancer, Pisces

PLANT	PHASE	SIGN
Beech trees	1st or 2nd	Virgo, Taurus
Beets	1st or 2nd	Cancer, Capricorn Pisces, Libra,
Biennials	3rd or 4th	
Broccoli	1st	Cancer, Pisces, Libra
Brussels sprouts	1st	Cancer, Scorpio, Pisces, Libra
Buckwheat	1st or 2nd	Capricorn
Bulbs	3rd	Cancer, Scorpio, Pisces
Bulbs for seed	2nd or 3rd	
Cabbage	1st	Cancer, Scorpio, Pisces, Libra, Taurus
Cactus		Taurus, Capricorn
Canes (raspberries, blackberries & gooseberries)	2nd	Cancer, Scorpio, Pisces
Cantaloupes	1st or 2nd	Cancer, Scorpio, Pisces, Libra, Taurus
Carrots	3rd	Taurus
Cauliflower	1st	Cancer, Scorpio, Pisces, Libra

PLANT	PHASE	SIGN
Celeriac	3rd	Cancer, Scorpio, Pisces
Celery	1st or 2nd	Cancer, Scorpio, Pisces
Cereals	1st or 2nd	Cancer, Scorpio, Pisces, Libra
Chard	1st or 2nd	Cancer, Scorpio, Pisces
Chicory	3rd	Cancer, Scorpio, Pisces
Chrysanthe-mums	1st or 2nd	Virgo
Clover	1st or 2nd	Cancer, Scorpio, Pisces
Corn	1st	Cancer, Scorpio, Pisces
Corn for fodder	1st or 2nd	Libra
Coryopsis	2nd or 3rd	Libra
Cosmos	2nd or 3rd	Libra
Cress	1st	Cancer, Scorpio, Pisces
Crocus	1st or 2nd	Virgo
Cucumbers	1st	Cancer, Scorpio, Pisces
Daffodils	1st or 2nd	Libra, Virgo
Dahlias	1st or 2nd	Libra, Virgo

PLANT	PHASE	SIGN
Deciduous trees	1st or 2nd	Cancer, Scorpio, Pisces, Virgo
Eggplant	2nd	Cancer, Scorpio, Pisces, Libra
Endive	1st	Cancer, Scorpio, Pisces, Libra
Flowers for:		
beauty	1st	Libra
abundance	1st	Cancer, Pisces, Virgo
sturdiness	1st	Scorpio
hardiness	1st	Taurus
Garlic	1st or 2nd	Cancer, Pisces
Gladiola	1st or 2nd	Libra, Virgo
Gourds	1st or 2nd	Cancer, Scorpio, Pisces, Libra
Grapes	2nd or 3rd	Cancer, Scorpio, Pisces, Virgo
Hay	1st or 2nd	Cancer, Scorpio, Pisces, Libra, Taurus
Herbs	1st or 2nd	Cancer, Scorpio, Pisces
Honeysuckle	1st or 2nd	Scorpio, Virgo
Hops	1st or 2nd	Scorpio, Libra
Horseradish	1st or 2nd	Cancer, Scorpio, Pisces

PLANT	PHASE	SIGN
House plants	1st	Libra (flowering), Cancer, Scorpio (vines), Pisces
Hyacinths	3rd	Cancer, Scorpio, Pisces
Iris	1st or 2nd	Cancer, Virgo
Kohlrabi	1st or 2nd	Cancer, Scorpio, Pisces, Libra
Leeks	1st or2nd	Cancer, Pisces
Lettuce	1st	Cancer, Scorpio, Pisces, Libra, Taurus (late sowings)
Lilies	1st or 2nd	Cancer, Scorpio, Pisces
Maple trees	1st or 2nd	Virgo
Melons	1st or 2nd	Cancer, Scorpio, Pisces
Moon vine	1st or 2nd	Virgo
Morning-glory	1st or 2nd	Cancer, Scorpio, Pisces, Virgo
Oak trees	3rd	Virgo
Oats	1st or 2nd	Cancer, Scorpio, Pisces, Libra
Okra	1st	Cancer, Scorpio, Pisces, Libra
Onion seeds	2nd	Scorpio, Cancer

PLANT	PHASE	SIGN
Onion sets	3rd or 4th	Libra, Taurus, Pisces
Pansies	1st or 2nd	Cancer, Scorpio, Pisces
Parsley	1st	Cancer, Scorpio, Pisces, Libra
Parsnips	3rd	Taurus, Capricorn, Cancer, Scorpio
Peach trees	3rd	Taurus, Libra
Peanuts	3rd	Cancer, Scorpio, Pisces
Pear trees	3rd	Taurus, Libra
Peas	2nd or 3rd	Cancer, Scorpio, Pisces, Libra
Peonies	1st or 2nd	Virgo
Peppers	1st or 2nd	Cancer, Pisces
Perennials	3rd	
Petunias	1st or 2nd	Libra, Virgo
Plum trees	1st or 2nd	Taurus, Virgo
Poppies	1st or 2nd	Virgo
Portulaca	1st or 2nd	Virgo
Potatoes	3rd	Cancer, Scorpio, Taurus, Libra, Capricorn, Sagittarius (for seed)
Privet	1st or 2nd	Taurus, Libra
Pumpkins	2nd	Cancer, Scorpio, Pisces, Libra

PLANT	PHASE	SIGN
Quinces	1st or 2nd	Capricorn
Radishes	1st or 2nd	Cancer, Libra, Taurus, Pisces Capricorn
Rhubarb	1st or 2nd	Cancer, Pisces
Rice	1st or 2nd	Scorpio
Roses	1st or 2nd	Cancer, Virgo
Rutabagas	3rd	Cancer, Scorpio, Pisces, Taurus
Saffron	1st or 2nd	Cancer, Scorpio, Pisces
Sage	3rd	Cancer, Scorpio, Pisces
Salsify	1st or 2nd	Cancer, Scorpio, Pisces
Shallots	2nd	Scorpio
Spinach	1st	Cancer, Scorpio, Pisces
Squash	2nd	Cancer, Scorpio, Pisces, Libra
Strawberries	3rd	Cancer, Scorpio, Pisces
String beans	1st or 2nd	Taurus
Sunflowers	3rd or 4th	Libra
Sweet peas	1st or 2nd	Cancer, Scorpio, Pisces

PLANT	PHASE	SIGN
Tomatoes	2nd, trans-plant in 3rd	Cancer, Scorpio, Pisces, Capricorn (if hot and dry)
Trees:		
shade	3rd	Taurus, Capricorn
ornamental	2nd	Libra, Taurus
erosion control	3rd	Cancer, Scorpio, Pisces, Taurus, Capricorn
Trumpet vines	1st or 2nd	Cancer, Scorpio, Pisces
Tubers for seed	3rd	Cancer, Scorpio, Pisces, Libra
Tulips	1st or 2nd	Libra, Virgo
Turnips	3rd	Cancer, Scorpio, Pisces, Taurus, Capricorn, Libra
Valerian	1st or 2nd	Virgo, Gemini
Watermelons	1st or 2nd	Cancer, Scorpio, Pisces, Libra
Wheat	1st or 2nd	Cancer, Scorpio, Pisces, Libra

COMPANION PLANTING

PLANT	HELPERS	HINDERED BY
Asparagus	Tomatoes, parsley, basil	
Beans	Carrots, cucumbers, cabbage, beets, corn	Onions, gladiola
Bush beans	Cucumbers, cabbage, strawberries	Fennel, onions
Beets	Onions, cabbage, lettuce	Pale beans
Cabbage	Beets, potatoes, onions, celery	Strawberries, tomatoes
Carrots	Peas, lettuce, chives, radishes leeks, onions	Dill
Celery	Leeks, bush beans	

PLANT	HELPERS	HINDERED BY
Chives		Beans
Corn	Potatoes, beans, peas, melons, squash, pumpkins, cucumbers	
Cucumbers	Beans, cabbage radishes, sunflowers, lettuce	Potatoes, aromatic herbs
Eggplant	Beans	
Lettuce	Strawberries, carrots	
Melons	Morning-glories	
Onions, leeks	Beets, chamomile, carrots, lettuce	Peas, beans
Garlic	Summer savory	
Peas	Radishes, carrots, corn, cucumbers, beans, turnips	Onions
Potatoes	Beans, corn, peas, cabbage, hemp, cucumbers	Sunflowers
Radishes	Peas, lettuce, nasturtium, cucumbers	Hyssop
Spinach	Strawberries	
Squash, pumpkins	Nasturtium, corn	Potatoes

PLANT	HELPERS	HINDERED BY
Tomatoes	Asparagus, parsley, chives, onions, carrots, marigold, nasturtium	Dill, cabbage, fennel
Turnips	Peas, beans	

PLANT	COMPANIONS AND USES
Anise	Coriander
Basil	Tomatoes; dislikes rue; repels flies and mosquitoes
Borage	Tomatoes and squash
Buttercup	Clover; hinders delphiniums, peonies, monkshood, columbines and others of this family
Chamomile	Small amounts help peppermint, wheat, onions and cabbage; destructive in large amounts;
Catnip	Repels flea beetles
Chervil	Radishes
Chives	Carrots; spray against apple scab and powdery mildew
Coriander	Hinders seed formation in fennel
Cosmos	Repels corn earworm
Dill	Cabbage; hinders carrots and tomatoes
Fennel	Disliked by all garden plants

Garlic	Aids vetch and roses; hinders peas and beans
Hemp	Beneficial as a neighbor to most plants
Horseradish	Repels potato bugs
Horsetail	Makes fungicide spray
Hyssop	Attracts cabbage fly away from cabbages; harmful to radishes
Lovage	Improves hardiness and flavor of neighbor plants
Marigold	Pest repellent; use against Mexican bean beetles and nematodes; makes spray
Mint	Repels ants, flea beetles and cabbage worm butterflies
Morning-glory	Corn; helps melon germination
Nasturtium	Cabbage, cucumbers, squash and melons; deters aphids, squash bugs and pumpkin beetles
Nettles	Increase oil content in neighbors
Parsley	Tomatoes, asparagus
Purslane	Good ground cover
Rosemary	Cabbage, beans and carrots; repels cabbage moths, bean beetles and carrot flies
Sage	Repels cabbage moths and carrot flies
Summer savory	Deters bean beetles
Sunflower	Hinders potatoes; improves soil

PLANT	COMPANIONS AND USES
Tansy	Roses; deters flying insects, Japanese beetles, striped cucumber beetles, ants and squash bugs
Thyme	Repels cabbage worm
Yarrow	Increases essential oils of neighbors

BREEDING ANIMALS &
SETTING EGGS

Eggs should be set and animals mated so that the young will be born when the Moon is increasing and in a fruitful sign (Cancer, Scorpio and Pisces). Young born in a fruitful sign are generally healthier, mature faster and make better breeding stock. Those born during a semi-fruitful sign (Taurus and Capricorn) will generally still mature quickly, but will produce leaner meat. The sign of Libra yields beautiful, graceful animals for showing and racing.

To determine the best date to mate animals or set eggs, subtract the number of days given for incubation or gestation from the fruitful dates given in the following tables. For example, cats and dogs are mated 63 days previous to the desired birth date; chicken eggs are set 21 days previous.

GESTATION AND INCUBATION

Animal	Number of Young	Gestation
Horse	1	346 days
Cow	1	283 days
Monkey	1	164 days
Goat	1-2	151 days
Sheep	1-2	150 days
Pig	10	112 days
Chinchilla	2	110 days
Fox	5-8	63 days
Dog	6-8	63 days
Cat	4-6	63 days
Guinea pig	2-6	62 days
Ferret	6-9	40 days
Rabbit	4-8	30 days
Rat	10	22 days
Mouse	10	22 days

Domestic Fowl	Number of Eggs	Incubation
Turkey	12-15	26-30 days
Guinea	15-18	25-26 days
Pea hen	10	28-30 days
Duck	9-12	25-32 days
Goose	15-18	27-33 days
Hen	12-15	19-24 days
Pigeon	2	16-20 days
Canary	3-4	13-14 days

BEST DATES FOR SETTING EGGS

Dates to be Born	Moon's Sign and phase	Set Eggs
Jan. 4, 4:49 PM– Jan 6, 11:57 PM	Pisces 1st qtr.	Dec. 14-16
Jan. 9, 10:58 AM– Jan. 11, 11:57 PM	Taurus 2nd qtr.	Dec. 19-21
Jan. 14, 12:20 PM– Jan. 16, 3:27 PM	Cancer 2nd qtr.	Dec. 24-26
Feb. 1, 3:05 AM– Feb. 3, 9:12 AM	Pisces 1st qtr.	Jan. 11-13
Feb. 5, 7:08 PM– Feb. 8, 7:44 AM	Taurus 1st qtr.	Jan. 15-18
Feb. 10, 8:17 PM– Feb. 13, 6:32 AM	Cancer 2nd qtr.	Jan. 20-23
Mar. 1, 6:48 AM– Mar. 2, 6:30 PM	Pisces 1st qtr.	Feb. 8-9
Mar. 5, 3:51 AM– Mar. 7, 3:56 PM	Taurus 1st qtr.	Feb. 12-14
Mar. 10, 4:41 AM– Mar. 12, 3:29 PM	Cancer 2nd qtr.	Feb. 17-19
Apr. 1, 11:59 AM– Apr. 3, 11:50 PM	Taurus 1st qtr.	Mar. 11-13
Apr. 6, 12:40 PM– Apr. 9, 12:16 AM	Cancer 1st qtr.	Mar. 16-19

Apr. 13, 1:20 PM– Apr. 15, 7:08 AM	Libra 2nd qtr.	Mar. 23-25
Apr. 29, 12:37 PM– May 1, 6:53 AM	Taurus 1st qtr.	Apr. 8-10
May 3, 7:45 PM– May 6, 7:55 PM	Cancer 1st qtr.	Apr. 12-15
May 10, 11:30 PM– May 13, 1:54 AM	Libra 2nd qtr.	Apr. 19-22
May 31, 1:59 AM– Jun. 2, 2:17 PM	Cancer 1st qtr.	May 10-12
Jun. 7, 8:14 AM– Jun. 9, 12:04 PM	Libra 2nd qtr.	May 17-19
Jun. 27, 7:51 PM– Jun. 29, 8:02 PM	Cancer 1st qtr.	Jun. 6-8
Jul. 4, 2:56 PM– Jul. 6, 8:19 PM	Libra 1st qtr.	Jun. 13-15
Jul. 31, 8:24 PM– Aug. 3, 2:29 AM	Libra 1st qtr.	Jul. 10-13
Aug. 28, 2:15 AM– Aug. 30, 7:51 AM	Libra 1st qtr.	Aug. 7-9
Sep. 7, 7:09 PM– Sep. 9, 11:15 PM	Pisces 2nd qtr.	Aug. 17-19
Sep. 24, 11:55 AM– Sep. 26, 2:20 PM	Libra 1st qtr.	Sep. 3-5
Oct. 5, 2:36 AM– Oct. 7, 7:42 AM	Pisces 2nd qtr.	Sep. 14-16
Nov. 1, 8:18 AM– Nov. 3, 2:21 PM	Pisces 2nd qtr.	Oct. 15-18

Nov. 5, 10:35 PM- Nov. 8, 8:55 AM	Taurus 2nd qtr.	Oct. 15-18
Nov. 28, 1:59 PM- Nov. 30, 7:51 PM	Pisces 2nd qtr.	Nov. 7-9
Dec. 3, 4:40 AM- Dec. 5, 3:35 PM	Taurus 2nd qtr.	Nov. 12-14
Dec. 25, 9:45 PM- Dec. 28, 2:06 AM	Pisces 1st qtr.	Dec. 4-7
Dec. 30, 10:22 AM- Jan. 1, 9:30 AM	Taurus 2nd qtr.	Dec. 9

CREATING A MOON GARDEN

By Carly Wall

My garden has always been a place from which I've drawn strength, peace, and connection to the Earth. Traditionally, gardens have been placed with the sun in mind. The warm sunshine, after all, was what the plants longed for to grow and thrive. Of course I enjoy the sun, and gardening in this way was always a pleasure, but secretly, I've always been taken with the Moon. So, when I learned that I could garden by the light of these silvery rays, I was thrilled.

I had to discover the secret, and secret it was. There are many blossoms that open at dusk, but I had never heard of them. Today, many gardeners are not free to enjoy their "daylight" gardens during the day—they have to work. By the time they do get a few moments of quiet reflection, the shadows of darkness have begun to fall. There are weekends, but responsibilities and weeding consume that time.

For busy gardeners, a Moon garden seems the perfect answer. Not only can you enjoy cool summer breezes after a hard work, but night-blooming flowers delight and amaze. Moon flowers have enticing scents. Why are these night plants filled with such heady perfume? Most are pollinated by night-flying insects, so they lure these creatures by smell instead of by sight.

Since these night flowers are often exotic plants, you may have to treat them as annuals unless you live where the climate is temperate. But for northern gardens, the extra work of planting them every year is worth it. There are a few hardier plants you can choose from to fill your special spot, too.

There are two ways to create your mystery garden. The first is the oldest and most natural: using the Moon to light the way. The second way is when you want to use artificial lighting to highlight the scene. Although I go for natural light most of the time, both ways have their advantages.

In the artificially illuminated garden, you may plan your setting anywhere you wish, and it need not be fully open to the sky. You don't need to be especially careful about your walkways, either, as you won't be walking around in the dark. You will want fragrant night flowers, though, as this is what the garden is all about, except that you can go for the showier blossoms in a range of colors, you don't have to stick with white. The only concern is the type of lighting used. You don't want too much light, as this detracts from the aura of the setting. After all, you don't want it to look like daylight — you'll be defeating your purpose. Visit a home center that sells all types of lights and lighting. There are some wonderful lights which can be used to illuminate paths, delicately lighting certain areas without being harsh. There are others that you can place at the garden's entrance to add a luminescent-shadowy glow to the rest of the tour; some with movement sensors, some battery-operated.

For the natural garden, the concern is mainly on the design and plant material, but there are a few things to consider. Here, safe footing must be ensured. Make pathways clear and smooth so there aren't any falls to ruin the enjoyment of the evening—and that includes paths which stay slippery—in heavy dew or rain. In plant choice, fragrance is the key, as moon-glow will sometimes be hidden by cloud cover.

The hard part is in planning. From my experience, I've learned that it is never wise, in garden plans, to start out large. Knowing this, I knew my Moon garden would have to be small, but large enough to be special. I decided to make the corner off my front porch my target. It was partially shaded, which most night-loving plants like, but it was open to the Moon. It would also be a good compact size, from the corner of the porch to the edge of the house, and it was easy to access (a step led down to that area).

Although you can choose the site and placement of your variety of plants, I will show you the plants I chose. I've also included some fragrant or pretty day plants and herbs to fill the garden out and give it an equally nice daytime look.

Here are a few plants you may want to include in your garden:

Night blooms

Moonflower (*I. noctiflora*): This is a brilliant white flower which is large and showy, somewhat like a large morning glory, but sweet-scented. It opens in early twilight, while the plant is vining, and reaches a height of 10 feet.

Flowering tobacco (*Nicotiana*): This is a genus of mostly native American plants grown in temperate climates, but they can be grown as annuals elsewhere. They are very fragrant, tubular flowers with a sweet honey scent not unlike jasmine. In the evenings, flowers will open around dusk, but on cloudy days you can also catch them coming out.

Night-blooming silene (*Silene noctiflora*): These plants have creamy white flowers with pink at the center. They grow to 3 feet tall.

Evening primrose (*Oenothera*): This is a really show-stopping night plant, which blooms all summer. Most have yellow flowers, but there is one variety with white (*O. trichocaly*). It blooms the first year from seed, opens its blooms at night, and stays open during the day. It releases its fragrance at night only, attracting moths to pollinate it. It is an easy grower and self-seeding, growing 4-6 feet tall.

Evening stock (*Matthiola bicornis*): A straggling, branchy annual with small, fragrant lilac blossoms which perfume the air as they open toward evening. It is hardy, grows 15 inches tall and blooms from July to September.

Night-blooming pea (*Multibloom tephrosia*): From the pea family, these snow white, pealike flowers open in late evening and close by morning. They grow up to 2 feet, but can sprawl and look "leggy."

Honeysuckle (*Heckrotti plan*): This is a vining plant, blooming spring and summer, with a great quantity of showy, fragrant night flowers.

Japanese daylily (*H. Thunbergii*): This is a late bloomer, opening in July and August with blossoms 2-3 inches long.

Tuberose (*Polianthes*): This is a rich-scented, waxy white flower which blooms late summer to fall. Northern gardeners must dig the bulbs in fall to store over the winter.

Oriental lily (*Casablanca*): This 10-inch fragrant flower is dazzling white, with auburn anthers 4-5 feet tall.

Fillers and other good plants for night gardening

White pampas grass (*Cortaderia selloana*): A very showy plant; good for dramatic effect in evening gardens. It has spear-leaves of a grass-like nature with powdery, feathery blooms. It blooms in late summer and is a perennial, growing 6-12 feet.

Ornamental sage (*Salvia*): There is a silver white variety that blossoms beautifully, growing 18 inches and covered with silvery white spikes. There are many other salvias in various colors to choose from, but for the night garden, the white is especially easy to see. Salvias have no strong scent, but are visual plants that blend well with other scents.

Sweet woodruff: This is a lovely groundcover, which blooms delicate white flowers in May and June. It has a distinct vanilla aroma when the leaves are dried. It fills out bare spots and gives the appearance of a woodland garden. Druids used this plant in their Mayday celebrations, and it was often used in medival times in tussie mussies and sachets.

Caladium (*White Queen*): This is a stunning plant with unusual leaves that simply glow at night. The leaves are white, shading to green, and stay beautiful all season. Dig the bulbs and store through winter. It likes semi-shade and grows 18-20 inches.

Dusty miller (*Cineraria*): This is an annual I chose for its silver foilage, which looks nice with the white flowers growing around it. It's easy to grow, and reaches only 8 inches in height.

Lavender cotton (*Santolina*): An aromatic with a feathery texture and a silvery gray-green color. This makes the perfect plant to use as a hedge to outline the night garden. It can grow up to 2 feet, and can be pruned lower.

Mystic Moon

★ **How to Find Your Moon Sign**
★ **Personal Moon Signs**
★ **Lunar Cycles**
★ **Moon Lore**

HOW TO FIND YOUR MOON SIGN

Every year we give tables for the position of the Moon during that year, but it is more complicated to give tables for the Moon position in any year because of its continuous movement. However, the problem was solved long ago by Grant Lewi in *Astrology for the Millions*, a do-it-yourself manual (available from Llewellyn). Here's Lewi's system:

1. Find your birth year in the Moon Tables.
2. Run down the left-hand column and see if your date is there.
3. If your date is in the left-hand column, run over this line until you come to the column under your birth year. Here you will find a number. This is your base number. Write it down, and go directly to the direction under the heading "What to Do with Your Base Number" on the next page.

4. If your birth date is not in the left-hand column, get a pencil and paper. Your birth date falls between two numbers in the left-hand column. Look at the date closest *after* your birth date; run over this line to your birth year. Write down the number you find there, and label it "top number." Having done this, write directly beneath it on your piece of paper the number printed just above it in the table. Label this "bottom number." Subtract the bottom number from the top number. If the top number is smaller, add 360 to it and then subtract. The result is your difference.

5. Go back to the left-hand column and find the date *before* your birth date. Determine the number of days between this date and your birth date. Write this down and label it "intervening days."

6. In the table of difference below, note which group your difference (found at 4, above) falls in.

Difference	Daily Motion
80-87	12 degrees
88-94	13 degrees
95-101	14 degrees
102-106	15 degrees

Note: If you were born in a leap year *and*

use the difference between February 26th and March 5th, use the following table:

Difference	Daily Motion
94-99	12 degrees
100-108	13 degrees
109-115	14 degrees
115-122	15 degrees

7. Write down the "daily motion" corresponding to your place in the proper table of difference above. Multiply this daily motion by the number labeled "intervening days" (found at step 5).

8. Add the result of 7 to your bottom number (under step 4). This is your base number. If it is more than 360, subtract 360 from it and call the result your base number.

WHAT TO DO WITH YOUR BASE NUMBER

Turn to the Table of Base Numbers and locate your base number in it. At the top of the column you will find the sign your Moon was in. At the left you will find the degree your Moon occupied at:

7 AM of your birth date if you were born under Eastern Standard Time.

6 AM of your birth date if you were born under Central Standard Time.

5 AM of your birth date if you were born under Mountain Standard Time.

4 AM of your birth date if you were born under Pacific Standard Time.

If you don't know the hour of your birth, accept this as your Moon's sign and degree.

If you do know the hour of your birth, get the exact degree as follows:

If you were born *after* 7 AM, Eastern Standard Time (6 AM Central Standard Time, etc.), determine the number of hours after the time that you were born. Divide this by two. Add this to your base number, and the result in the table will be the exact degree and sign of the Moon on the year, month, date and hour of your birth.

If you were born *before* 7 AM Eastern Standard Time (6 AM Central Standard Time, etc.), determine the number of hours before the time that you were born. Divide this by two. Subtract this from your base number, and the result in the table will be the exact degree and sign of the Moon on the year, month, date and hour of your birth.

TABLE OF BASE NUMBERS

	Aries (13)	Taurus (14)	Gemini (15)	Cancer (16)	Leo (17)	Virgo (18)	Libra (19)	Scorpio (20)	Sagittarius (21)	Capricorn (22)	Aquarius (23)	Pisces (24)
0 deg.	0	30	60	90	120	150	180	210	240	270	300	330
1 deg.	1	31	61	91	121	151	181	211	241	271	301	331
2 deg.	2	32	62	92	122	152	182	212	242	272	302	332
3 deg.	3	33	63	93	123	153	183	213	243	273	303	333
4 deg.	4	34	64	94	124	154	184	214	244	274	304	334
5 deg.	5	35	65	95	125	155	185	215	245	275	305	335
6 deg.	6	36	66	96	126	156	186	216	246	276	306	336
7 deg.	7	37	67	97	127	157	187	217	247	277	307	337
8 deg.	8	38	68	98	128	158	188	218	248	278	308	338
9 deg.	9	39	69	99	129	159	189	219	249	279	309	339
10 deg.	10	40	70	100	130	160	190	220	250	280	310	340
11 deg.	11	41	71	101	131	161	191	221	251	281	311	341
12 deg.	12	42	72	102	132	162	192	222	252	282	312	342
13 deg.	13	43	73	103	133	163	193	223	253	283	313	343
14 deg.	14	44	74	104	134	164	194	224	254	284	314	344
15 deg.	15	45	75	105	135	165	195	225	255	285	315	345
16 deg.	16	46	76	106	136	166	196	226	256	286	316	346
17 deg.	17	47	77	107	137	167	197	227	257	287	317	347
18 deg.	18	48	78	108	138	168	198	228	258	288	318	248
19 deg.	19	49	79	109	139	169	199	229	259	289	319	349
20 deg.	20	50	80	110	140	170	200	230	260	290	320	350
21 deg.	21	51	81	111	141	171	201	231	261	291	321	351
22 deg.	22	52	82	112	142	172	202	232	262	292	322	352
23 deg.	23	53	83	113	143	173	203	233	263	293	323	353
24 deg.	24	54	84	114	144	174	204	234	264	294	324	354
25 deg.	25	55	85	115	145	175	205	235	265	295	325	355
26 deg.	26	56	86	116	146	176	206	236	266	296	326	356
27 deg.	27	57	87	117	147	177	207	237	267	297	327	357
28 deg.	28	58	88	118	148	178	208	238	268	298	328	358
29 deg.	29	59	89	119	149	179	209	239	269	299	329	359

		1901	1902	1903	1904	1905	1906	1907	1908	1909	1910
Jan.	1	55	188	308	76	227	358	119	246	39	168
Jan.	8	149	272	37	179	319	82	208	350	129	252
Jan.	15	234	2	141	270	43	174	311	81	213	346
Jan.	22	327	101	234	353	138	273	44	164	309	84
Jan.	29	66	196	317	84	238	6	128	255	50	175
Feb.	5	158	280	46	188	328	90	219	359	138	259
Feb.	12	241	12	149	279	51	184	319	90	221	356
Feb.	19	335	111	242	2	146	283	52	173	317	94
Feb.	26	76	204	326	92	248	13	136	264	60	184
Mar.	5	166	288	57	211	336	98	229	21	147	267
Mar.	12	249	22	157	300	60	194	328	110	230	5
Mar.	19	344	121	250	24	154	293	60	195	325	105
Mar.	26	86	212	334	116	258	22	144	288	69	192
Apr.	2	175	296	68	219	345	106	240	29	155	276
Apr.	9	258	31	167	309	69	202	338	118	240	13
Apr.	16	352	132	258	33	163	304	68	204	334	115
Apr.	23	96	220	342	127	267	31	152	299	77	201
Apr.	30	184	304	78	227	354	114	250	38	164	285
May	7	267	40	177	317	78	210	348	126	249	21
May	14	1	142	266	42	172	313	76	212	344	124
May	21	104	229	350	138	275	40	160	310	85	210
May	28	193	313	87	236	2	123	259	47	172	294
Jun.	4	277	48	187	324	88	219	358	134	258	30
Jun.	11	11	151	275	50	182	322	85	220	355	132
Jun.	18	112	238	359	149	283	48	169	320	93	218
Jun.	25	201	322	96	245	11	133	267	57	180	304
Jul.	2	286	57	197	333	97	228	8	142	267	40
Jul.	9	21	160	283	58	193	330	94	228	6	140
Jul.	16	121	247	7	159	291	57	178	330	102	226
Jul.	23	209	332	105	255	18	143	276	66	188	314
Jul.	30	295	66	206	341	105	239	17	151	275	51
Aug.	6	32	168	292	66	204	338	103	237	17	148
Aug.	13	130	255	17	168	301	65	188	339	111	234
Aug.	20	217	341	113	265	27	152	285	76	197	323
Aug.	27	303	77	215	350	113	250	25	160	283	62
Sep.	3	43	176	301	75	215	346	111	246	27	157
Sep.	10	139	263	27	176	310	73	198	347	121	242
Sep.	17	225	350	123	274	35	161	294	85	205	331
Sep.	24	311	88	223	358	122	261	33	169	292	73
Oct.	1	53	185	309	85	224	355	119	256	35	166
Oct.	8	149	271	36	185	320	81	207	356	130	250
Oct.	15	233	359	133	283	44	169	305	93	214	339
Oct.	22	319	99	231	7	130	271	42	177	301	83
Oct.	29	62	194	317	95	233	5	127	266	44	176
Nov.	5	158	279	45	193	329	89	216	5	139	259
Nov.	12	242	6	144	291	53	177	316	101	223	347
Nov.	19	328	109	239	15	140	280	50	185	311	91
Nov.	26	70	203	325	105	241	14	135	276	52	185
Dec.	3	168	288	54	203	338	98	224	15	148	268
Dec.	10	251	14	155	299	61	185	327	109	231	356
Dec.	17	338	118	248	23	150	289	59	193	322	99
Dec.	24	78	213	333	115	249	23	143	286	61	194
Dec.	31	176	296	61	213	346	107	232	26	155	277

		1911	1912	1913	1914	1915	1916	1917	1918	1919	1920
Jan.	1	289	57	211	337	100	228	23	147	270	39
Jan.	8	20	162	299	61	192	332	110	231	5	143
Jan.	15	122	251	23	158	293	61	193	329	103	231
Jan.	22	214	335	120	256	23	145	290	68	193	316
Jan.	29	298	66	221	345	108	237	32	155	278	49
Feb.	5	31	170	308	69	203	340	118	239	16	150
Feb.	12	130	260	32	167	302	70	203	338	113	239
Feb.	19	222	344	128	266	31	154	298	78	201	325
Feb.	26	306	75	231	353	116	248	41	164	286	60
Mar.	5	42	192	317	77	214	2	127	248	26	172
Mar.	12	140	280	41	176	311	89	212	346	123	259
Mar.	19	230	5	136	276	39	176	308	87	209	346
Mar.	26	314	100	239	2	124	273	49	173	294	85
Apr.	2	52	200	326	86	223	10	135	257	35	181
Apr.	9	150	288	51	184	321	97	222	355	133	267
Apr.	16	238	14	146	286	48	184	318	96	218	355
Apr.	23	322	111	247	11	132	284	57	181	303	96
Apr.	30	61	208	334	96	232	19	143	267	43	190
May.	7	160	296	60	192	331	105	231	4	142	275
May.	14	246	22	156	294	56	192	329	104	227	3
May.	21	331	122	255	20	141	294	66	190	312	105
May.	28	69	218	342	106	240	29	151	277	51	200
Jun.	4	170	304	69	202	341	114	240	14	151	284
Jun.	11	255	30	167	302	65	200	340	112	235	11
Jun.	18	340	132	264	28	151	304	74	198	322	114
Jun.	25	78	228	350	115	249	39	159	286	60	209
Jul.	2	179	312	78	212	349	122	248	25	159	293
Jul.	9	264	39	178	310	74	209	350	120	244	20
Jul.	16	349	141	273	36	161	312	84	206	332	123
Jul.	23	87	237	358	125	258	48	168	295	70	218
Jul.	30	187	321	86	223	357	131	256	36	167	302
Aug.	6	272	48	188	319	82	219	360	129	252	31
Aug.	13	359	150	282	44	171	320	93	214	342	131
Aug.	20	96	246	6	133	268	57	177	303	81	226
Aug.	27	195	330	94	234	5	140	265	46	175	310
Sep.	3	281	57	198	328	90	229	9	138	260	41
Sep.	10	9	158	292	52	180	329	102	222	351	140
Sep.	17	107	255	15	141	279	65	186	312	91	234
Sep.	24	203	339	103	244	13	149	274	56	184	319
Oct.	1	288	68	206	337	98	240	17	148	268	52
Oct.	8	18	167	301	61	189	338	111	231	360	150
Oct.	15	118	263	24	149	290	73	195	320	102	242
Oct.	22	212	347	113	254	22	157	284	65	193	326
Oct.	29	296	78	214	346	106	250	25	157	276	61
Nov.	5	26	177	309	70	197	348	119	240	7	161
Nov.	12	129	271	33	158	300	81	203	329	112	250
Nov.	19	221	355	123	262	31	164	295	73	202	334
Nov.	26	305	88	223	355	115	259	34	165	285	70
Dec.	3	34	187	317	79	205	359	127	249	16	171
Dec.	10	138	279	41	168	310	89	211	340	120	259
Dec.	17	230	3	134	270	40	172	305	81	211	343
Dec.	24	313	97	232	3	124	267	44	173	294	78
Dec.	31	42	198	325	87	214	9	135	257	25	181

		1921	1922	1923	1924	1925	1926	1927	1928	1929	1930
Jan.	1	194	317	80	211	5	127	250	23	176	297
Jan.	8	280	41	177	313	90	211	349	123	260	22
Jan.	15	4	141	275	41	175	312	86	211	346	123
Jan.	22	101	239	3	127	272	51	172	297	83	222
Jan.	29	203	325	88	222	13	135	258	34	184	306
Feb.	5	289	49	188	321	99	220	359	131	269	31
Feb.	12	14	149	284	49	185	320	95	219	356	131
Feb.	19	110	249	11	135	281	60	181	305	93	230
Feb.	26	211	334	96	233	21	144	266	45	191	314
Mar.	5	297	58	197	343	107	230	8	153	276	41
Mar.	12	23	157	294	69	194	328	105	238	6	140
Mar.	19	119	258	19	157	292	68	190	327	104	238
Mar.	26	219	343	104	258	29	153	275	70	200	323
Apr.	2	305	68	205	352	115	240	16	163	284	51
Apr.	9	33	166	304	77	204	337	114	247	14	149
Apr.	16	130	266	28	164	303	76	198	335	115	246
Apr.	23	227	351	114	268	38	161	285	79	208	331
Apr.	30	313	78	214	1	123	250	25	172	292	61
May.	7	42	176	313	85	212	348	123	256	23	160
May.	14	141	274	37	173	314	84	207	344	125	254
May.	21	236	359	123	277	47	169	295	88	217	339
May.	28	321	88	222	11	131	259	34	181	301	70
Jun.	4	50	186	321	94	220	358	131	264	31	171
Jun.	11	152	282	45	182	324	93	215	354	135	263
Jun.	18	245	7	134	285	56	177	305	96	226	347
Jun.	25	330	97	232	20	139	268	44	190	310	78
Jul.	2	58	197	329	103	229	9	139	273	40	181
Jul.	9	162	291	54	192	333	101	223	4	144	272
Jul.	16	254	15	144	294	65	185	315	104	236	355
Jul.	23	338	106	242	28	148	276	54	198	319	87
Jul.	30	67	208	337	112	238	20	147	282	49	191
Aug.	6	171	300	62	202	341	110	231	15	152	281
Aug.	13	264	24	153	302	74	194	324	114	244	4
Aug.	20	347	114	253	36	157	285	65	206	328	95
Aug.	27	76	218	346	120	248	29	156	290	59	200
Sep.	3	179	309	70	213	350	119	239	25	161	290
Sep.	10	273	32	162	312	83	203	332	124	252	13
Sep.	17	356	122	264	44	166	293	75	214	337	105
Sep.	24	86	227	354	128	258	38	165	298	70	208
Oct.	1	187	318	78	223	358	128	248	35	169	298
Oct.	8	281	41	170	322	91	212	340	134	260	23
Oct.	15	5	132	274	52	175	303	85	222	345	115
Oct.	22	97	235	3	136	269	46	174	306	81	216
Oct.	29	196	327	87	232	7	137	257	44	179	307
Nov.	5	289	50	178	332	99	221	349	144	268	31
Nov.	12	13	142	283	61	183	313	93	231	353	126
Nov.	19	107	243	12	144	279	54	183	315	91	225
Nov.	26	206	335	96	241	17	145	266	52	189	314
Dec.	3	297	59	187	343	107	230	359	154	276	39
Dec.	10	21	152	291	70	191	324	101	240	1	137
Dec.	17	117	252	21	153	289	63	191	324	99	234
Dec.	24	216	343	105	249	28	152	275	60	199	322
Dec.	31	305	67	197	352	115	237	9	162	285	47

		1931	1932	1933	1934	1935	1936	1937	1938	1939	1940
Jan.	1	60	196	346	107	231	8	156	277	41	181
Jan.	8	162	294	70	193	333	104	240	4	144	275
Jan.	15	257	20	158	294	68	190	329	104	239	360
Jan.	22	342	108	255	32	152	278	67	202	323	88
Jan.	29	68	207	353	116	239	19	163	286	49	191
Feb.	5	171	302	78	203	342	113	248	14	153	284
Feb.	12	267	28	168	302	78	198	339	113	248	8
Feb.	19	351	116	266	40	161	286	78	210	332	96
Feb.	26	77	217	1	124	248	29	171	294	59	200
Mar.	5	179	324	86	213	350	135	256	25	161	306
Mar.	12	276	48	176	311	86	218	347	123	256	29
Mar.	19	360	137	277	48	170	308	89	218	340	119
Mar.	26	86	241	10	132	258	52	180	302	69	223
Apr.	2	187	334	94	223	358	144	264	34	169	315
Apr.	9	285	57	185	321	95	227	355	133	264	38
Apr.	16	9	146	287	56	178	317	99	226	349	128
Apr.	23	96	250	18	140	268	61	189	310	80	231
Apr.	30	196	343	102	232	7	153	273	43	179	323
May.	7	293	66	193	332	103	237	4	144	272	47
May.	14	17	155	297	64	187	327	108	235	357	139
May.	21	107	258	28	148	278	69	198	318	90	239
May.	28	205	351	111	241	17	161	282	51	189	331
Jun.	4	301	75	201	343	111	245	13	154	280	55
Jun.	11	25	165	306	73	195	337	117	244	5	150
Jun.	18	117	267	37	157	288	78	207	327	99	248
Jun.	25	215	360	120	249	28	169	291	60	200	339
Jul.	2	309	84	211	353	119	254	23	164	289	64
Jul.	9	33	176	315	82	203	348	125	253	13	160
Jul.	16	126	276	46	165	297	87	216	336	108	258
Jul.	23	226	8	130	258	38	177	300	69	210	347
Jul.	30	317	92	221	2	128	262	33	173	298	72
Aug.	6	41	187	323	91	211	359	133	261	21	170
Aug.	13	135	285	54	175	305	97	224	346	116	268
Aug.	20	237	16	138	267	49	185	308	78	220	355
Aug.	27	326	100	232	10	136	270	44	181	307	80
Sep.	3	49	197	331	100	220	8	142	270	31	179
Sep.	10	143	295	62	184	314	107	232	355	125	278
Sep.	17	247	24	147	277	58	194	317	89	228	4
Sep.	24	335	108	243	18	145	278	55	189	316	88
Oct.	1	58	206	341	108	229	17	152	278	40	188
Oct.	8	151	306	70	193	322	117	240	4	134	288
Oct.	15	256	32	155	287	66	203	324	100	236	13
Oct.	22	344	116	253	27	154	287	64	198	324	98
Oct.	29	68	214	350	116	239	25	162	286	49	196
Nov.	5	161	316	78	201	332	126	248	12	145	297
Nov.	12	264	41	162	298	74	212	333	111	244	22
Nov.	19	353	125	262	36	162	296	73	207	332	108
Nov.	26	77	222	0	124	248	33	172	294	58	205
Dec.	3	171	325	87	209	343	135	257	19	156	305
Dec.	10	272	50	171	309	82	220	341	120	253	30
Dec.	17	1	135	271	45	170	306	81	217	340	118
Dec.	24	86	231	10	132	256	43	181	302	66	214
Dec.	31	182	333	95	217	354	142	265	27	167	313

		1941	1942	1943	1944	1945	1946	1947	1948	1949	1950
Jan.	1	325	88	211	353	135	258	22	165	305	68
Jan.	8	50	176	315	85	219	348	126	256	29	160
Jan.	15	141	276	50	169	312	87	220	340	123	258
Jan.	22	239	12	133	258	52	182	303	69	224	352
Jan.	29	333	96	221	2	143	266	32	174	314	75
Feb.	5	57	186	323	95	227	358	134	265	37	170
Feb.	12	150	285	58	178	320	96	228	349	131	268
Feb.	19	250	20	142	267	62	190	312	78	234	359
Feb.	26	342	104	231	11	152	274	43	182	323	83
Mar.	5	65	196	331	116	236	8	142	286	46	179
Mar.	12	158	295	66	199	328	107	236	10	139	279
Mar.	19	261	28	150	290	72	198	320	102	243	8
Mar.	26	351	112	242	34	161	281	53	204	332	91
Apr.	2	74	205	340	125	244	16	152	294	55	187
Apr.	9	166	306	74	208	337	117	244	19	148	289
Apr.	16	270	36	158	300	81	206	328	112	252	17
Apr.	23	360	120	252	42	170	290	63	212	340	100
Apr.	30	83	214	350	133	254	25	162	302	64	195
May	7	174	316	82	217	346	127	252	27	158	299
May	14	279	45	166	311	90	215	336	123	260	26
May	21	9	128	261	50	179	299	72	221	349	110
May	28	92	222	1	141	263	33	173	310	73	204
Jun.	4	184	326	91	226	356	137	261	36	168	307
Jun.	11	287	54	174	322	98	224	344	134	268	34
Jun.	18	17	137	270	60	187	308	81	231	357	119
Jun.	25	102	231	11	149	272	42	183	318	82	213
Jul.	2	194	335	99	234	7	145	269	44	179	316
Jul.	9	296	63	183	332	106	233	353	144	277	43
Jul.	16	25	147	279	70	195	318	89	241	5	129
Jul.	23	110	240	21	157	280	52	192	327	91	224
Jul.	30	205	343	108	242	18	153	278	52	190	324
Aug.	6	304	71	192	341	115	241	3	153	286	51
Aug.	13	33	156	287	80	203	327	98	251	13	138
Aug.	20	119	250	30	165	289	63	201	336	99	235
Aug.	27	216	351	117	250	28	162	287	61	200	332
Sep.	3	314	80	201	350	125	249	13	161	296	59
Sep.	10	41	165	296	90	211	336	108	260	21	146
Sep.	17	127	261	39	174	297	74	209	345	107	246
Sep.	24	226	359	126	259	38	170	295	70	209	341
Oct.	1	323	88	213	358	135	257	22	170	306	67
Oct.	8	49	174	306	99	220	344	118	269	30	154
Oct.	15	135	272	47	183	305	84	217	353	116	256
Oct.	22	236	8	134	269	47	180	303	80	217	351
Oct.	29	333	95	220	7	144	265	31	179	315	75
Nov.	5	58	181	317	107	229	352	129	277	39	162
Nov.	12	143	283	55	192	314	94	225	1	125	265
Nov.	19	244	18	141	279	55	189	311	90	225	0
Nov.	26	343	104	229	16	153	274	39	189	323	84
Dec.	3	67	189	328	115	237	360	140	284	47	171
Dec.	10	153	292	64	200	324	103	234	9	136	274
Dec.	17	252	28	149	289	63	199	319	100	234	9
Dec.	24	351	112	237	27	161	282	47	199	331	93
Dec.	31	76	198	338	123	246	9	150	293	55	180

		1951	1952	1953	1954	1955	1956	1957	1958	1959	1960
Jan.	1	194	336	115	238	6	147	285	47	178	317
Jan.	8	297	67	199	331	107	237	9	143	278	47
Jan.	15	30	150	294	70	200	320	104	242	9	131
Jan.	22	114	240	35	161	284	51	207	331	94	223
Jan.	29	204	344	124	245	17	155	294	55	189	325
Feb.	5	305	76	207	341	116	246	18	152	287	56
Feb.	12	38	159	302	80	208	330	112	252	17	140
Feb.	19	122	249	45	169	292	61	216	340	102	233
Feb.	26	215	352	133	253	27	163	303	63	199	333
Mar.	5	314	96	216	350	125	266	27	161	297	75
Mar.	12	46	180	310	91	216	351	121	262	25	161
Mar.	19	130	274	54	178	300	86	224	349	110	259
Mar.	26	225	14	142	262	37	185	312	72	208	356
Apr.	2	324	104	226	358	135	274	37	169	307	83
Apr.	9	54	189	319	100	224	360	131	271	34	170
Apr.	16	138	285	62	187	308	97	232	357	118	269
Apr.	23	235	23	150	271	46	194	320	82	217	5
Apr.	30	334	112	235	6	146	282	46	177	317	91
May	7	62	197	330	109	232	8	142	279	42	177
May	14	146	296	70	196	316	107	240	6	127	279
May	21	243	32	158	280	54	204	328	91	225	15
May	28	344	120	244	15	155	290	55	187	326	100
Jun.	4	71	205	341	117	241	16	153	288	51	186
Jun.	11	155	306	79	204	325	117	249	14	137	288
Jun.	18	252	42	166	290	63	214	336	101	234	25
Jun.	25	354	128	253	26	164	298	63	198	335	109
Jul.	2	80	214	351	125	250	24	164	296	60	195
Jul.	9	164	315	88	212	335	126	259	22	147	297
Jul.	16	260	52	174	299	72	223	344	110	243	34
Jul.	23	3	137	261	37	173	307	71	209	343	118
Jul.	30	89	222	2	134	258	33	174	304	68	205
Aug.	6	174	324	97	220	345	134	268	30	156	305
Aug.	13	270	62	182	308	82	232	353	118	254	42
Aug.	20	11	146	269	48	181	316	79	220	351	126
Aug.	27	97	232	11	143	267	43	183	314	76	215
Sep.	3	184	332	107	228	355	143	278	38	166	314
Sep.	10	280	71	191	316	92	241	2	127	265	50
Sep.	17	19	155	278	58	189	325	88	230	359	135
Sep.	24	105	242	20	152	274	54	191	323	84	225
Oct.	1	193	341	116	237	4	152	287	47	174	324
Oct.	8	291	79	200	324	103	249	11	135	276	58
Oct.	15	27	163	287	68	198	333	98	239	8	143
Oct.	22	113	252	28	162	282	64	199	332	92	235
Oct.	29	201	350	125	245	12	162	295	56	182	334
Nov.	5	302	87	209	333	114	256	19	144	286	66
Nov.	12	36	171	297	76	207	341	109	247	17	150
Nov.	19	121	262	37	171	291	73	208	341	101	244
Nov.	26	209	0	133	254	20	173	303	65	190	345
Dec.	3	312	95	217	342	124	265	27	154	295	75
Dec.	10	45	179	307	84	216	348	119	255	27	158
Dec.	17	129	271	46	180	299	82	218	350	110	252
Dec.	24	217	11	141	263	28	184	311	73	199	355
Dec.	31	321	103	225	352	132	273	35	164	303	84

		1961	1962	1963	1964	1965	1966	1967	1968	1969	1970
Jan.	1	96	217	350	128	266	27	163	298	76	197
Jan.	8	179	315	89	217	350	126	260	27	161	297
Jan.	15	275	54	179	302	86	225	349	112	257	36
Jan.	22	18	141	264	35	189	311	74	207	359	122
Jan.	29	105	225	1	136	275	35	173	306	85	206
Feb.	5	188	323	99	225	360	134	270	35	171	305
Feb.	12	284	64	187	310	95	235	357	121	267	45
Feb.	19	26	150	272	46	197	320	81	218	7	130
Feb.	26	113	234	11	144	283	45	182	315	93	216
Mar.	5	198	331	109	245	9	142	280	54	180	313
Mar.	12	293	73	195	332	105	244	5	142	277	54
Mar.	19	34	159	280	71	205	329	90	243	15	139
Mar.	26	122	243	19	167	291	54	190	338	101	226
Apr.	2	208	340	119	253	18	151	290	63	189	323
Apr.	9	303	82	204	340	116	252	14	150	288	62
Apr.	16	42	167	288	81	213	337	99	253	23	147
Apr.	23	130	253	28	176	299	64	198	347	109	235
Apr.	30	216	349	128	261	27	161	298	71	197	333
May	7	314	90	213	348	127	260	23	158	299	70
May	14	51	176	298	91	222	345	109	262	32	155
May	21	137	263	36	186	307	74	207	357	117	245
May	28	225	359	137	270	35	172	307	80	205	344
Jun.	4	325	98	222	357	137	268	31	168	309	78
Jun.	11	60	184	308	99	231	353	119	270	42	163
Jun.	18	146	272	45	195	315	82	217	6	126	253
Jun.	25	233	10	145	279	43	183	315	89	214	355
Jul.	2	336	106	230	6	147	276	40	178	318	87
Jul.	9	70	191	318	108	241	1	129	279	51	171
Jul.	16	154	281	56	204	324	91	227	14	135	261
Jul.	23	241	21	153	288	52	193	323	98	223	5
Jul.	30	345	115	238	16	156	286	47	188	327	97
Aug.	6	79	200	327	116	250	10	138	288	60	180
Aug.	13	163	289	66	212	333	99	238	22	144	270
Aug.	20	250	32	161	296	61	203	331	106	233	14
Aug.	27	353	124	246	27	164	295	55	199	335	106
Sep.	3	88	208	336	126	259	19	147	297	68	189
Sep.	10	172	297	77	220	342	108	249	30	152	279
Sep.	17	260	41	170	304	72	212	340	114	244	23
Sep.	24	1	134	254	37	172	304	64	208	344	115
Oct.	1	97	217	344	136	267	28	155	308	76	198
Oct.	8	180	306	88	228	351	117	259	38	161	289
Oct.	15	270	50	179	312	82	220	350	122	254	31
Oct.	22	10	143	262	47	182	313	73	217	353	123
Oct.	29	105	226	352	146	275	37	163	318	84	207
Nov.	5	189	315	97	237	359	127	268	47	168	299
Nov.	12	281	58	188	320	93	228	359	130	264	39
Nov.	19	19	151	271	55	191	321	82	225	3	131
Nov.	26	113	235	1	157	282	45	172	328	92	215
Dec.	3	197	326	105	245	7	138	276	55	176	310
Dec.	10	291	66	197	328	102	237	7	139	273	48
Dec.	17	30	159	280	63	202	329	91	234	13	139
Dec.	24	121	243	11	167	291	53	183	337	101	223
Dec.	31	204	336	113	254	14	149	284	64	184	320

		1971	1972	1973	1974	1975	1976	1977	1978	1979	1980
Jan.	1	335	109	246	8	147	279	56	179	318	90
Jan.	8	71	197	332	108	243	6	144	278	54	176
Jan.	15	158	283	69	207	328	93	240	18	139	263
Jan.	22	244	20	169	292	54	192	339	102	224	4
Jan.	29	344	117	255	17	156	288	64	188	327	99
Feb.	5	81	204	342	116	253	14	153	287	63	184
Feb.	12	167	291	79	216	337	101	251	26	147	271
Feb.	19	252	31	177	300	62	203	347	110	233	14
Feb.	26	353	126	263	27	164	297	72	199	334	109
Mar.	5	91	224	351	124	262	34	162	296	72	204
Mar.	12	176	312	90	224	346	122	262	34	156	293
Mar.	19	261	55	185	309	72	226	356	118	243	37
Mar.	26	1	149	270	37	172	320	80	208	343	130
Apr.	2	100	233	360	134	270	43	170	307	80	213
Apr.	9	184	320	101	232	355	131	273	42	164	302
Apr.	16	271	64	194	317	82	235	5	126	254	46
Apr.	23	9	158	278	47	181	329	88	217	352	139
Apr.	30	109	242	8	145	278	52	178	318	88	222
May	7	193	329	111	240	3	141	282	50	173	312
May	14	281	73	203	324	92	243	14	134	264	54
May	21	19	167	287	55	191	337	97	226	3	147
May	28	117	251	16	156	286	61	187	328	96	231
Jun.	4	201	339	120	249	11	151	291	59	180	323
Jun.	11	291	81	213	333	102	252	23	143	273	63
Jun.	18	29	176	296	64	201	346	106	234	13	155
Jun.	25	125	260	25	167	295	69	196	338	105	239
Jul.	2	209	349	129	258	19	162	299	68	188	334
Jul.	9	300	90	222	341	111	261	32	152	282	72
Jul.	16	40	184	305	72	212	354	115	243	24	163
Jul.	23	133	268	35	176	303	78	206	347	114	248
Jul.	30	217	0	137	267	27	172	308	77	197	344
Aug.	6	309	99	230	350	120	271	40	161	290	83
Aug.	13	51	192	314	81	223	2	124	252	34	171
Aug.	20	142	276	45	185	312	86	217	356	123	256
Aug.	27	225	10	146	276	36	182	317	86	206	353
Sep.	3	317	109	238	360	128	281	48	170	299	93
Sep.	10	61	200	322	90	232	10	132	262	43	180
Sep.	17	151	284	56	193	321	94	228	4	132	264
Sep.	24	234	20	155	284	45	191	326	94	215	2
Oct.	1	325	120	246	9	136	291	56	179	308	103
Oct.	8	70	208	330	101	241	19	140	273	51	189
Oct.	15	160	292	66	202	330	102	238	12	140	273
Oct.	22	243	28	165	292	54	199	336	102	225	10
Oct.	29	334	130	254	17	146	301	64	187	318	112
Nov.	5	79	217	338	112	249	27	148	284	59	197
Nov.	12	169	300	76	210	339	111	247	21	148	282
Nov.	19	253	36	175	300	63	207	347	110	234	18
Nov.	26	344	139	262	25	156	310	73	195	329	120
Dec.	3	87	226	346	122	257	36	157	294	67	206
Dec.	10	177	310	84	220	347	121	255	31	156	292
Dec.	17	261	45	185	308	72	216	356	118	242	28
Dec.	24	355	148	271	33	167	318	81	203	340	128
Dec.	31	95	235	355	132	265	44	166	303	76	214

		1981	1982	1983	1984	1985	1986	1987	1988	1989	1990
Jan.	1	226	350	129	260	36	162	300	71	205	333
Jan.	8	315	89	225	346	126	260	36	156	297	72
Jan.	15	53	188	309	73	225	358	119	243	37	168
Jan.	22	149	272	35	176	319	82	206	348	129	252
Jan.	29	234	0	137	270	43	172	308	81	213	343
Feb.	5	324	98	234	354	135	270	44	164	306	82
Feb.	12	64	196	317	81	236	6	128	252	48	175
Feb.	19	157	280	45	185	328	90	217	356	138	260
Feb.	26	242	10	145	279	51	182	316	90	222	353
Mar.	5	332	108	242	15	143	280	52	185	313	93
Mar.	12	74	204	326	104	246	14	136	275	57	184
Mar.	19	166	288	55	208	337	97	227	19	147	268
Mar.	26	250	20	154	300	60	191	326	111	230	1
Apr.	2	340	119	250	24	151	291	60	194	322	103
Apr.	9	84	212	334	114	255	22	144	286	66	192
Apr.	16	175	296	66	216	346	106	237	27	156	276
Apr.	23	259	28	164	309	69	199	336	119	240	9
Apr.	30	349	130	258	33	160	302	68	203	331	113
May	7	93	221	342	124	264	31	152	297	75	201
May	14	184	304	75	225	355	114	246	36	165	285
May	21	268	36	175	317	78	207	347	127	249	18
May	28	358	140	266	41	170	311	76	211	341	122
Jun.	4	102	230	350	135	272	40	160	307	83	210
Jun.	11	193	313	84	234	3	123	255	45	173	294
Jun.	18	277	45	185	325	87	216	357	135	258	27
Jun.	25	8	149	275	49	180	320	85	219	352	130
Jul.	2	110	239	359	146	281	49	169	317	92	219
Jul.	9	201	322	93	244	11	133	263	55	181	304
Jul.	16	286	54	196	333	96	225	7	143	266	37
Jul.	23	19	158	284	57	191	328	94	227	3	138
Jul.	30	119	248	7	155	290	57	178	327	101	227
Aug.	6	210	331	101	254	19	142	272	66	189	313
Aug.	13	294	64	205	341	104	236	16	152	274	48
Aug.	20	30	166	293	66	202	337	103	236	13	147
Aug.	27	128	256	17	164	299	65	187	335	111	235
Sep.	3	218	340	110	264	27	151	281	75	197	321
Sep.	10	302	75	214	350	112	247	24	160	282	59
Sep.	17	40	174	302	74	212	345	112	245	23	156
Sep.	24	138	264	26	172	309	73	197	343	121	243
Oct.	1	228	349	119	274	36	159	292	84	206	329
Oct.	8	310	86	222	359	120	258	32	169	291	70
Oct.	15	50	183	310	84	220	354	120	255	31	165
Oct.	22	148	272	35	181	319	81	206	352	130	251
Oct.	29	234	357	130	282	44	167	303	92	214	337
Nov.	5	318	96	230	8	129	268	40	178	300	79
Nov.	12	58	193	318	93	229	4	128	265	39	175
Nov.	19	158	280	44	190	329	90	214	2	139	260
Nov.	26	243	5	141	290	53	175	314	100	223	345
Dec.	3	327	106	238	16	139	277	49	185	310	88
Dec.	10	66	203	326	103	237	14	136	274	48	185
Dec.	17	167	288	52	200	337	98	222	12	147	269
Dec.	24	252	13	152	298	62	184	324	108	232	355
Dec.	31	337	114	248	24	149	285	59	193	320	96

		1991	1992	1993	1994	1995	1996	1997	1998	1999	2000
Jan.	1	111	242	15	145	281	53	185	317	92	223
Jan.	8	206	326	108	244	16	136	279	56	186	307
Jan.	15	289	54	210	337	99	225	21	147	270	37
Jan.	22	18	158	299	61	190	329	110	231	2	140
Jan.	29	119	252	23	155	290	62	193	326	101	232
Feb.	5	214	335	116	254	24	145	287	66	193	315
Feb.	12	298	63	220	345	108	235	31	155	278	47
Feb.	19	29	166	308	69	201	337	119	239	12	148
Feb.	26	128	260	32	164	299	70	202	335	111	240
Mar.	5	222	356	124	265	32	166	295	76	201	337
Mar.	12	306	87	229	354	116	259	39	164	285	72
Mar.	19	39	189	317	77	211	360	128	248	22	170
Mar.	26	138	280	41	172	310	90	212	343	121	260
Apr.	2	230	5	133	275	40	175	305	86	210	345
Apr.	9	314	98	237	3	123	270	47	173	294	83
Apr.	16	49	198	326	86	220	9	136	257	31	180
Apr.	23	148	288	50	180	320	98	221	351	132	268
Apr.	30	238	13	143	284	48	183	315	95	218	353
May	7	322	109	245	12	132	281	55	182	302	93
May	14	57	207	335	95	228	18	144	267	39	190
May	21	158	296	59	189	330	106	230	1	141	276
May	28	247	21	154	292	57	191	326	103	227	1
Jun.	4	330	119	253	21	141	291	64	190	311	102
Jun.	11	66	217	343	105	236	28	152	276	48	199
Jun.	18	168	304	68	199	340	114	238	11	150	285
Jun.	25	256	29	165	300	66	199	337	111	236	10
Jul.	2	339	129	262	29	150	300	73	198	321	111
Jul.	9	74	227	351	114	245	38	160	285	57	209
Jul.	16	177	313	76	210	348	123	246	22	158	293
Jul.	23	265	38	175	309	75	208	347	120	245	19
Jul.	30	349	137	272	37	160	308	83	206	331	119
Aug.	6	83	237	359	123	255	48	169	293	67	218
Aug.	13	186	322	84	221	356	132	254	33	166	302
Aug.	20	273	47	185	318	83	218	356	129	253	29
Aug.	27	358	146	282	45	169	317	93	214	340	128
Sep.	3	93	246	7	131	265	56	177	301	78	226
Sep.	10	194	331	92	231	4	141	263	43	174	311
Sep.	17	281	56	194	327	91	228	5	138	261	39
Sep.	24	8	154	292	53	178	326	102	223	349	137
Oct.	1	104	254	16	139	276	64	186	310	89	234
Oct.	8	202	339	101	241	13	149	273	53	183	319
Oct.	15	289	66	202	337	99	238	13	148	269	49
Oct.	22	32	164	301	61	187	336	111	231	357	148
Oct.	29	115	262	25	148	287	72	195	318	100	242
Nov.	5	211	347	111	250	22	157	283	61	193	326
Nov.	12	297	76	211	346	107	247	22	157	277	58
Nov.	19	24	174	309	70	194	346	119	240	5	159
Nov.	26	126	270	33	156	297	80	203	328	109	251
Dec.	3	220	355	121	258	31	165	293	69	202	334
Dec.	10	305	85	220	355	115	256	31	165	286	67
Dec.	17	32	185	317	79	203	357	127	249	13	169
Dec.	24	135	278	41	166	306	89	211	338	117	260
Dec.	31	230	3	131	266	41	173	303	78	211	343

YOUR PERSONAL MOON SIGN

By Gavin Kent McClung

The Moon is the point of life potential through which we contact the universe at the "gut level" of experience. Here is where we unthinkingly absorb nourishment from outside ourselves and where we instinctively give sustenance to others. The Moon represents life at the wavelength of feeling and mothering. Both men and women must fulfill this role or operate at this frequency from time to time.

ARIES MOON

Anyone who knows an Aries Moon also knows the boost of feelings associated with a person of high emotional aspiration. This active, often impetuous force is powered by a keen imagination and a compass-like search for the "true north" of inward, person-to-person situations. This may result in a shy appearing or jumpy person, always ready to be off and away from close confrontations.

Here, the first impulse that occurs is likely to be adopted. There is clearly something chancy, something risky about this person's approach. Sparks may sometimes fly, if one is not so quick to start up as an Aries Moon. They may know they are right, whether they know what they are right about or not. Once the relative steadiness of maturity has arrived, the Aries Moon can be a supportive dynamo for the less adventurous.

Severance from anything that is perpetually binding is likely to tempt them rather sooner than later. The emotional level is transient, yet ever ready to extend the hand of reconciliation. The Aries Moon automatically reassigns him or herself to new tasks and challenges, and it is wise not to interfere with this constant process of renewal.

TAURUS MOON

A personal goal for this person is to establish practical results, concrete expression wherever this is appropriate in connection with his or her feelings and emotions, and sometimes where it may *not* be so appropriate. Pie in the sky is not enough to provide satisfaction here. For Taurus Moon, the pie should be on the table, on a plate, and in ample supply. The search for true value in life may be this person's best contribution to society. They can forcibly supply the rest of us with the drive to integrate the idea of "pie in the sky" with the reality of "plate on the table."

Taurus Moon will generally tend to see things

in summation, to demand that one's position in life be made manifest in reality. The orientation to material values is primary. The source of all this inward solidity is probably the deep-rooted and persistent imagination of this person, which does not allow him or her to accept substitutes in life, but drives ever onward to obtain "the real thing."

GEMINI MOON

This Moon sign is perpetually drawn toward life itself, living it, feeling it, breathing it in. This, in turn, gives the effect of breathing life into life itself. Quickness and versatility are exceptional here, though others may sometimes construe these traits as being deceptive. But this perception may simply reflect two persons operating at two different speeds. Gemini adapts very fast, and relatively unjudgmentally, to whatever he or she faces.

There is a mental approach to the feeling level here, but these feelings are the same as everyone else's, and Gemini Moon is quite aware of their presence within. But he or she does not feel bound to dwell on things too long. The result can be a tendency to work things over a little at a time—for a long, long time. It would be a little contradictory for this Moon sign not to be a little contradictory.

With Gemini Moon, a basic assumption is that everything in life is imminent; is about to happen. This sense of urgency presses them into a constant search for the true body of experience, and they manage to acquire much knowledge as they go along through life.

CANCER MOON

Contacting a Cancer Moon will nearly always result in an unusual expansion of what was meant earlier by "gut level" experience in life, for Cancer is itself ruled by the Moon. Everything lunar functions at high pitch in this sign. Moods are enlarged dramatically; sensitivity and changeability may be exaggerated in some way.

This person "lives to feel." The need to nurture others is great. If you need a bowl of chicken soup, the Cancer Moon will usually provide at least a gallon of it. The problem is generally one of keeping things in perspective. For Cancer Moon, it may take some hard work.

There is the sense of "summation" with a Cancer Moon, but powered here by a real feeling for the group need, which he or she will home in on quite naturally and almost always try to satisfy. They strive to offer every encouragement for development to others in their sphere of activity. Generosity as such is almost an obligation and sometimes he or she will nearly demand to help you, as if it were their inborn right. The effects of constructive flux or change for the better that a Cancer Moon produces can benefit all who chance to fall beneath his or her goodwill beams.

LEO MOON

This person has a positive feel for leadership and a sense of preeminence in emotion as well, which they and others must take into account. The air of assurance is always present to some degree, regarding the relative importance of his or her personal position in a given situation.

Where give and take are involved, there is a notable freedom of giving, and the taking is understood since Leo feels that what is his is *his*, no questions asked. There is a great air of vitality and fire and also some stubbornness about changing one's way or altering one's position. Yet Leo Moon tends to sense the overall purpose in emotional situations and often takes the lead in resolving them.

Leo Moon communicates a kind of sufficiency to others that is often unmistakable, as if karma or inevitable forces had put this person into the place he or she occupies. Sometimes the appearance of overconfidence is a relatively transparent cover for the need of respect from others that may lie deep within the psyche. Leo Moon demands its due in deference from others, and pays for this in kindness and concern for others' ultimate welfare.

VIRGO MOON

Assimilation to the world as it is, the accommodation of reality—"the way things are"—is a power that activates this person. Virgo Moon will bend and give, in all the right places, to handle whatever comes his or her way, but this is not to suggest that they themselves are able to "feel" adaptively, better than most. In fact, they are often so well organized that small discrepancies are easily detected, and seem more aggravating to them.

The same mental component that allows Gemini to feel intensely present in the moment is applied by Virgo in terms of mastering technique and routine. Virgo Moon wants to be ready for all eventualities, and may be overly analytical about how to meet them, over-planning for the future. This may drive those around them crazy, but it certainly is a force for order in general. Organization as an actual feeling is paramount.

This Moon sign is well equipped to make intuitive choices, and the craftsmanship with which they pursue life is often a source of amazement for others. For Virgo Moon, prudence is prudent.

LIBRA MOON

This person has emotional identification with the concept of equality or equivalence, as such. They are forever testing the winds of every situation to see what is needed to bring things into alignment.

They have the acquisitiveness of Taurus, but this force runs more toward aesthetic harmonies than toward materialistic realizations. There is a positive repulsion for things that are out of tune, and the only area where Libra Moon can go overboard is in the rejection of extremism itself. Their sensitive openness to others must not be infringed upon, or they may "turn off" completely.

A sort of dialectic process is forever operative within the breast of the Libra Moon, and thus their alert attendance upon the value of "rightness" in life. They have a special appreciation for poignancy of emotion, and feel a real sense of presence in the life that expresses these in a measured way. The Libra Moon sense of relaxed poise is based on a true fidelity to past experience, which always sees them prepared for newer ventures.

SCORPIO MOON

These people know the value of true creativity in making active application of some of life's stronger impulses. This comes from a determination and control that is always oriented toward bringing unused or neglected facets of life into fuller expression. Others may be surprised or even "turned off" by the results, but they will seldom fail to be attracted in one way or another.

Scorpio Moon has the ability to take the initiative in direct and sometimes unsettling ways. There is notable power to focus single-mindedly, even obsessively, on specific goals. It may be difficult for other people to relate to this kind of intensity.

As a product of their drive toward emotional maturity, this Moon sign often appears to be overindulgent when from a certain point of view they are actually "testing the limits," and busily separating the "wheat from the chaff" of experience. Few know sooner than this person when a situation has lost its merit, or has become outmoded. Scorpio Moon can provide the transmutation of experience through a great power to lift even if the lifting involves a sudden "drop."

SAGITTARIUS MOON

Sagittarius Moon has a broad spectrum of contact with its surroundings, and prefers not to be held to any specific point for very long. There may be a tendency here to take an overview approach emotionally, or to view present resources as the means to possibly very distant ends.

A level of enthusiasm is present here that carries over into warm and spontaneous feelings. The imagination is open to stimulation, and there is often a sense of great buoyancy. This can sometimes produce a certain fitfulness that must be recognized as being more natural for this person than for most others. One must not expect to pin down a Sagittarius Moon very easily.

The relativity of standpoint is important to a Sagittarius Moon. That is, this person will strive to find out where another person is "coming from" in order to fix or to understand their own position better. There is very little desire, however, to "corral" another person emotionally. The inner liberty of Sagittarius is itself sufficient motivation to allow full freedom for others, and this person expects to receive an equal measure of the leeway he or she gives in return. The secret of the Sagittarius Moon is its fluidity.

CAPRICORN MOON

An essential function of this placement is discrimination, and not necessarily in the negative sense.

Here also is the power to know imaginatively and instinctively what is discriminating in the sense of being distinctive or "high class." As long as this does not become an obsession, the Capricorn Moon can become the model of emotional class and style.

There is a high sensitiveness to the correct way of providing structure to life, of getting things in proper order, making them work right. Filling in all the blanks in life is important to a Capricorn Moon, and they may be rather quick to point out where others have failed to do so. As long as they apply the hard rules of life to themselves, then their sense of authority in guiding others is not without constructive foundation.

This Moon sign has a great drive to express completion in life, and may suffer a secret fear of the inadequacy of all of us in the face of extremely high ideals or standards in life. Truly adult and responsible guidance of life's course is a major orientation here. If this person consciously or unconsciously calls our attention to some deficiency in ourselves, perhaps we should heed the implicit advice that is being offered.

AQUARIUS MOON

The "friendship" potential of this Moon sign will seldom fail to manifest itself. There is a constant opening up and reaching out, which often will provide an inventive twist to his or her relationships. But to maintain a steady course, Aquarius Moon will usually remain somewhat objective.

Sensitivity to the right of independence in others is usually high in this person's awareness. This is a practice that most of us try to follow, but none with more sincerity than an Aquarius Moon. There may be ingenious or unconventional results, or unusual associations that are often viewed as being ahead of their time somehow. A substantial ability to make feelings have real effects in the world will be seen here.

Aquarius Moon will tend to penetrate to the heart of any emotional dilemma rather quickly, and often this person is a fine reader of character. There is a particular felicity of detachment here, which will successfully avoid becoming separated from others. This is because this combination is almost an embodiment of the term "humanitarian," in the best and truest sense of that word.

PISCES MOON

This combination has exceptionally sympathetic openness to whatever is taking place in one's surroundings. A constant, subtle "all-surrounding" impulse is at work. Sometimes the Pisces Moon feels so many things at once that there is a muddle in trying to identify them all. There may be a kind of passivity that is based on gentleness or kindliness. But passivity is still passivity.

This Moon sign has an inward leading that requires constant clarification of one's obligations or responsibilities to oneself and to other persons. This means guarding against any unusual lapse into simply letting important things take care of themselves. The beauty of life is highly appreciated, and steps to make oneself part of the action will be taken by the Pisces Moon.

What really drives the Pisces Moon onward is the sense of incompleteness it seems to see in all directions in life. It is a privilege for this individual to sustain others who may themselves have lapsed into vacillation. The constructive sacrifice that does not infringe upon one's own integrity attracts this person. Simple argument will seldom force them out of their position, partly because this position is seldom very clearly known itself.

LUNAR CYCLES

• Your **lunar high** occurs when the Moon is in the same sign as your natal Sun. If you are a Sagittarius, for example, your lunar high will occur when the Moon is in Sagittarius. The result would be a time of inspiration, when new ventures could be successfully implemented. It is a day when you are most emotionally like your Sun sign. It is a day when your thinking is most sound.

• Your **lunar low** occurs when the Moon is in the sign opposite your natal Sun. If you are a Taurus, your lunar low would occur when the Moon is in Scorpio. Since you are least sure of your decisions on this day, try to postpone major decisions. You will run into opposition in whatever you may start. This is, however, a good day to exchange ideas since you are much more aware of other people. You may feel restless and will want to keep busy. Plan constructive (but not demanding) projects.

• If you know the sign and degree of the Moon at the time of your birth, you can determine your **lunar birthday**—when the transiting Moon is conjunct (in the same sign as your natal Moon). If your natal Moon is in Gemini, your lunar birthday is when the Moon is in Gemini. This is a time when you respond rather than initiate. You might be absorbed in feelings and sensations. You will often want to be in the company of women on this day.

• If you know the positions of your natal planets, you can plot the Moon's passage over these points.

Mercury: A good day for ideas and communications.

Venus: Go out and have a good time.

Mars: Work hard. You may be irritating or irritated.

Jupiter: Don't overindulge. You feel optimistic and self-confident.

Saturn: Look into yourself. You are realistic and feeling serious today.

Uranus: Surprises and excitement. A good day to explore and experiment.

Neptune: You are very emotional. You may forget things and feel lost.

Pluto: You want to be alone.

MOONLORE

By Verna Gates

Circling the Moon as surely as it circles the earth is a world of folklore and fantasy. Many practices and stories have grown up to explain, as well as honor, the Moon in all of her (or his, in some cultures) glorious phases.

Child of Earth and Night

The people of the Mission Indians rejoiced as they saw Wyot, Guardian of All Things, cross the Mississippi. This child of Night and Earth brought sad news, however. He foretold his own death, to occur some ten months hence. It would come when "the great star rises over the high grass."

Wyot planned to guard his people until his own end, and beyond. He issued instructions for his funeral. Ten months passed. Wyot remained alive. Glad of his time spent on the Earth, he stopped to refresh himself with a drink from a spring. As he reached the water, a frog awaited the touch of his lips to the water.

In those days, frogs were considered beautiful creatures. With white flesh and red markings, and of course, large eyes, they graced pond and stream. Their only flaw appeared to be their legs, scrawny and misshapen, not beautiful like human legs.

Resenting her ugly nether-parts, the frog watched Wyot lean over for a drink, then spat poison three times into the water. All the while, she cursed him with her vanity.

It was the appointed time, and Wyot passed from earthly life. The Indians gathered to send his spirit on. As his body burned, his spirit transcended the fire and rose into the sky to become the Moon. His body became the oak tree, a guardian.

If you look closely at the Moon, you can see that he took the spiteful little frog with him and her bulging eyes still stare down at the lovely legs of the creatures below.

Revelation

The God of Israel took a moment to explain to the Moon its own significance. The dual lights represented the two sides of life: this world and the world beyond, the dwelling of the afterlife. The polarity of the two lights was to serve as a constant reminder of God's plan for humanity.

The Moon, honored to represent the heavenly afterlife, hastily suggested that since he ruled the greater realm, he should shine the brightest light. This was a grave error made in haste.

The Lord spoke. Since the Moon had been so ready to supersede the Sun, he would never equal him. Instead it would live as the smaller orb, sustained only by the reflected light of the Sun.

The Moon was repentant. He pleaded with God to be restored. For a few thoughtless words, so harsh a punishment!

The Lord heard and promised the moon that on the last day of the world, at the Last Judgment, he would grow as big as the sun, and shine once again as his twin light. However, the changing time must occur during an eclipse, as that lunar event is cited in the Old Testament as the harbinger of Judgment Day.

Tower of Babel

The Moon is responsible for the many tongues spoken across the world. At least, that's what they say in Indochina.

A long time ago, everyone lived in one big village. They all ate the same food, followed the same customs and spoke the same language. They all loved the night-time celebrations of the Full Moon; it was right according to their beliefs.

One evening, during a council session, someone proposed having more Full Moons. Didn't the children of Earth deserve a bright night to enjoy as the day? The Moon was wrong in denying itself to them. After all, at the New Moon, the dishonorable among them stole cattle and pottery. As the Moon waxed, quarreling and warfare increased along with it. The changing Moon should be stopped. As they talked, the people became angry at the Moon, and decided to kidnap it and force it to face them forever in its full, rounded glory.

To implement their plan, the people decided to build a tower to the Moon. Soon, it stood so tall that people stopped coming down to the village at night. Families began staying on their own level in the tower. Food and water were passed up the levels; messages were passed down. After a while, each level developed its own way of doing things. Its own way of thinking. Its own way of speaking.

Before long, the tower reached so far up into the sky, that the Moon could look down in it and hear the people talking. When the Moon realized the plans, his anger rose higher than the tower. He called up a violent storm, one to match his temper.

The tower tumbled to ruins. The people fell far and wide. Those who landed back on earth built new villages, using their new customs and new languages. You can see the tower for yourself. It still lies as the mountains that separate Burma from the Bay of Bengal.

The Searcher

Back in the Dreamtime, a brave young hunter lived with his lovely wife and beloved little son. The hunter, named Japara, killed many kangaroos and other game, keeping his family and village well-fed.

Japara spent days out on the plain, hunting. His wife spent days alone with her son. One day, while Japara hunted, Parukapoli strolled by, and finding the wife, settled down to tell her stories.

Japara's wife listed to the spinning tales and lost herself in laughter. During one particularly amusing story, she lost sight of her young son.

He toddled to the bank of the stream. The next sound after the laughter subsided was a hollow splash. Japara's wife knew its meaning. She rushed to the stream and pulled her baby out. Too late! The boy was dead. She sat there, by the stream for many hours, holding her son's lifeless body and waiting for her husband's return.

Japara did not take the news well. He accused his wife of neglecting his son and in his anger, he killed her. Then he sought out Parukapoli for the same fate. They fought hard and fierce, for many hours. Both were nearly dead from injuries, but Parukapoli succumbed to the stronger man's blows. Through his wounded body and soul, Japara mourned his son. In spite of his agony, the village still came to him in anger for killing his wife over an accident. Japara knew in his heart that they were right. He rushed to find the dead bodies of his wife and son. But they were gone.

Kind spirits had taken them into the sky. Now Japara roams endlessly across the sky, looking for his lost family. The Moon is his campfire. The scars of the Moon show his wounds from the battle with Parukapoli. Some say he's found his loved ones, and they explore the sky together. Others say his eyes are still looking.

World Events

★ International Predictions
★ Weather Predictions
★ Earth Changes
★ Moonlighting the Economy

International Predictions
NEW HEADLINERS CLOSE
THE MILLENNIUM:

By Noel Tyl

China: Normally hidden from western scrutiny, this nation is emerging into modern history with an extraordinarily new and different image, the world's largest population, and an economy burgeoning at double-digit growth rates. China has achieved tremendous poise, as was seen early in 1994 when China stood up to the United States on several issues. In early 1993 it was not accidental that China made news regarding human rights issues and trade status, and as an intermediary with North Korea and the nuclear weapons issue. China has a plan of re-emergence, of making history, of touching as much of the world as it can economically, with a philosophy keyed to gradualism (Saturn in Virgo, perigrine).

Thanks to the research of British astrologer Nicholas Campion (see his *The Book of World Horoscope*, The Aquarian Press: England, 1988), many national birth dates and times are now catalogued and open to serious testing by mundane astrologers; astrologers studying the affairs of nations and history. We know that the Chinese Peoples' Political Consultative Conference opened in Peking on September 21, 1949, and established the Peoples' Republic of China. Over the following week, the Conference debated and designed a new constitution and system of government for China. On September 30, Mao Tse-Tung was elected Chairman, and the process was completed on October 1, 1949. We have a time of 3:15 in the afternoon in Peking for the "birth" of Communist China, attributed to England's Charles Carter, the great astrologer-scholar. This time is holding up well with astrologers' study of events for modern China.

The China horoscope immediately shows the contradiction China represents to western eyes. With the Sun in Libra and the Moon in Aquarius, rising at the Ascendant, we expect a true "People's Republic." These are the Sun-Moon signs of the true romantic and humanitarian, showing love and affection as a banner of identity or coat-of-arms. There is also, however, a powerfully twisted, involuted, angry aspect formation of Venus in Scorpio squared the conjunction of Mars and Pluto in the 7th House; this is what the public sees easily. This is reinforced by the subtle but undeniable measurement of the Aries Point equalling the midpoint of Saturn/Node; a loner position with a serious appearance and much kept under wraps.

China's basic image is going to change now over a period that climaxes in the summer of 1997, upon China's assimilation of Hong Kong, scheduled for midnight, July 1, 1997. The astrology of it all is literally Earth-shaking, and the process, the plan and the growth will have already begun to take shape in 1995.

The year should start with a high China-profile. I think China will make a tremendously important business announcement, or deploy a major international promotion program to increase trade and attract foreign investment. As part of this business image-effort, in response as well to unrest among its people, it is entirely possible that China will have changed leadership; that new, younger leaders with high business/marketing sophistication will have taken over the country's energies, poised for grand leadership in the transition to the 21st century (as its Sun arcs to its Midheaven). The key times for these developments will have been May-July 1994 and and October-December 1994; with the leadership changes most likely during the May-June period. This country-wide shift to capitalism and individualism is indeed a revolution of enormous importance for China's next centuries.

China will look past its own new year to the new year for the West, and market its new capitalist thrust in ways that will startle all other nations. Response by foreign investors within the world community will be highest in July 1995. There will be a curious development, probably on October 8 or 9, 1995, which will be financial in strategy but inscrutable or deceptive in long-range significance. I can't help but see the deception of the United States, preoccupied at that time surely with armed force-support on the Israel-P.L.O. front. What else will be forming in China's grand plan at that time, as the United States hurries back to its own problems?

Korea: My predictions, made in the December 1993 issue of *New Worlds of Mind and Spirit*, stated it simply, "North Korea has the BOMB!" I cited Western conjecture about that status as very strong around March 12 (actual newsdate focus was March 22). I made further projections for international strategic positioning and plans between April 16 and 24, 1994, and in the third week of August.

We can be sure about this explosive news because transiting Pluto (the symbol for atomic energy) is exactly conjunct Korea's national Ascendant (27 Scorpio 19) and, in the national chart (September 12, 1948, noon in Pyongyang), Pluto squares the exact midpoint of Sun and Moon, and Mars is exactly conjunct the Mars of the "Atomic Energy" horoscope (December 2, 1942 at 2:25 PM, Chicago). It is fascinating to see why China is so involved as well. Its Midheaven (27 Scorpio 09) is almost precisely the Ascendant of North Korea!

Where will North Korea have gone with all of this nuclear tension throughout 1994 and into 1995? With its collapsing economy, North Korea desperately needs a better market position to be taken seriously for the times ahead. The country knows where China is heading with its gradual and grand plan, and wants to be right along with its ally. Together, these two countries and their resources for weaponry and stoic diplomacy are formidable.

North Korea surely will dominate the news in April 14-24 and throughout the month of May, staying just on the safe side of real trouble (they are not yet ready). Then, in the period of August 15 to December 1994 (especially October 20-November 1 and the third week of December), this small country will have been "clarified." Their idealized outlook will have been exposed in their own terms, and the rest of the world will know how to deal with them. In my opinion, they will be very closely allied to the plans being made by China. Just look at a map of the Far East: see China, en route to formal annexation of Hong Kong (July 1997), then Nationalist China (Taiwan), and North Korea in an embrace of power, and all of these facing Japan— with its increasing political and economic disarray (watch March-May 1995 especially)—across the Sea of Japan, we have a formidable picture of China's powerful position by 1999. The Korean peninsula is of critical importance to whomever wants hegemony of the heretofore named "Japanese Basin."

I do not see a clash between North and South Korea. Much will depend on how the world receives North Korean developments in October-November 1994. There is a peacefulness being established in the midst of conjectural maelstrom late in December 1994. Then, North Korea begins rebuilding its economy with new stature in the world: watch the last week of January 1995, the first weeks of April, and especially the first two weeks of June 1995 for major development. China will not let North Korea break up its identity. 1995 is a tough, tough year for North Korea. The rebuilding efforts will start to produce respectable results in Spring 1996.

India: The Republic of India (January 26, 1950, at 10:15 AM in New Delhi) faces some extraordinary upset, which will have begun and made news probably in July-August 1994. We can time the major focus of this to the month of March 1995, with the most conspicuous development probably March 18-19 (SA Uranus conjunct Pluto and transiting Saturn conjunct Saturn Cycle Chart Mercury at the Ascendant in New Delhi; see "Iran" below for "Cycle Chart" explanation). India is not geared for change; it likes to stay as it is, to be remote within to the changes of time and to persist in a weakened but inscrutably self-rationalized state. This will become impossible in the light of the approaching millennium, the national changes everywhere, and, specifically, its exploding population and its extreme insecurity on every front, including health, housing, and income per capita. The revolt could very easily be stimulated by a health crisis in tuberculosis or some form of paralysis.

The spring of 1995 is the first phase, probably involving the youth of India, a student force, perhaps, protesting social conditions and the government in power. Students may block transportation routes and communications networks to dramatize their position. The situation will involve a tremendous upset of the status quo. This will have repercussions in November-December 1995.

The next phase of this extraordinary unrest in India will be in the spring and summer of 1996, March-July, when national elections will probably occur. The build-up of one year of protest will reorganize India in a way not imaginable at this time.

Iran: In Iran, we can expect that an outburst against the party in power will have occurred strongly (even with firepower) May 18-21, 1994. This is a beginning of a show of the people's discontent.

The astrology here is most interesting, based on hard-and-fast rules involving what is called a "Cycle Chart," drawn for the moment a particular planet enters northern declination from the south. In the Mars Cycle Chart (April 17, 1994 at 8:27 P.M., GMT), we can see that the Sun is almost precisely at the Nadir (fourth cusp) of the chart drawn for Teheran (-3:30 H). It is squared by Uranus-Neptune rising (and the Moon is in Cancer in the 7th). When the planet that "owns" the particular Cycle Chart (in this case, Mars) transits particular planet positions in the Cycle Chart in real future time, we can expect major occurrences on Earth where these planets are placed.

Transiting Mars conjoins the Cycle Chart Sun in 27 Aries on May 20, 1994, suggesting an uprising against the party in power (the 4th House against the 10th). The public involvement is suggested by the Moon in Cancer in the 7th. Many other measurements then rush into play. The Cycle Chart stays in force until the next one; the Cycle Charts for Mars, Jupiter, and Saturn are most telling in mundane astrology.

Extending transits from the Mars Cycle Chart further into the world and into future time, we see Mars conjoining Cycle Chart Moon in the first week of September 1994 in Dar Es Salaam, Tanzania, and in Yemen. Working with the eclipsed Full Moon on April 15, 1995 (12:08 PM, GMT), we can put Tanzania on revolutionary alert all spring and summer 1995, from April 15 through August. A similar alert in the same span of time is registered for Ethiopia, Turkey (an eruption of civil rights issues and the pressures to abandon old ways and join the European Community), Panama, and San Salvador.

Italy: The elections in Italy have been hailed as the burial of the Fourth Republic (June 10, 1946, at 6:00 PM CED, in Rome). Silvio Berlusconi, the public media tycoon, has won, but he represents a conservative three-party alliance and is not an out-and-out victor. In other words, with the bitter, quarrelsome air among his coalition partners, the tensions are not yet resolved. Italy still is in a tremendous period of change, which began some 10 years ago, with all the financial double-dealings top to bottom in its society, focusing most strongly 4 years ago (with SA Neptune upon the Ascendant).

A further step to resolution of the dissonance depends on who will be named new Prime Minister by Italy's president Oscar Luigi Scalfaro. This will have taken place around April 28, 1994. Berlusconi will probably be named. Between then and August 1994, there will be much wheeling and dealing in Italy's extremely complex political machinery. Another crank of the gears will have taken place November 16-December 15, 1994. The plans that settle things down among all the factions should be strong in June, late August, and early October 1995. It will take just about that long for the volatile atmosphere to stop crackling. Just before Christmas 1995, a more mature Italy, with "post-fascist" voices quieted and with the leader of the right-wing National Alliance, Gianfranco Fini, working well within the coalition, will emerge. Government policy will be quite changed with regard to the Mafia: campaign promises to crack down on illegalities and crime will be the prime agenda for the new government.

France: France (The Fifth Republic, October 5, 1958, at 00:00 AM in Paris) is starting to show its love of revolution, rock throwing, and government bashing out front in the public eye. The young are very powerful in France (Moon in Gemini; Mercury conjunct Sun), and early in 1994, students successfully forced withdrawal of government plans to tamper with the guaranteed minimum wage. Astrologically, this was a symptom of revolt and force in France growing to adjust the strictures of government; to trade in the old and conventional for the new and more individualistic. Many measurements forming now in 1994 echo those that dominated the French chart in 1968, when a major student uprising occurred.

In May, June, July, and October 1994, all of this should have broken out into the open. New individual perspectives, with a characteristic French emotionalism, will be aimed at reform of the bankrupt social structure of that country.

The target date is May 1995 (when the Solar Arc picture Uranus=Sun/Mars sums it all up). High excitability, sudden impulses and events, forceful adjustment of new circumstances, militarism, overexertion causing a breakdown of efficiency and troubles with authority will be the themes of that time. There will be powerful demonstrations, underhanded dealings unmasked in the government (how the public has been duped; transiting Neptune on the Descendant), and deceptive tactics will run amok. International policies will suffer until all of this settles. Fuel prices will soar.

Make note that May 1995 is the time of national elections in France. The laws being questioned will be pivotal in those elections. The outcome of the elections will be doubted and mistrusted; there will probably be a rebellious outburst again on October 13-16, 1995 (transiting Mars conjunct Cycle Chart Pluto; see "Iran," above), and it will take one month to be resolved.

Mexico: With the assassination of Mexico's leading presidential candidate on March 23, 1994, Mexico's national profile is at its lowest and most confused in many years. The chart of the Mexican Constitution appears to be valid for January 31, 1917, at 4:05 PM, LMT in Queretaro, Mexico. March 1994 shows Solar Arc Saturn opposed the Midheaven, SA Midheaven conjoining Pluto, SA Neptune square the Ascendant, and transiting Uranus opposed Saturn. This will be very difficult business, with total reform in the offing.

I do not see progress out of the reorganization confusion until early 1995. Perhaps on January 16 or 17 major plans will be made public; a new year, a new regime, a new projection into a better future. Education programs will become extremely important to lift up the Mexican people's standard of living. Mexico will resurrect a national pride. There will be fire-power pockets of revolt in May-June 1995. June and/or August 1995 will be the worst time of the change, with all the revolutionaries put down. There will be every effort then to get away from militarism as the way of government, and peace will soon prevail.

Israel and the P.L.O.: In *New Worlds* (June-July 1994), I explained and presented a profile of violence based on 20 years of research, and on the reliability of the Israel chart (May 14, 1948 at 4:00 PM, EET in Tel Aviv). Those 1994 dates were around February 25 (when the Hebron massacre occurred), March 4, May 14, June 24, July 17, August 21-30, October 27-November 9, and December 1-4. These are times of extreme vulnerability to violent eruption.

I hesitate to project these times into 1995 because of the extreme nature of the activities that will have closed 1994. The civil turmoil caused by Israel's people railing against government liaison with the P.L.O. and the fight against the civil dissidents on the P.L.O. side threaten terribly in June 1994 and finally in December 1994. From November 18 through December 1994, the fighting is at its worst.

Israel will probably make a major proclamation between January 14 and January 28. This should be a pronouncement of Israel's new position in the Middle East chaos after the dust has settled. It will involve the enduring pact with the P.L.O., the emergence of peaceful accords with Syria, and all the violence that plagues every step of development.

Still another cloud arises in March 1995, around the 15th, but again Israel's might will prevail and see stabilization in May at its 45th birthday (a very important time of the accumulated Solar Arc semisquare, exact to the month).

My predictions in these pages were exact with the specifics of the signing with the P.L.O. (September 13, 1993 at 11:43 AM, EDT in Washington, D.C.), the interruption by the Hebron violence, and the resumption in "early April 1994." August 1994 represents a major time of fulfillment in the talks, but we come again from this perspective to the bombast and chaos of December 1994. This extends with great difficulty into April 1995, and coincides with Israel's identity adjustment in May

1995 as well. These are very difficult times. There is every possibility that the talks break down completely if they can not survive the militarism at the close of 1994, and in April 1995. The next steps of the talks are severely threatened in September 1995 and January 1996.

United States: The United States horoscope (July 4, 1776 at 2:13 AM, LMT in Philadelphia) is tightly tied to the chart of Israel. There is little doubt that the United States will be involved with international militarism between September and the end of 1994, and that that militarism will be to aid Israel in the Middle-East crisis, involving fulfillment of the peace pact with the P.L.O. for Palestinian self-rule. This will again raise the American outcry to keep U.S. attention at home and to stop policing the world.

The people will have their way, and I feel that the United States will adopt formal policies of non-intervention, framed in April-June and between September and October 1995.

Bill Clinton is under siege almost constantly throughout 1994, as predicted long ago. His wife will have been dragged into the arena with him, especially in May-June 1994. Bill Clinton will wonder why anyone would want his job during his worst times, June-September 1994. The application of force during the Middle East violence actually rescues his success profile.

Hillary Rodham Clinton (October 26, 1947, at 8:00 PM in Chicago) has extraordinary astrological upheaval from September 1995 through November 1996. It is as if she will propel her husband's drive to be reelected in the campaign of 1996.

Hillary is powerful throughout the second half of 1995 and into the spring and summer of 1996. With the health plan basically defeated as she and the President have formulated it, there will be a new plan of different design adopted, and this will have to be the vehicle for her to express the 6th House power (with transiting Pluto conjunct Jupiter in Sagittarius) in her horoscope. As long as the cause Hillary serves remains "noble," the more of a winner she will be.

Bill Clinton's horoscope calms down in 1995. Indeed, he will have really been "through it," with all the investigation of his personal finances (the ending of Pluto's transit of Clinton's 2nd House), and I think we can anticipate a maturation evident in March 1995. The success of his militarism at the end of 1994 will have buoyed him with a reinforced confidence and optimism in the light of the nation's demand for attention to domestic problems. Clinton will mellow in the spring of 1995. He will begin feeling that he need not run for reelection in 1996 to fulfill himself further, but in September and November 1995, he will indeed make the resolve to run in 1996 for another term as President.

As poised and affable as Bill Clinton is, Hillary's growing power fuels his energies, invigorates his strategies and makes decisions for him. Her power can begin to intimidate him as well. Bill and Hillary are going to have to come up with some codes of conduct to keep their relationship as apparently efficient as it is.

In the long term, Bill Clinton will run again, and will enjoy an enormously positive April and May 1996, the key months of his campaign.

Republican Senator Robert Dole (July 22, 1923, at 00:10 AM in Russell, KS) will be there, too! I believe Dole will announce his run for the presidency early in October 1995, perhaps on the 8th. Throughout 1995, Dole is on fire, so to speak, with particularly grand times of success in June and July.

• •

ZONE CHART FOR WEATHER PREDICTIONS

WEATHER PREDICTIONS

By Nancy Soller

NOVEMBER 1994

ZONE 1: Seasonable temperatures are forecast for this zone. The northeast may be dry. Most areas south will have normal precipitation. Florida, however, could have some very dry areas. Dates most likely to result in precipitation include the 8th, 9th and 10th; also the 13th and 28th. Weather patterns in effect now should continue through December.

    ZONE 2: Slightly dry weather is forecast for most areas in this zone in November. Temperatures should be seasonable. Rainfall is very likely on the 8th, 9th and 10th; rainfall is also likely on the 13th and 28th. Weather patterns set this month are likely to continue through the rest of the year. Areas near the Mississippi will see an unusual amount of blue sky for the season.

ZONE 3: Slightly dry weather is forecast for most areas near the Mississippi. Skies will be unusually blue for the season. Areas in the far west of this zone will be chill and unusually damp. Precipitation will be likely on the 2nd; precipitation will also be likely on the 8th-10th, 13th, 18th and 24th. Snowfall is likely November 27th and 28th. Dry weather near the Mississippi will continue into December.

ZONE 4: Eastern portions of this zone may be cold and damp, but most areas here will be dry, with temperatures above normal. Dates most likely to result in precipitation include the 2nd, 8th, 9th, 10th and 13th; also the 18th, 24th, 27th and 28th. Weather patterns in effect in this zone this month should continue throughout most of the month of December.

ZONE 5: Seasonable temperatures and generous amounts of precipitation are forecast for this zone in November. Watch for rainfall on the 2nd, and more precipitation on the 9th, 10th, 13th and 14th. Snow is possible the 18th, 24th and 26th. Weather patterns in effect this month should continue through December. Desert areas will remain dry south.

ZONE 6: The Alaskan Panhandle will be wet this month, but central parts of the state will be dry. Western Alaska will have seasonable weather. Hawaii will have a pleasant, normal month. November 2nd, 8th-10th, 13th, 14th and 18th. The 24th, 26th, 27th and 28th should be wet also.

Dates to Watch

Watch for winds November 4th, 7th, 12th, 13th, 14th, 18th, 20th, 24th and 27th-29th.

Watch for rain November 2nd, 8th, 10th, 11th, 13th and 14th.

Watch for snow November 18th, 19th and 26th-28th.

DECEMBER 1994

ZONE 1: Normal temperatures and normal precipitation patterns are forecast for this zone in December. The Northeast may be subjected to some sudden, heavy snows. Watch for snow December 3rd, 8th and 9th. Snowfall is also due December 23rd and 30th. Snowfall on the 23rd may stick to the ground, creating a beautiful, white Christmas in widespread areas in this zone.

     ZONE 2: Seasonable precipitation and seasonable temperatures are forecast for this zone in December. Skies may be unseasonably blue in the west. Watch for snowfall on the 3rd, 8th and 9th; areas south could see rain on these dates. The 23rd and 30th could see snowfall in wide spread areas in this zone. Snowfall on the 23rd may stick, causing a white Christmas in many areas.

     ZONE 3: Normal temperatures and normal precipitation patterns are forecast east in this zone, but areas west are likely to be wet and chill. Watch for precipitation west on the 2nd, and snow in wide spread areas on the 3rd, 8th and 9th. Snow on the 23rd and 30th may stick, making both Christmas and New Year's Day white and festive.

ZONE 4: Areas in the eastern Rockies will be chill and unusually damp, but central and western portions of this zone will be dry, with temperatures markedly above normal. Watch for generous snowfall on the 2nd and, again, on Christmas Day. Eastern portions of this zone may see snow on other dates, but the rest of this zone will be relatively snow-free.

ZONE 5: Temperatures will be seasonable this month, with many areas in this zone having generous amounts of precipitation. Snowfall should usher in the month north and there should be generous snowfall Christmas Day. Other dates should see precipitation originating over the Pacific and reaching land a bit later; dates for precipitation in ZONE 6 should tell when.

ZONE 6: Parts of the Alaskan Panhandle will be very wet, and the central and western portions of the state should have some sudden, heavy snowfall. Central parts of the state will be warmer than normal for this time of year. Watch for snowfall on the 2nd south, the 3rd, 8th, 9th and 17th, the 23rd and the 25th, 29th and 30th. Hawaii should have a pleasant month.

Dates to Watch

Watch for winds December 1st-4th, 6th, 7th, 14th, 20th, 23rd and 24th.

Watch for snow December 3rd, 4th, 8th, 9th, 18th, 23rd, 25th, 29th and 30th.

JANUARY 1995

ZONE 1: A mild month with little precipitation is forecast for northern portions of this zone. Southern areas, however, will have much precipitation. Watch for snow north on the 6th, 8th and 13th. The same dates should result in rain and chill south. Snow is also likely on the 15th, 17th and 23rd. January 4th and 8th should bring chill winds to widespread areas in this zone.

ZONE 2: Much snow is forecast north, and there should be ample cold rain south in this zone in January. Cincinnati and points directly north and south will see the greatest amounts of precipitation. Watch for snowfall on the 6th, 8th, 13th, 15th, 17th and 23rd. The same dates will bring cold rains south. Sharp winds are forecast for the 4th and 8th, with drifting on the 8th.

ZONE 3: The wettest portion of this zone will be along the Mississippi River. Most areas to the west will be drier although sudden, heavy snowfall will be likely throughout this zone all winter. Heavy snow is likely north January 4th, 6th and 8th. Watch for snow also January 9th, 13th and 15th. Other snow dates include the 16th, 17th, 23rd and 27th.

ZONE 4: Normal precipitation and seasonable temperatures are predicted for this zone in January. Watch for snow January 2nd; also January 9th, 14th and 16th. Precipitation is also likely January 27th. Snows in the eastern portions of this zone are likely to be sudden and heavy, and this pattern is likely to continue throughout the winter. Wind will accompany many snows.

ZONE 5: Dry, cold and windy is the forecast for this zone in January. Temperatures will be below normal. Dates most likely to result in precipitation include the 2nd, 6th, 9th and 14th; also the 15th, 16th and 27th. Winds in this zone north will be especially chill, and some temperatures south may set record lows. January weather patterns should continue all winter.

ZONE 6: The Alaskan Panhandle will have seasonable weather, but central parts of the state will be unusually chill and extremely snowy. Western portions of the state will have seasonable weather. Watch for snows January 2nd, 6th, 7th, 14th-16th and again in the last days of the month. Hawaii will have a pleasant, normal month preceding a pleasant, normal winter.

Dates to Watch

Watch for winds January 2nd, 4th, 5th, 6th, 7th-10th, 11th, 13th, 15th, 16th, 22nd, 27th and 30th.

Watch for snow January 2nd, 6th, 7th, 9th, 13th-17th, 23rd and 27th.

FEBRUARY 1995

ZONE 1: Dry weather north and wet weather south is the forecast for this zone in February. Temperatures north should be mild. Watch for precipitation February 1st and 4th; February 15th and 26th should see ample snowfall north and rain south.

Other dates may see precipitation, but it will originate far to the west and may be almost spent before it arrives.

ZONE 2: Wet, snowy weather is predicted for this zone in February. Temperatures should be seasonable. The month should open with snow north and rain south; other dates likely to result in precipitation include February 4th, 7th and 15th. The end of the month will likely see precipitation originating far to the west. This could blanket the north and wet the south thoroughly.

ZONE 3: Seasonable temperatures and normal amounts of precipitation are likely in this zone in February, but snow, when it comes, is likely to be sudden and heavy. The month should open with snow north and rain south; other dates which should result in precipitation include February 4th, 7th and 15th. Snowfall originating west should arrive after the 22nd and 26th.

ZONE 4: Seasonable temperatures and normal total precipitation are predicted for this zone in February, but snowfall will be very heavy and come on relatively few dates. Watch for snow February 4th and 7th; also February 15th and 22nd. Precipitation originating farther west may reach this zone after the 19th and 26th. Strong winds are predicted February 6th.

ZONE 5: Chill winds and low temperatures will mark this zone in February, and there will be little precipitation. Even desert areas of the Southwest will feel a little chill. Precipitation is most likely February 7th, possibly on the 15th and likely on the 19th, 22nd and 26th. Winds are likely February 6th. March weather should continue patterns set this month.

ZONE 6: Very cold weather with much snow is forecast for the central parts of Alaska; most of the rest of the state will see normal temperatures and normal snowfall. Much snow is likely on relatively few dates. Watch for snow on the 1st, 4th, 15th and 26th. Hawaii will have a nice month with no weather anomalies. The central freeze should continue well into March.

Dates to Watch

Watch for winds February 1st, 3rd, 6th, 9th, 11th and 19th.

Watch for snow February 1st, 4th, 7th, 15th, 16th, 19th, 22nd and 26th.

MARCH 1995

ZONE 1: Northern portions of this zone will be dry, with temperatures above normal for the season. Southern portions of this zone will be wet with seasonable temperatures. The month will open with precipitation north, and with more precipitation due on the 9th, 15th, 22nd, 24th, 25th and 28th in many parts of this zone. The last week of the month will bring a rise in temperature.

ZONE 2: This zone will be marked with much precipitation in March. The number of days likely to result in rain is not unusually great, but generous precipitation is forecast for days resulting in rain. Watch for rain or snow to open the month, and watch for more precipitation on the 9th, 15th, 22nd, 24th, 25th and 28th. Precipitation is also possible west on the 14th.

ZONE 3: The wettest portions of this zone will be areas near the Mississippi, but the entire zone can expect some sudden, heavy rainfall this month. The end of the month should see especially heavy rainfall throughout this zone. Watch for snow north on the 1st; more precipitation is due on the 3rd, 14th, 15th, 25th, 26th and 28th. A tornado is possible March 3rd.

ZONE 4: Normal temperatures and normal amounts of precipitation are forecast for this zone in March. Areas in the extreme east, however, may deal with several sudden, heavy downpours. Precipitation is likely west March 1st and 3rd. Watch for zone-wide precipitation March 5th, 15th, 17th, 23rd and 30th. Seasonable winter weather in this zone precedes more seasonable weather throughout the spring.

ZONE 5: Chill winds north and dry weather throughout this zone are forecast for March. Southern portions of this zone will have below-normal temperatures. Best days for precipitation are the 1st, 3rd, 5th, 9th and 15th. Watch also the 17th, 23rd, 24th and 30th. Rainfall coming on these days will not be very heavy or long-lasting. A beautiful spring lies ahead.

ZONE 6: The Alaskan Panhandle will see normal March weather, but central portions of this state will have extremely heavy snow and markedly below-normal temperatures. Watch for precipitation on the 1st, 3rd, 5th, 9th, 15th and 17th; watch also the 22nd, 23rd, 24th, 25th and 28th. Moist weather in March will be followed by a dry spring. Hawaii will see beautiful weather.

Dates to Watch

Watch for winds March 2nd, 3rd, 9th, 14th, 15th, 20th, 21st, 22nd, 24th, 26th, 28th and 30th.

Watch for snow March 1st, 3rd, 6th, 9th, 14th and 15th.

Watch for rain March 16th, 17th, 22nd, 23rd, 26th, 28th and 30th.

APRIL 1995

ZONE 1: A dry, warm month is predicted for most of this zone in April, but New England and the Canadian East Coast may see some excessive moisture. The first week of the month will be dry, but rainfall is due April 8th, 10th and 12th. Watch for more precipitation April 15th, 18th, 21st and 27th. Dry weather south may last throughout the entire spring season.

ZONE 2: Dry, warm weather is predicted for this zone in April. Precipitation, when it comes, however, should be sudden and heavy. Watch for rainfall April 8th, 10th and 12th, and also the 15th. Rainfall is also due April 18th, 21st and 27th. Dry weather this month begins a dry spring. Temperatures will be above normal, especially in the eastern portions of this zone.

ZONE 3: A normal month is expected in this zone in April, with the possible exception that rainfall, when it comes, will be sudden and heavy. The month will open with dry weather, but there will be rainfall April 8th, 9th, 14th, 15th and also April 18th, 21st, 22nd and 27th. Weather patterns in effect this month should continue throughout the entire season.

ZONE 4: Normal temperatures and a normal precipitation pattern are predicted for this zone in April. The month will open with dry weather, but rainfall is predicted for the 9th, 14th and 15th. Watch also April 18th, 21st and 22nd. Springtime in the Rockies should be pleasant this year. April's weather patterns should continue throughout the spring.

ZONE 5: A pleasant month is predicted for this zone in April. Temperatures will be unusually mild north and precipitation patterns normal throughout this zone. Dry weather is forecast the first week of the month, but rainfall is due April 9th, 10th and 13th-15th. Watch also for rainfall April 21st. Nice weather in this zone this month should continue all month.

ZONE 6: A pleasant month is predicted for the Alaskan Panhandle and dry, chill weather with wind is predicted for the central part of the state. The extreme west may see generous amounts of precipitation. Watch for rainfall April 8th-10th, 12th-15th, the 18th, 21st, 22nd, 27th and 29th. Hawaii will have a pleasant month, but there may be very generous amounts of rainfall.

Dates to Watch

Watch for winds April 2nd, 3rd, 9th, 10th, 12th, 14th, 15th, 17th, 20th-22nd, 24th, 26th, 27th and 29th.
Watch for rain April 8th-10th, 12th-16th, 18th 21st, 22nd, 27th and 29th.

MAY 1995

ZONE 1: Generous rainfall north and dry, unseasonably warm weather south are forecast for this zone this May. May 3rd could result in rain in parts of this zone; watch also the 7th, 13th, 16th, 17th and 21st. Temperatures will be seasonable north. A continuation of May weather should last throughout most of June. May 2nd may see some strong, destructive winds in some parts of this zone.

ZONE 2: Dry, warm weather is forecast for this zone in May. Areas near the Mississippi, however, may see some sudden dumping of precipitation on some rain dates. Sharp, cold winds are due on the 2nd, which is also a possible tornado date. Watch for precipitation on the 3rd, on the 7th east, the 13th, 16th, 21st and 24th. May 30th should be chilly and windy.

ZONE 3: Normal temperatures are forecast for this zone in May, but precipitation is likely to be sudden and heavy. Dates most likely to result in rainfall include the 3rd, 12th, 13th and 21st. Sharp, cold winds are possible May 2nd, 21st and 24th; also the 30th. These dates could also result in tornadoes. May weather patterns should continue throughout most of June.

ZONE 4: Normal temperatures and season-able precipitation patterns are predicted for this zone in May. Relatively dry weather is predicted for the first two weeks of the month, but watch for generous rainfall mid-month or a little before. Watch also for rain on the 16th and 21st. Weather patterns in effect this month should precede similar weather patterns in June.

ZONE 5: Beautiful blue skies and pleasant temperatures are forecast for this zone in May. The 3rd of the month should bring rain, as should the 12th, 13th and 16th. Watch for more rain on the 24th. A storm originating over the ocean could extend rainfall through the 14th and 15th as well. Nice weather this month should continue through-out the month of June.

ZONE 6: Weather on the Alaskan Panhandle will be beautiful, but central portions of the state will be dry, windy and chilly. To the west, temper-atures will be normal. Watch for precipitation on the 3rd, the 7th and the 12th-14th; also the 16th, 17th, 21st and 24th. Hawaii will have a pleasant month. May weather patterns should continue throughout most of the month of June.

Dates to Watch

Watch for winds May 2nd, 5th, 12th, 17th, 20th, 21st, 23rd, 24th and 30th.

Watch for rain May 3rd, 7th, 12th, 13th, 15th-17th, 21st and 34th.

JUNE 1995

ZONE 1: Wet north and dry, and hot south is the forecast for this zone in June. The last week of the month may be extremely hot and dry, starting a weather pattern that could continue throughout the rest of the summer. Watch for rainfall June 5th and 6th; also June 9th, 10th and 12th. Rain is also likely on the 15th, 17th, 19th, 21st and 30th. Rainfall south is likely to be scant and short-lived.

ZONE 2: Dry, hot weather is forecast for this zone in June, but areas close to the Mississippi will have normal or greater than normal precipitation. Rain is likely June 5th and 6th, June 9th, 10th and 12th, June 15th, 17th and 19th; also June 21st, 27th and 30th. Rainfall in most of this zone will be short-lived and scant. Rain coming on the 10th should be accompanied by winds. Rain on June 30th could be generous.

ZONE 3: Rainfall in this zone this month should range from normal to generous; temperatures will be seasonable. Precipitation here may be best described as sudden, and on occasion, very heavy. Watch for precipitation June 5th, 6th, 9th, 10th and 12th; also June 15th, 17th, 27th and 30th. Rains June 10th will be accompanied by winds. Rainfall patterns in effect this month should last throughout the rest of the summer.

ZONE 4: Normal precipitation and normal temperatures are forecast for this zone in June. Areas in the very easternmost sections of this zone, however, may see some sudden, generous rainfall.

Watch for precipitation June 5th and 6th, June 10th east, June 15th; also the 17th and 30th. Weather patterns begun in this zone this month should continue throughout the summer.

ZONE 5: The forecast for this zone in June is for beautiful, blue skies, enough moisture to benefit agriculture and comfortable temperatures at most locations. Rain is likely on the 5th; also the 15th and 27th. Storms originating to the west over the ocean may reach land on or after the 10th and 18th. Other moisture originating to the west is also likely. Good weather this month forecasts a pleasant summer and fall.

ZONE 6: Nice weather is predicted for the Alaskan Panhandle this month, but the interior of the state will be cool, dry and windy. Watch for precipitation in some parts of the state on the 5th, 6th, 9th, 10th, 12th and 15th; also the 17th-19th, 21st and 30th. A rise in temperature may occur the last week of the month. A pleasant, normal month is forecast for Hawaii.

Dates to Watch

Watch for winds June 5th, 9th, 10th, 13th, 15th, 18th, 21st and 27th.

Watch for rain June 5th, 6th, 9th, 10th, 13th, 15th, 17th-19th, 21st, 27th and 30th.

JULY 1995

ZONE 1: Very hot, dry weather is predicted for the northern portions of this zone this month; to the south normal temperatures and normal amounts of precipitation should prevail. Watch for rainfall July 7th, July 11th and 12th; also the 15th-17th. Rainfall is also likely July 19th, 23rd, 24th and 27th. July 7th should bring winds as well as rain, as should the 15th and 20th. Wind only is predicted the 21st.

ZONE 2: Normal precipitation and seasonable temperatures are forecast for this zone in July. Near the Mississippi, however, a pattern of sudden, heavy rainfall is likely. Watch for precipitation on the 7th east, the 11th, 12th and 16th; also the 17th, 19th and 20th. The 23rd-25th should yield precipitation also. Nice weather this month should continue all summer, but fall will be chilly.

ZONE 3: This month will set a pattern of sudden, heavy precipitation in this zone which should continue through the summer. Rain is likely July 1st; watch also the 7th east, the 8th, the 11th east and the 12th. July 23rd is likely to result in rain, as is the 25th and 27th. Temperatures in this zone should be normal for the season. Weather patterns in effect this month should continue into August.

ZONE 4: Rain is likely to be heavy and sudden east, but the rest of this zone should have normal precipitation and seasonable temperatures in July. Watch for rainfall July 1st, July 8th east, July 12th and July 17th. More precipitation is due July 19th, 24th, 25th and 27th. The July moisture pattern is forecast to continue well into August, and may last through much of September.

ZONE 5: Normal amounts of precipitation and seasonable temperatures are forecast for this zone in July. Watch for rainfall July 1st, July 5th, July 12th and July 17th. Precipitation is also likely July 19th east and July 25th. Some strong and possibly destructive winds are possible July 3rd, 12th, 18th, 22nd and 27th. August should continue July's weather patterns.

ZONE 6: Below-normal temperatures are predicted for the Alaskan Panhandle, but the interior of the state will have temperatures considerably higher than normal. Precipitation near Juneau will range from normal to generous, but the interior should be very dry. Rainfall is most likely in some part of the state July 5th, 7th, 11th, 12th, 15th-17th, 20th and 22nd; also the 25th, 27th and 28th. Hawaii will have a nice month.

Dates to Watch

Watch for winds July 3rd, 7th, 9th, 12th, 15th, 17th, 18th, 20th-22nd, 23rd, 24th, 26th, 27th, 28th and 30th.

Watch for rain July 1st, 5th, 7th-9th, 12th, 13th, 15th-17th, 19th, 20th, 22nd-25th, 27th and 28th.

AUGUST 1995

ZONE 1: New England and neighboring areas will be extremely hot and dry; to the south this zone will have seasonable temperatures and normal precipitation. Rainfall is most likely on the 3rd, 6th, 9th and 17th; also the 24th and 27th. The 31st may bring rainfall to the extreme north of this zone. Hot weather in the north this month should continue throughout much of September.

ZONE 2: Temperatures will be normal and precipitation will range from normal to generous in this zone in August. Areas near the Mississippi will have the greatest amounts of precipitation. Watch for rainfall August 3rd, 6th, 10th and 17th; also the 23rd and 27th. August 9th, 13th, 17th, 21st and 26th may see strong winds. Tornado activity is still possible during this month.

ZONE 3: Temperatures will be seasonable in this zone in August; precipitation will range from normal to generous. Rainfall will be likely to be sudden and heavy when it comes. This month will likely have the heaviest rains of the summer. Watch for precipitation August 3rd, 6th, 10th and 20th; also August 23rd. Sudden rainfall is a pattern that should continue well into the fall.

ZONE 4: Normal August weather is forecast for this zone this month. There will likely be nothing unusual about either temperatures or precipitation. Watch for rainfall August 6th, 10th, 17th, 20th, 21st and 23rd. Strong winds are forecast August 8th and 17th. The weather patterns in effect this month are likely to continue throughout most of September, but the rest of the fall will bring chilly, wet weather.

ZONE 5: Seasonable temperatures and normal amounts of precipitation are predicted for this zone in August. Rainfall is likely August 6th and 10th; also the 17th, 21st and 28th. Storm activity, originating over the ocean, could affect this zone on other dates. The weather patterns of August should continue into September, making that month a seasonable month also. However, dry weather is likely in the fall.

ZONE 6: The Alaskan Panhandle will probably see normal weather for the month, but the interior of the state will be dry, with temperatures above normal. Western Alaska will also be dry. Watch for precipitation August 3rd, 6th, 9th and also the 17th, 20th, 21st, 24th and 27th. Hawaii will see some nice weather, but temperatures may be a little above normal and there may be less rain than usual.

Dates to Watch

Watch for winds August 2nd, 6th, 7th, 8th, 9th, 13th, 17th, 21st, 23rd, 24th, 26th and 27th.
Watch for rain August 3rd, 6th, 9th, 11th, 17th, 20th, 21st, 23rd, 24th, 26th-28th and 31st.

SEPTEMBER 1995

ZONE 1: September will be a dry, hot month in the north with normal September weather in the south. Watch for rainfall September 2nd and 8th; also September 16th. The last week of the month may bring a chill both north and south, and the testimony for dry weather will be strengthened north and introduced south. Wind is likely to play a prominent part in fall weather.

ZONE 2: September will see normal weather in much of this zone, but areas near the Mississippi may see sudden, heavy precipitation on occasion. Watch for rain on the 2nd, 5th and 6th, the 8th and 10th; also the 13th, 14th, 16th and 23rd. Notice that the last part of the month will be mostly dry. Next month, however, is likely to be much wetter. Again, winds may be prominent.

ZONE 3: The forecast for this zone in September calls for seasonable temperatures and normal amounts of precipitation. Rainfall is likely September 2nd, 5th, 9th, 13th and 14th; also September 23rd and 29th. The last week in the month may see a rise in temperatures, setting a pattern of mild temperatures that should continue throughout most of the fall. October should be dry.

ZONE 4: Normal temperatures and normal precipitation patterns are forecast for this zone in September, with the exception of the most eastern portions of this zone where rainfall will likely be sudden and heavy. Watch for rain September 5th, 6th, 13th, 14th and 16th east; also the 23rd, 29th and 30th. The end of the month will bring zone-wide temperature dips and heavy precipitation.

ZONE 5: The forecast for this zone in September calls for seasonable temperatures and normal amounts of precipitation. Rainfall is likely September 2nd, 5th, 9th, 13th and 14th; also September 23rd and 29th. The last week of the month may see a rise in temperatures, setting a pattern of mild temperatures that should continue through most of the fall.

ZONE 6: Eastern Alaskan weather will range from wet to normal, but central and western parts of the state will have dry weather with temperatures markedly above normal. Watch these dates when rain is most possible: September 2nd, 5th, 6th, 8th-10th and 13th; also the 14th, 16th, 23rd, 29th and 30th. Hawaii should have a pleasant month, but temperatures may be up slightly.

Dates to Watch

Watch for winds September 2nd, 3rd, 5th, 8th, 13th, 14th, 20th, 21st and 29th.

Watch for rain September 2nd, 5th, 9th, 10th, 13th, 14th, 16th, 23rd, 29th and 30th.

OCTOBER 1995

ZONE 1: Dry, chilly, and windy is the forecast for most of this zone in October. The exceptions may be New England and the extreme south, where normal to excessive moisture is possible. Watch for rainfall on the 2nd, 6th, 8th-10th and 15th; also the 16th, 25th, 28th and 30th. Wind is likely October 3rd, 5th, 6th, 12th and 19th; also the 24th, 25th, 30th and 31st.

ZONE 2: Wet weather with normal temperatures is forecast for this zone in October. Rainfall should be often and heavy. Watch for precipitation on the 2nd, 4th-6th, 8th-10th, the 15th, the 16th, the 21st and 25th; also the 28th and 30th. Winds are likely the 3rd, 5th, 6th, 10th and 12th; also the 19th, 24th, 25th, 30th and 31st. October weather patterns should continue throughout the fall.

ZONE 3: The weather in this zone in October will range from nice and normal near the Mississippi to wet and chilly to the west. Precipitation is likely October 2nd, October 4th-7th, October 15th and 21st; also the 25th, 28th and 30th. Winds will be frequent, but not as strong as those to the east. Wet weather this month should continue into the month of November.

ZONE 4: Eastern portions of this zone will be wet and chilly; to the west temperatures will be milder than usual and precipitation will be normal. Watch for rainfall October 2nd-4th, October 5th east, October 6th and 7th; also the 28th east and the 30th in widespread areas in this zone. Winds will be a feature this month, but they will not be as strong as they will be in the eastern part of the country.

ZONE 5: Blue skies are forecast for much of this zone this month with temperatures higher than usual. Some areas may experience some extremely dry conditions. Watch for rainfall October 2nd, October 4th east, October 5th, 6th, 9th, 10th and 25th; also the 28th east. The 30th may also result in rain. The weather of October will precede similar weather patterns throughout November.

ZONE 6: Dry weather can be predicted for most of Alaska this month; temperatures should be markedly above normal. Dates most likely to result in rain include October 9th and 10th, October 15th and 16th, the 25th, 28th and 30th. In addition, precipitation in some parts of the state is likely during the first week of the month. Hawaii will see normal, pleasant weather, but some areas may be drier than usual.

Dates to Watch

Watch for winds October 2nd-5th, 6th, 7th, 10th, 12th, 15th, 19th, 20th, 21st, 24th, 25th, 30th and 31st.

Watch for rains October 1st-7th, 9th, 10th, 15th, 16th, 21st, 25th, 28th, 30th and 31st.

NOVEMBER 1995

ZONE 1: Dry, chilly and windy weather is predicted for most of this zone in November; New England and Florida may be the exceptions with some sudden, heavy precipitation. Likely dates for rain include November 2nd, 5th, 10th and 11th; also the 15th, 17th, 22nd, 23rd and 26th. The 27th could result in snow south. The chill should intensify during the month and continue into December.

   ZONE 2: Wet weather with seasonable temperatures is predicted for this zone in November. Thanksgiving may be white north and wet south. Watch for precipitation November 2nd, 5th, 6th and 10th; also the 11th, 15th, 17th east, 22nd and 23rd. The 26th and 27th should be wet also. Winds will also be an important feature this month and drifting could be a problem where it snows north.

   ZONE 3: Mild weather with normal precipitation patterns is forecast east, but most of the western portions of this zone will be wet and cold. Watch for precipitation November 5th east and November 6th and 10th throughout other areas in this zone. The 11th, 13th, 15th and 18th could bring precipitation as well as the 23rd, 27th and 29th. Chilly winds are predicted west.

ZONE 4: Wet, cold weather is predicted for eastern portions of this zone in November, but areas west will be dry and mild with some beautiful blue skies. Watch for precipitation east on November 6th, 7th and 10th, the 11th east, the 13th-15th; also the 17th, 18th, 21st, 26th and 29th. Winds will be a feature of the weather this month, making the chill in this zone even colder.

ZONE 5: Mild temperatures and normal amounts of precipitation are forecast for this zone in November. North is likely to be unusually mild. Watch for precipitation November 6th and 7th, November 13th and November 17th and 18th. The 21st, 23rd, 26th and 29th will also be likely to result in precipitation. Winds here will not have as much bite as they will farther east.

ZONE 6: The Alaskan Panhandle will have mild weather this month and most of the rest of the state will be unusually warm and dry. Dates most likely to result in precipitation include the 2nd, 5th-7th, 10th and 11th; also the 13th and 15th, 17th-19th, 21st-23rd, 26th, 27th and 29th. Snowfall, when it comes, is likely to be local and scant. Hawaii will have a pleasant, mild month.

Dates to Watch

Watch for winds November 2nd, 6th, 13th, 15th, 18th, 19th, 20th, 21st-24th, 27th and 28th.

Watch for rain November 2nd, 5th, 6th, 8th, 10th, 11th, 13th and 15th.

Watch for snow November 17th, 18th, 19th, 22nd, 23rd, 26th and 29th.

DECEMBER 1995

ZONE 1: Dry, bitterly chill weather north and more seasonable temperatures south are forecast for this zone in December. Precipitation south is likely to be unseasonably heavy. Watch for snowfall December 4th, December 8th and the 10th, 15th and 16th; watch also the 20th, 22nd, 25th and 27th. Winds north will be strong, and snowfall coming on or around Christmas Day may be unusually heavy.

ZONE 2: Cold, dry weather is forecast for the eastern portions of this zone this month. Areas near the Mississippi, however, should have an unusually great amount of snowfall. Watch for snow December 4th and 8th, the 10th, the 15th-16th; also December 20th, 22nd, 24th and 25th. December 27th could also result in a storm. Snow near on the 24th and 25th could interfere with holiday travel.

ZONE 3: Heavy precipitation is forecast for this zone in December. Areas east should have mild temperatures, but western portions of this zone should be bitterly chill. Watch for snowfall December 4th and 12th, December 15th, 16th and 22nd, December 24th in all areas and December 28th west. Snowfall north on the 24th may be so heavy that it interferes with holiday travel. Winds are predicted on this date also.

ZONE 4: Chilly, wet weather east and mild temperatures west are forecast for this zone in December. Areas west are likely to see little snowfall. Dates most likely to result in snow are the 4th and 12th, December 15th and 22nd; also December 24th and 28th. Snow on the 24th will involve winds, so drifting is likely and holiday traffic may be impeded. A white Christmas is forecast for most of this zone.

ZONE 5: Mild temperatures, unusually blue skies and relatively dry weather will mark this zone this month. Dates most likely to result in precipitation include the 12th and 15th, 16th and 22nd, 24th and 28th. Snowfall north on Christmas Eve will involve winds, making drifting likely. Not only is a white Christmas predicated north, but also temperature dip.

ZONE 6: A month with dry weather and unseasonably warm temperatures is forecast for most of the state of Alaska. Snowfall will be most likely December 4th, 7th and 8th, December 10th and 12th, December 16th and also the 20th, 22nd, 24th and 25th. The 27th and 28th could also result in snowfall. Snow will be scant and short-lived on many snow dates. Hawaii will have a pleasant month.

Dates to Watch

Watch for winds December 3rd, 4th, 8th, 20th, 22nd-25th and 27th-29th.

Watch for snow December 4th, 7th, 8th, 10th, 12th, 15th, 16th, 20th, 22nd and 24th-28th.

EARTH CHANGES

By Nancy Soller

Everybody knows that the Sun is our source of heat and light, and in school children learn that the Moon and the Sun together rule the tides, but astrometeorology knows that even the planets play an important part in earth changes.

Astrometeorology is the study of weather prediction by means of planetary positions. The planets predict the weather in several different ways. Planets prominent on a seasonal ingress chart predict the kind of weather that will occur at a given location for the season. In addition, planets, as they form major aspects to each other and the sun, indicate important temporary weather changes such as storms and winds. Also, the conjunctions of the slow-moving outer planets coincide with dramatic and long-lasting changes in air pressure, which cause the jet stream and trade winds to alter their normal paths, resulting in freakish weather. In addition, planets indicate specific types of weather by sign and declination.

The seasonal ingress chart used for predicting a season's weather is a horoscope drawn for a particular location for the moment the sun enters Aries (spring), Cancer (summer), Libra (fall) and Capricorn (winter). Planets are considered prominent on this chart if they form a 0, 90, or 180° earth-centered angle to the mid-heaven of the chart, plus or minus 8°. If no planets form a hard angle to the mid-heaven, then planets in the 1st, 4th, 7th and 10th houses are considered prominent.

On a seasonal ingress chart, Venus, Saturn and Neptune indicate wet weather, with Saturn indicating below-normal temperatures as well.

Mercury and Uranus indicate dry weather with below-normal temperatures and wind. Mars and Pluto indicate dry weather with above-normal temperatures.

Jupiter usually brings good weather and the same may also be true of Chiron, the planetoid discovered in 1977.

Horoscopes also indicate whether weather-changing aspects of one planet to another or the sun are likely to affect a given locality. If either a planet, or a planet and the Sun, are prominent on a chart set for a given locality, the moment the aspect is perfect the weather changes will affect that locality. Venus, Saturn and Neptune are indicative of precipitation; Mercury, Mars, Uranus and Pluto are indicative of wind. In addition, Saturn, Mercury and Uranus tend to lower temperatures; Mars and Pluto tend to raise them.

Conjunctions of the slow-moving outer planets tend to coincide with abnormal weather conditions that last for one year or more. These conditions last as long as it takes these planets to form a conjunction and then begin to separate. We are tempted to say that a particular type of conjunction creates drought or abnormally high amounts of precipitation because they may do this in the United States, but in truth, a global picture of the effects of these great conjunctions would show both drought and deluge. The total amount of air above the earth remains constant; a dry, high-pressure area at one location is likely to result in a wet, low-pressure area elsewhere.

In addition, planets traveling through water signs tend to bring moisture; planets traveling through fire signs tend to bring heat and dry conditions.

Not all weather changes are indicated by planets. The Moon at its quarters is likely to result in precipitation, and the day following a Full Moon is likely to result in a sudden, heavy dumping of precipitation.

Not only do the planets influence and/or predict the weather, but they can also be used to predict earthquake activity as well. There are several different kinds of earthquake-sensitive degrees and planets. Striking these degrees in their travels can trigger earthquake activity as well. Usually, several different earthquake-sensitive degrees have to be triggered at the same time for a really big quake to occur.

It has long been known that recent solar and lunar eclipse-points constitute earthquake-sensitive degrees. To this we add the solstice and equinox points, the mid-points between them and the mid-points between those. In addition, the heliocentric (sun-centered) planetary nodes also constitute earthquake-sensitive degrees. This is true whether the planet strikes, squares or opposes a node in either geocentric (earth-centered) or heliocentric angles. Venus and Mars are the most common triggers; in addition, the Sun can be a trigger if an earth-centered angle is involved, and the earth can be a trigger if a sun-centered angle is involved.

Most big earthquakes not only involve several different earthquake-sensitive degrees, but other factors can enter as well. Some quakes occur when the moon crosses or squares its nodes, or when Mars and Neptune are in hard aspect to each other. It should also be noted that a planet conjunct the Sun at the time of an eclipse can trigger a quake felt in or near the eclipse area, or at least in the same hemisphere.

The January 17, 1994, San Fernando Valley quake involved both eclipse points and heliocentric planetary nodes where its timing was concerned. On the 16th of January, Mars was opposing Pluto's heliocentric planetary node of 20° Cancer, Jupiter was squaring Neptune's heliocentric planetary node of 11° Leo, and the Earth was making a heliocentric opposition to the January 5th, 1991, eclipse point of 25 Capricorn, with the sun and Venus conjuncting this eclipse-point geocentrically. Notice that there was a lag between the time these aspects occurred and the quake itself. Earthquake timing is more predictable now than earthquake locations. Recent studies appear to indicate that some locations are earthquake-sensitive to planets located in certain signs, but much more study has to be done on this.

Volcanic activity is much less frequent than earthquake activity, but recent volcanic activity can be studied for relevant planetary positions. The May 18, 1980, 8:32 AM (PST) eruption of Mount Saint Helen's shows some interesting planetary positions. Pluto, named for the Roman god of the underworld, was located at nineteen degrees of Libra. This conjuncts the October 12, 1977, solar eclipse-point of 19° of Libra, and squares its own heliocentric north node of 19° 57' of Cancer. In addition, the sun at 27° of Taurus was squaring its February 2, 1980, eclipse-point of 27° of Aquarius. Chiron, at 14° of Taurus, was less than the 1.5° from the 15° of Taurus mid-point between 0° of Aries and 0° of Cancer. It appears that a thorough study of the timing of volcanic activity would likely show some similarities to earthquake charts.

There have been many conjectures as this century draws to a close that some big earthquakes are due. If some really big quakes occur, they may be due in part to the August 11, 1999, solar eclipse at 18° of Leo. While this eclipse will not conjunct a planet, Uranus at 14° of Aquarius will oppose the eclipse-point, while Mars and Saturn at 16° of Scorpio and Taurus respectively oppose each other and square the eclipse-Uranus axis. Notice that the four arms of this giant cross all conjunct 15° of the fixed signs, earthquake-sensitive degrees. Dramatic earthquake activity could accompany this eclipse or occur later as planets strike the earthquake-sensitive degrees.

Below are dates when at least two earthquake-sensitive degrees are aspected:

January: 8th, 15th, 16th, 19th, 21st and 23rd.

February: 8th, 13th, 14th, 20th and 26th.

March: 2nd, 7th, 12th, 13th, 16th, 19th, 20th and 29th.

April: 3rd, 4th, 6th, 10th-12th, 25th and 30th.

May: 3rd, 8th-10th, 11th, 12th, 13th, 16th, 22nd and 26th.

June 1st, 2nd, 3rd, 4th, 10-13th, 16th, 18th, 23rd, 24th, 25th, 26th, 27th and 30th.

July: 6th, 8th, 13th, 21st, 23rd, 24th and 27th.

August: 1st, 7th, 18th, 13th, 14th, 15th and 23rd.

September: 3rd, 16th, 17th, 19th and 24th.

October: 2nd, 4th, 7th, 9th, 17th, 19th, 21st, 23rd and 26th-28th.

November: 1st, 4th, 9th, 10th, 12th, 14th, 16th, 17th and 20th.

December: 5th, 13th, 14th-16th, 18th, 27th, 29th and 31st.

BIBLIOGRAPHY

Calder, Nigel. *The Weather Machine*. New York, NY: Viking Press, 1976.

Goodavage, Joseph E. *Our Threatened Planet*. New York, NY: Pocket Books, 1978.

Michelsen, Neil F. *The American Ephemeris: 1991-2000*. San Diego, CA: ACS Publications, 1980.

Michelson, Neil F. *The American Ephemeris for the Twentieth Century*. San Diego, CA: ACS Publications, 1980.

Michelson, Neil F. *The American Heliocentric Ephemeris: 1901-2000*. San Diego, CA: ACS Publications, 1982.

Rosenberg, Diana K. "Stalking the Wild Earthquake," *The Astrology of the Macrocosm*. St. Paul, MN: Llewellyn Publications, 1990.

MOONLIGHTING THE ECONOMY

By Barbara Koval, D. F. Astrol. S.

The Moon rules the tides of earth and man. It stirs the fortunes of day traders and consumers, raises price, lowers it, increases demand, increases indifference. In Chaos Theory, the only segment of modern science that bears any resemblance to the astrological paradigm, the Moon would be called a strange attractor. A strange attractor stirs up the matrix of reality to create diversity and change. In the Solar Field, bounded by the Ecliptic, the Equator and the Nodes, and represented by the array of planets on a 360° graphic ephemeris, we see the Moon slashing through the double helix of Mercury and Venus, pumping the hearts of humans to buy and sell.

In timing monthly purchases or trades, remember that prices rise from New Moon to Full;

from the Moon conjunct the South Node to the North Node, and from extreme South Declination to extreme North. Prices often receive a minor jolt at zero declinations and quarter moons.

Astrological charts depict what really happens, not simply what appears in the news. Nor do they reflect only consensus opinions on events and their meanings. In a year where reality and propaganda are working against one another, when data can be manipulated to make things appear other than they are, read the news on the inner pages and compare. In 1995, with Jupiter conjunct the U.S. Ascendant, our situation will appear much better than it is. Indeed, it will be better than most. But, economic hardship is brewing. The U.S. will be in group denial. If you look into the future and beyond, you will protect your assets and prosper.

MAJOR ASTROLOGICAL EVENTS

Pluto in and out of Sagittarius dances on the United States Ascendant. Pluto will raise interest rates, debt, taxes, violence, and fear in the population. Its backtracking into Scorpio will give us a brief respite from rising interest rates. The rest continues to create victims and crime. Jupiter square Saturn impedes worldwide recovery, and necessitates hard choices if prosperity and growth are to return. The mutual reception between Saturn and Neptune enables us to scheme and plot around many of our problems. The oil glut continues to drive energy prices unbelievably low to mask increasing taxes on production, heat, and transportation. Phony programs and regulations give an illusion of growth and protection and a promise of better times, but will be in reality an inflationary mirage that evaporates when Saturn enters Aries, and Uranus and Neptune take inflation out of the financial markets and put it into domestic economy.

The Economic News looks good on the surface because the population has more money to spend. Employment numbers look better. Though prices are rising, they are not rising enough to make people nervous. Underneath the news the real United States indebtedness is growing. The multiplier effect of previous borrowing begins to show in the consumer price sector.

Good investments for the year: communications, travel, mature companies, insurance, environmental cleanup, and repair companies.

JANUARY 1995

Mars retrograde and Pluto in Sagittarius bodes ill for peace or prosperity. Interest rates rise. The citizens of the United States scurry to borrow before they go higher. We begin to feel the tax bite of previous economic policies and programs as they show themselves in everyday life. Jupiter reigns, however, and the public remains confident that prosperity is just around the corner.

1 New Moon in Capricorn

The New Moon occurs close to the Mutation Jupiter Saturn conjunction. The focus is on the economy and the impact of trade, particularly exports, on the financial health of the United States. It is opposite the Sun of the U.S. Chart and in the 2nd House of domestic wealth. The President is challenged to address the deficit, rising inflation, burgeoning imports and the imbalance of trade. Expect fighting words.

16 Full Moon in Cancer

The Full Moon sets across the Mercury and Pluto of the U.S. Chart. The spotlight is on the President and his State of the Union message. Expect many explanations and revelations about debt, taxes, and the bureaucracy. The United States Uranus is also strongly activated. For the economy it means heavy activity in domestic trade and exports, but combined with warring Mars and Pluto could signal the breaking of a treaty or agreement.

Expect the peak in stock market averages at the Full Moon. The market should take a substantial fall on or immediately after the 16th. This is a good time to take your money out of mutual fund and park it in a money market fund for a week or two after the shakeout. Since Venus is in a bull market for most of this year, the averages will rise, and most mutual funds along with them.

Uranus and Neptune on the U.S. Pluto indicate a domestic debt that is getting out of control. This is reinforced by the Uranus Neptune conjunction to the Full Moon across the U.S. Mercury/Pluto opposition. Our trading partners are getting less and less receptive to our primary export, inflation.

Lots of speculative activity will take place this month on the New York Stock Exchange, but the Mars Retrograde will lose the gains of earlier rises.

Uranus in the degrees of the Mutation Venus shows instability in the copper and financial markets, especially banks, worldwide. Expect wide fluctuations in currency. Land values are shaken up. The United States confronts broken agreements and possibly severe reversal in the balance of trade.

CAUTION: Though the Full Moon usually brings a revelation, don't believe everything you hear. Saturn and Neptune in mutual reception indicates that world trade numbers will be used to mask the not so palatable reality.

25 Mercury Retrograde

Mercury's change of direction indicates a normal correction and a downtrend in all markets. Price levels in the second half of January are down.

30 Blue Moon 10 Aquarius

The second New Moon of the month is close to the U.S. Nodes, and in the degree of the transiting Nodes and the Mercury of the Mutation Chart. Expect the inevitable and perpetual chatter about our trade situation and the status of our paper money. Nodes are fate. Events are getting beyond our control.

FEBRUARY

3 Mercury Conjunct Sun

Mercury moves into the buy phase of its synodic cycle. In a Venus bull everybody wants to buy. Nobody wants to sell. Early in the Venus cycle it can mean a sluggish market. By mid-cycle it usually drives the market up. With the Jupiter Saturn square, we can expect the market to slow.

11 Sun opposite Mars

Interest rates and debt numbers reach an intermediate peak.

15 Full Moon in Leo

There is only one Lunation February in the degree of the United States Moon, in the 3rd House of trade, ruler of the 8th of taxes and debt, natural ruler of foodstuffs and consumer goods. Despite the continued passage of Saturn in Pisces, this looks like a bullish report for home sales and housing starts. More likely it means a short term peak in price.

16 Mercury Stationary Direct—Market Upturn

The Mercury station is on the U.S. Nodes in the import/export houses, conjunct the Sun of the

Mutation Chart, and the Uranus of the Federal Reserve Chart. The combination suggests an impact on the dollar in international trading, the price of gold, and inflation-generating debt. Expect the Fed to add liquidity in order to keep interest rates down. Adding liquidity means the Fed borrows from itself, the modern way to print money. Since Mercury rules paper and is the fundamental facilitator of trade, and the Sun rules gold, this could be bullish for the price of gold. At the very least, the price of gold at this time is a significant number to watch as an indicator of the relative value of U.S. currency.

Jupiter Square Saturn

The most significant planetary aspect in effect this month is Jupiter square Saturn, significator of an economic downturn. Factors restrict growth and expansion and make it more costly. While this aspect comes very close to exact this month, it never makes it. Disaster is averted. While the United States is less affected than most, the world economy will correct between now and November of this year, completing the first phase of the restructuring that began at the Jupiter/Saturn oppositions of 1989 through 1992. The prospect is schizophrenic for the U.S.; Saturn square the ruling planet limits growth, even as the Jupiter in Sagittarius keeps the population confident and optimistic. Saturn in the 4th House denotes difficulties in the land, which suggests poorer than expected crops. Consumer needs and consumer prices are the focus of this combination in the United States. Look for rising prices and slowing growth.

MARCH

1 New Moon 10 Pisces

Saturn rising on the New Moon Chart suggests a burdened population cheered up by the powers that be. We see a widening gap between our government's confident projections and the increasing costs of living. We could hear some news about forced retirements, cuts in retirement benefits and pension funds, or new laws to that effect.

The effect on the U.S. chart is mainly in the land/crop area, which is also the house of the opposition to the president. The president suffers heavy criticism and opposition for most of the year. Despite natural disasters, the Neptune Saturn mutual reception continues to lower prices for food and oil. If the environment doesn't kill the farmer, low prices will. Although some farm groups may try to protest, fix prices or ask for subsidies, public opinion and the government are not behind them.

The Saturn of this New Moon is on Mars, ruler of the Mutation Chart. Expect a fall in steel production, lowering of interest rates, and increasing joblessness for the month. The United States will not have as good a month economically as the rest of the world. With the singleton Mars of this chart on the Mutation Neptune, speculation and inflation are likely to be stimulated.

3 Pluto retrograde in 15.56 Aquarius

Pluto retrograding close to the U.S. Ascendant puts lots of pressure on the population. Because Jupiter is on the First House relative to equal houses from the MC, people are not terribly upset about their government. They still believe the government can take action to solve the problem. The Pluto on the House of the population bespeaks murder and mayhem, increasing debt burden, and increasing numbers on the dole, be it unemployment, welfare, or Medicaid.

5 Sun conjunct Saturn 15.01 Pisces

Sun conjunct Saturn correlates to a rise in the Dow and a number to watch throughout the year. Saturn is a sign of limitation and usually defines a trading range. In a Venus bull market, such as this one, it could be an underlying low. Because the Saturn—Sun conjunction is on the Mutation Neptune, we can also expect an oil price limit to be set at this time. With oil, Saturn usually indicates a high. Home heating oil prices will rise to this conjunction and a bit beyond. Expect our trading partners and foreign governments to demand that we control U.S. inflation by raising our interest rates. We could also see disruptions or curtailments in the flow of international oil and natural gas.

17 Full Moon 25 Pisces/Virgo

The Full Moon on the 17th in Virgo/Pisces lies across the houses of the government/presidency and our natural resources, and close to the U.S. Neptune. Environmental issues are raised to mask some of the natural and economic difficulties farmers are experiencing with the Saturn passage through the U.S. Fourth. Saturn is also transiting the Mars of the stock market chart. Speculation is discouraged, whether by increased regulation or stiffer margin requirements. Less of our debt created money flows into the stock market this period. The chart itself puts the focus on labor, police and military, the bureaucracy and health care. Great pains are taken to keep the true costs hidden from sight or the true state of employment.

24 Mars Direct in 13.10 of Leo

Mars retrograde is bearish side for markets. Mars direct is a turn up. Conjunct the stock market Uranus it could cause electronic problems, or break up trading groups or informal cartels. Don't forget that the stock market is dominated by pension funds and mutual funds, both of which put tremendous amounts of group money into the hands of a select few money managers. There could be a little flurry of scandal or crisis.

The station occurs very near opposition to the Mutation Mercury Neptune: this means a bit of hyperactive speculation in the currency markets.

31 Blue Moon 9 Aries

This second New Moon of the month hovers near the Sixth House. A Mars singleton tops the chart.

What was not newsworthy at the Mars station erupts here. While we would not call it a workers' revolt, unemployment is a big issue. Police and crime are equally strong. With Jupiter in the Second people will spend, despite the continued restriction of the Saturn square. Consider it pent-up buying urges.

Venus on the Seventh of the stock market bodes well for Wall Street. Aries is conducive to speculative fever and market rises. The New Moon is the low of the period. Expect new issues and speculation to grow till mid April. Very bullish for gold.

APRIL 1995

1 Jupiter Retrograde 15.23 Sagittarius; Uranus enters Aquarius

April starts off with a bang. Expect a big spending surge at the station. Market prices rise, too. We might call this one a last-minute reprieve. Since the Jupiter turnabout avoids the Saturn square, we can breathe easier. Uranus into Aquarius indicates a new face for group excitement and fads, all of which can mean an inventive year, a new age year, or just a year of marketplace silliness. If it is a gadget, preferably electronic, invest.

14 Mercury conjunct Sun 24 Aries

Expect a short rise in the stock market. This marks a short hop from the Mercury buyer's market to the Mercury seller's market. Because Venus is in her bull phase, we should have a healthy supply of buyers and sellers until Mercury goes retrograde in May.

15 Lunar Eclipse

The positive movement is quickly capped by the eclipse reversal. Eclipses are contrary. Just when you think you have them figured out they go the other way. Trading on eclipses is for the intrepid. Aries/Libra is a significator of new issues, young entrepreneurial companies, and consulting groups. Expect a shakeup and a peaking of this movement that began with Jupiter in Libra. This eclipse hits the Jupiter/Neptune to Saturn opposition of the New York Stock Exchange.

While the position does not seem particularly important in national and world events, it could be a blowout in New York. Possibilities here are for a large absorption of inflationary or foreign funds, and/or a movement for new and greater regulation. Up or down, the market is under a severe strain. Lunar eclipses tend to be climaxes or revelations. Scandal and stock manipulation could be revealed. We could hear of a big pension or mutual fund might not meet its obligations. Expect a topping of gold and silver. Small cap stocks and IPOs could take a hit.

21 Pluto into Scorpio

Pluto into Scorpio exerts a downward pull on interest rates. On the New York Stock Exchange MC, it brings the possibility of scandal or increased rules and regulations. Pluto in the degree of the Moon of the Mutation Chart signals price rises in food commodities and a downturn for the price of silver.

27 Neptune stationary retrograde 25 Capricorn

The presidency and U.S. trade agreements are in disarray.

29 Solar Eclipse

The markets reset themselves to reality. Difficult financial times usually accompany Taurus/Scorpio eclipses. They are bad for the financial industry and for banks worldwide. This one occurs trine the Mutation and close to the New York Seventh of the Great Mutation Chart. Trade partnerships start or end. At the very least, a change in our relationship to the international banking system will affect money going into the Stock Market. The inflationary tendencies in the U.S. chart create barriers to agricultural exports, and the solvency of our banks. It should be one of those seemingly minor shocks or attacks that we can work our way around.

Mercury, ruler of the Second, dominates the Eclipse chart, itself a contract or agreement about money. The Eclipse occurs in the Ninth of imports and law. The Ascendant is exactly opposite the U.S. Moon. Because of the simultaneous entrance of Uranus into the U.S. Third of exports, we may see our balance of trade growing exceedingly worse. Uranus brings foreign goods into our domestic markets and indicates a rejection of goods we try to export. Neptune is simultaneously opposite the Mercury of the U.S. chart, signifying an undermining of the President and the presidency, the dilution of our paper money, and cheating partnerships. It looks as if bootlegging is back in style, and not just of drugs.

Part of the export problem, despite a weakening dollar that makes our products more affordable throughout the world, is that to control consumer inflation we buy more abroad. In effect, we have priced ourselves out of our own market. Since nobody consumes as much as we do, there is no competition. In the long term, the Uranus and ultimately Neptune passage through the U.S. Third House may bring our currency sufficiently low to make imports unattractive. When that happens, we can expect to see double digit inflation at home.

MAY 1995

5 Uranus Retrograde 0 Aquarius

May is a relatively quiet month, where the market averages slowly climb and culminate around the Full Moon. Uranus retrograde puts a damper on the silly and the outrageous, but the falling off in new age electronics is temporary. We can expect a bit of good news about trade deficit problems but the effect is only temporary.

14 Full Moon 23 Scorpio/Taurus

The Full Moon Pluto conjunction is very bearish for silver, probably an annual low. Since the lunation sits in the Second/Eighth House area, money and banks are the focus. A new bankruptcy hits the news. The Mercury Jupiter opposition across the Third and Ninth Houses brings legal action, and a lot of talk in the media about the balance of trade and consumer price rises, even as sales fall. Saturn in the Sixth in mutual reception with Neptune in the Fourth indicates the true unemployment figures are both better and worse than they appear. Farmers may be leaving the farms and people without jobs may be leaving the country. The month of May will see increased applications for unemployment compensation and for jobs.

Saturn on the U.S. Neptune trims our agricultural output and adds to the federal debt while appearing to cut it. Beware of off-budget items like the old S and L failures and health care. Mars remains opposite the U.S. Moon, creating aggravation and agitation among the population. The Full Moon hits the Mercury of the NYSE. New figures are released on trade, money exchange and trading practices.

24 Mercury Retrograde 18.22 Gemini

Expect a downturn in most markets. Don't expect any pact, bill, or agreement signed while Mercury is retrograde to last, and don't believe everything you hear. Mercury is on the 7th MC Equal House.

The government is likely to be negotiating an agreement with a neighbor, trading partner or enemy. Don't expect anything solid until Mercury hits this degree again in early July.

29 New Moon 7 Gemini

This New Moon starts a very unstable period with Saturn, Jupiter, Mercury, Mars, the Sun and Moon in Mutable Signs. The Stock Market always makes a major correction when either Jupiter or Saturn are in Mutables and other Mutable planets reinforce. Markets are destabilizing, subject to unusual highs and lows. At this time of year, they are more likely to go high.

The New Moon rises opposite Jupiter and square Mars in the Fourth. A new spending spree is about to start. Conditions with trading partners improve, as does activity in the domestic markets. Saturn in a market degree portends a rise in the stock market. Saturn in the Eleventh signifies a decline in corporate profits. Expect agitation for protectionist regulation to ease the blow.

On the United States Chart, the stellium hits Uranus and Mars in the Seventh. Expect a lot of self-righteous moralizing against the unfair tactics of our partners and neighbors (and theirs about ours). Mars conjunct the 10th Equal House from the first brings fighting words out of the White House. Saturn opposing Neptune, and in Mutual reception with transiting Neptune on the U.S. Pluto brings talk of anti-inflationary policies and deficit cutting, but the activity lets the debt run more and more out of control. It works as long as Saturn is in Pisces. Venus in the 6th produces encouraging employment numbers.

The Stock Market Chart has Mars moving into the First. Good for heavy speculation and trouble, but not just yet. There are no other major contacts outside the continuing transit of Saturn to Uranus. Expect stress and contraction in real estate and agriculture, and a gradual withdrawal of foreign funds from our speculative markets.

JUNE 1995

1 Sun opposite Jupiter 10.31 Gemini

The Sun/Jupiter opposition and the Sun Mercury conjunction foster some interesting highs in the stock market the first week in June. Note the numbers at the Sun/Jupiter opposition. They are significant relative to annual market highs and lows.

Activity slows a bit when Uranus goes back into Capricorn. There are moves to forestall corporations setting up shop abroad, but the corporate exodus will begin again in earnest when Uranus reenters Aquarius.

5 Mercury conjunct Sun 14.07 (r) Gemini
8 Uranus leaves Aquarius (to Capricorn)
13 Full Moon 21 Gemini Sagittarius

Jupiter conjunct the 10th on the Lunation chart should bring a grand speech from our president about our moral superiority, our nasty competitors, our wonderful natural resources and agriculture ,and our import/export condition. The offering is a new program of education and job counseling to counteract the not-so-nice employment figures this chart represents: more workers, fewer jobs, and greater competition.

The Sun, Moon and Saturn hover in the Neptune degree of the U.S. Chart. Don't believe what you hear. Saturn continues its relentless trek through the nation's Fourth House of land and homes. We hear cries to make homes more affordable. Pluto is moving back toward the square to the United States Moon. The national mood is dour. It takes more and more money to buy less and less. Mars is square the Uranus, a minor skirmish or a major argument.

Most of the activity is in the degree of the Mutation Uranus. This is another marker that international money is leaving our speculative markets. Pluto opposite the MC of the Stock Market Chart suggests shakeups in the accounting system or some revelations of wrongdoing.

17 Mercury direct 9:49 Gemini

Since Mercury will be on the U.S. Uranus, we can expect a shocking message from our partners and/or about our domestic trade and exports. This message will probably concern a new record imbalance.

28 New Moon 5 Cancer

The chart looks positive for our getting around the export problem, maybe accompanied by threats to take action on imports.

For a change, there is some good news. The lunation is the U.S. Jupiter, positive for a victory and for hope of prosperity and problems solved.

The New Moon is opposite the Mutation itself, which portends a new direction in international economic affairs, relative to American exports. Because Uranus is opposite the Moon and conjunct the Nodes of this chart, expect a major move in silver and rising commodity prices. Since Uranus is a reversal, we could have a jump and fall. Occurring in the Third of the U.S. version of the Mutation, we could find ourselves successfully blocking the import of food.

JULY 1995

6 Saturn Retrograde 24.45 Pisces
10 Mars Opposite Saturn 24.44 Virgo

The convergence of a number of oppositions, Mars/Saturn, Sun with Uranus and Neptune, suggest highs in the stock market. These are reinforced by the convergence of Moon, Sun and Mercury which produces up markets and starts the selling phase of the Mercury/Sun cycle. The Mercury sell phase this late in a Venus bull market tends to push the market towards new highs. Sun in Cancer dur-

ing the first part of the month is bullish for silver.
The Sun's entrance into Leo is bullish for gold.

12 Full Moon 19 Cancer/Capricorn

The Moon in Capricorn is the end of the silver
rise. The Twelfth House/Sixth House emphasis of
the lunation chart pushes health, hospitals, workers, welfare into the news. The Saturn Mars opposition falls right across the Third and Ninth
Houses. Trouble in the export import markets is
reaching a peak and a conclusion. Regulations
concerning the work force are an attempt to pump
up domestic trade and stop the flood of imports.
The end result is more burdens on the work force,
further erosion of jobs, and increased flight to
imports in order to save money. Whatever the
government tries to do, the net result will be an
export of jobs or of people seeking them. Health
care mandates likewise shrink the market for people looking for work. Jupiter in the Fifth indicates
increasing speculation.

The Full Moon transits fall across the Second
and Eighth Houses of the U.S. chart, the frantic
search for more ways to handle inflation, taxes, and
debt. Raising the minimum wage is the perennial
solution for protecting the constituency against the
government's misuse of public funds and public
trust.

The Saturn-Mars opposition is just beyond
the U.S. Neptune. Expect talk of wage and price
controls, but they are unlikely to do any good.

Mars-Saturn across the Fourth and Ninth Houses
bring an end or a slowdown to some of the agricultural problems we face. Expect debate on farm
subsidies. Whatever is decided will be dealt away
in conference.

This lunation straddles the Third/Ninth
House of the U.S. Mutation chart, reinforcing the
export/import problem of the U.S. in the world
economy. In addition, it is exactly on the Ascendant of the Federal Reserve Board. The Fed tight-
ens the money supply it has previously been
trying to ease.

16 Sun Opposite Neptune; 21 Sun Opposite Uranus

While both of the above push the markets to new
highs, they especially jolt the gold averages.

23 Sun enters Leo

Bullish for gold

27 Mercury conjunct Sun; New Moon 4 Leo

The activity occurs in the Eleventh House of the
Lunation chart, indicating much activity in the
marketplace, with a focus on profits and selling
prices. Expect some good news on corporate
profits.

Mars conjunct the Ascendant is contentious,
but in this case may indicate collusion between
rivals or enemies. Jupiter in the Third is good for

lots of positive activity in the domestic economy. Good news for retailers and travel agents.

This New Moon occurs on the North Node of the U.S. chart in the Ninth of law and imports. We could enact another agreement that allows more imported goods into the country, whether or not this is the intention. Whatever the long-term implications, the immediate effect will be positive for the U.S.

The lunation is on the Sun, ruler of the U.S. Mutation. The emphasis is still export/import and may bring the president or the courts into focus. It looks strong for some sort of international agreement regarding trade. Since the dollar tends to parallel the movement of the Sun, we may see a gradual decline in the value of the dollar, which lowers the price of our exports for other nations. We may see a stimulus to a more favorable balance of trade.

31 North Node leaves Scorpio

Because Scorpio/Taurus eclipses are negative for a healthy economy, we should be relieved at this first indicator of change. The Aries/Libra emphasis has more to do with getting new enterprises started than with shaking out those that are already in play.

AUGUST 1995

2 Jupiter Direct 5 Sagittarius

Jupiter direct is strong for the stock market, and especially strong for the price of gold. Gold should take a big leap at its entrance into Leo and through most of August, but especially during the Full Moon on the Houses of the Tenth of the month.

8 Pluto direct 27.50 Scorpio

Pluto direct on the Eighth squares the U.S. Moon, which casts a certain amount of gloom over the public. Burdened by taxes and debt, they feel squeezed, but Jupiter in Sagittarius still creates hope for the future. On a positive note, we could see some reduction in the federal debt and a possible rise in interest rates, which makes debt less desirable.

10 Full Moon 17 Leo

The Full Moon chart has Pluto rising. Debt and interest rates dominate the mood as does the Lunation across the Third/Ninth houses. The emphasis is on export/imports, regulation, and domestic trade. Expect a message from the President designed to pump up confidence. Uranus and Neptune in the Third indicates imports still flood our domestic markets. We see renewed attempts to use our foodstuffs and natural resources to balance our international trade.

Because this Full Moon occurs on the midpoint of Mars and Saturn on the U.S. chart, we may hear of the death of a person beloved by the American people. Uranus is smack on the U.S. Pluto. Congress votes another extension of the size of the federal debt, or the Fed manipulates interest rates. Uranus tends to be lawbreaking or law-changing. Be prepared for developments concerning debt, interest rates, and bankruptcies. Pluto is also in the degree of the U.S. radical Pluto, which suggests debt piled on debt. Jupiter quincunx U.S. Jupiter means more unhealthy expansion. Mercury on the Equal House Tenth confirms a message from the leader/President on the lunation chart. Mars moving to a conjunction of Saturn suggests transient trouble with banks and money. While the net effect of this Full Moon is favorable because of the conjunction with Venus, the underlying factors and the continued manipulation of Saturn and Neptune suggests ongoing inflationary policies and deceptive expansion.

The lunation occurs close to the Neptune of the Mutation chart, which brings the focus to inflation and oil. This marks the end of an oil price move and some revelations about supply. Oversupply is more likely than shortages. Jupiter in the degree of the Mutation Sun confirms the price rise in gold in international markets. Jupiter on the Uranus of the Federal Reserve Board confirms a legal manipulation of the debt/interest rate structure.

The Pluto of this chart is opposite the Sun of the Stock Exchange. The Full Moon occurs close to its Pluto/Uranus wide opposition in the Sixth/Twelfth. We could hear of trading scandals and/or proposals for reform.

20 Venus conjunct Sun 27 Leo

Although the bear market doesn't get into full force until Venus reappears in the sky, we are in the technical Venus bear. Even more noteworthy, it occurs square to Pluto of debt and square the Sun of the stock market and trine its Neptune. It is also quincunx Uranus, all of which presages serious corrections ahead. The interest on the federal debt is eating up our tax base and most of the discretionary money that used to go into the stock market. The degree is also the Pluto of the U.S. chart and the Neptune of the Federal Reserve Board chart. Attempts to pump up the money supply are only going to create more debt, and at best an illusion of wealth by higher numbers. In reality there will be a serious erosion of value.

26 New Moon Virgo 2

This New Moon presages a slip in the trading averages. Saturn dominates, putting the President and the regulators under severe pressure. It also represents difficulties for manufacturers trying to sell their goods. Conversely, the Lunation conjunct Venus in the Third is temporarily good for domestic trade. The combination suggests that the consumer will be picky and retailers will have to lower their prices. New goods coming on line may find a less than enthusiastic reception. Saturn opposite the ruler of the chart also puts burdens and cautions into the public and the purchaser. It looks as if major purchases will be necessities. Uranus and

Neptune in the Eighth are indicators of mounting debt. Companies will try to borrow their way out of their difficulties and may cry for protection against imports.

This Lunation is conjunct the U.S. Tenth of the President. Expect a hopeful message from the President, full of positive statistics. But, the Ascendant of the chart is conjunct the U.S. Mars. The rebuttal from loyal opposition is hostile. Criticism from our trading partners, competitors, and enemies is equally harsh. The long passage of Uranus and Neptune opposite the U.S. Mercury, ruler of the government in general and the President in particular, represents a gradual and persistent distrust and undermining of the office. Although U.S. citizens remain confident and proud, and although our domestic economy appears to be doing better than most, the reputation and integrity of the government is steadily declining worldwide. Nobody believes what the government says, not even the citizenry. From this point on, markets get shaky.

SEPTEMBER 1995

3 Mars conjunct North Node 27 Libra

Mars conjunct the North Node on the Third indicates an intermediate topping of interest rates. In 27 Libra square the U.S. Moon we see one last punch at the mounting federal and corporate debt. The stock market Neptune takes a hit, indicating some frenzied speculation, and the Venus and Moon of the Mutation chart indicate a downward move for copper and food commodities. Since the Moon rules homes, and this position is not far from a trine to the U.S. Moon, we could see a topping out in mortgages and new home construction.

9 Full Moon; 16 Virgo Pisces

The Full Moon chart of the Ninth occurs in a Fourth/Tenth House square to the Ascendant and solidly in the Tenth House on any system. Expect new revelations of the burdens of the presidency, the Neptune/Saturn mutual reception deals, and the increasing inability to keep anything under control.

As usual, agriculture and natural resources save us. While bullish for commodities, the position is not great for manufactured goods. Expect talk of protectionist measures against imports as joblessness reaches critical proportions. Pluto in the Sixth destroys jobs. Jupiter in the sixth creates them. Though new jobs will be created, more jobs will be lost.

On the U.S. chart, the Tenth/Fourth House emphasis gives us reassuring words of continued support for the farmers and for people who have suffered natural calamities. We hear of new programs to encourage home building and buying. In the U.S. the theme of this Full Moon is "The government is your friend."

On the Mutation, the Full Moon and Venus/Saturn configurations stimulate the Mars/

Uranus conjunction in 15 and 21 Pisces. Expect skirmishes in the Middle East, where Pisces is one of the dominant rising signs of localized Mutation charts. Oil prices could be jolted up a bit. The Mars of the stock exchange chart is somewhat agitated, which signifies a short spurt of trading frenzy. The stock market could reach an annual high this month, followed by a fall.

14 Sun opposite Saturn 21 Virgo

The Sun opposite Saturn equates to a limiting high in the financial markets. The degree is especially critical because it stimulates the Uranus of the Mutation chart, the Mars square Neptune of the U.S. chart, and is just beyond the Mars of the stock exchange chart. All are strong indicators of troubles and reversals. Expect a strongly declining stock market through the last quarter. Not only are we in a Venus Bear Market, but we are reestablishing the Jupiter Saturn square and about to face Mercury retrograde, all of which tend toward a market slide.

22 Mercury retrograde 20 Libra

The station is trine the U.S. Mars, which could produce a message from Congress about debt, interest rates, or pending legislation designed to pump up domestic trade, encourage entrepreneurship, or provide tax breaks or low interest rates on federal programs. The more significant contact is opposite the Mutation Pluto, square the Federal Reserve

Mars, and opposite the stock exchange Moon. Interest rates are definitely affected. The news brings more people back into the market. The Mutation chart suggests some unpleasant news about U. S. employment.

24 New Moon at one degree Libra

We see yet another Tenth-Fourth House straddle. The President takes a new and more activist tack, and enters into a new pact or agreement with Congress as the Lunation falls in the 11th House of the U.S. chart. With Mercury retrograde, expect many changes and adjustments before it reaches final form. The message is well received. Most likely we are seeing an attempt to bring balance, both to the domestic economy and to our international trade.

In the Twelfth House of the Mutation Chart we see the result of secret negotiations, or of activity that could undermine our status in the world economy. Mars hits the Mutation Ascendant, so we appear belligerent to the rest of the world. The President will attempt to shore up the value of the dollar against increasing demands from outside to control U.S. indebtedness worldwide. We will not regain our status as a creditor nation any time soon.

This New Moon occurs on the North Node of the Stock Exchange chart and conjunct its Second House cusp. The government's policy has an irresistible and inevitable impact on the assets and financial stability of our major market. The continued battering by Pluto, Saturn, Uranus, and Neptune to all the vital planets on this chart suggests that the news will be an evanescent hope at best, and another nail at worst. Let us not forget that the stock market is where the fortunes of American industry are traded. If our industrial base erodes, the stock market becomes merely a vehicle of speculation, not one of investment. The wider thrust of the stock market throughout this year is to eliminate the corruption speculation inevitably bestows.

OCTOBER 1995

4 Neptune direct 22.47 Capricorn

The Neptune station is trine the U.S. Neptune, increasing inflation; square the Stock Exchange Jupiter, excessive speculation and overreach, sextile the Mutation Uranus overreaching activity, and conjunct the Jupiter of the Federal Reserve. It looks as if we are in for a bout of money creation. Electronic and cutting edge technology should get a big boost. Money that floods into the stock exchange is not investment in business, only in activity that is parasitical on business. Speculation creates neither prosperity nor jobs. The configuration is positive for foreign exchanges and international markets. Mercury conjunct Sun at 11 Libra gives an upward boost to a market in decline.

8 Full Moon Eclipse at 14.54 Aries/Libra

This Eclipse is on the Saturn of the U.S. Chart. The last Lunar Eclipse in this degree occurred in October of 1987. This is a very bad sign for the financial assets of the people of the United States, and is a danger signal for the banking system and for a general loss of wealth. However, the Lunation chart itself is quite positive, with Jupiter rising and the Sun in the Tenth. Looks as if we will have more encouraging moves from the White House. The bad news will be on the last page of your morning paper.

The stock market is relatively unaffected by this eclipse, so it would appear that the effect is not primarily on Wall Street, but in the banking system. Since the Eclipse on Saturn falls in the Eleventh House and conjunct the ruler of the Second, we may find legislation that exerts greater control on banks, on the financial assets of the people, or adds more pressure in the way of fees and taxes. This sort of thing is often hidden from public view, but impacts wealth nevertheless. Saturn opposite the Tenth on the U.S. chart indicates much opposition to government policies from business, housing interests, and agricultural lobbies, but they can be bought off with promises of subsidies and special treatment.

The eclipse is in the area of Pluto of the Mutation Chart which inclines as always toward debt, employment and tax crisis. It brings talk of environmental pollution/cleanup issues. With the Saturn opposite the U.S. MC and conjunct the Mutation Uranus, ruler of the Fourth, matters connected to the land and hardships in the land dominate this period.

13 Mercury Direct 5 Libra

Mercury trine the Mutation Sun brings important news relative to the price of gold; it will probably be up. It squares the U.S. Jupiter, suggesting a piece of legislation or good news concerning the availability of mortgages to an ever greater number of applicants. New statistics tell us the state of housing, farm output and population demographics.

18 Mars conjunct Pluto 29 Scorpio

While not a major mundane configuration, it correlates to an act of violence that galvanizes the population into a more militant anti-crime stance; a major default or tax evasion that raises cries for reform; a tax increase that spurs a tax revolt or an attack against our laws that raises cries for more fundamental values. Though anti-tax in nature, the incidents of this period have long-term implications for increasing violence, increasing authoritarian control, and an increasing debt burden on the citizens of the country. Your best financial ploy is protection. Anything that proposes to keep people from harm—personal, financial, environmental—will prosper and sell. Consider this a preview on the order of the Rodney King case. Rodney King is the Rosa Parks of the nineties.

20 Sun conjunct North Node

This signals an annual gold high and a general market movement down.

23 New Moon Eclipse in 0 Scorpio

This is the last of the financial market eclipses. The eclipse occurs conjunct the Fourth House of the Lunation chart, more emphasis on land, real estate, crops, and homes. The Fourth is also opposition to the President. The needs of the people are behind a program to help them rebuild, renovate, and refinance their homes. In the event that the events of this year reveal both a burgeoning federal debt/deficit and increasing consumer inflation, we will see activities that attempt to counteract the effect both of government irresponsibility and nature's wrath.

Zero Scorpio is the U.S. Twelfth House of hospitals, prisons and institutions, and the bureaucracy. Expect new programs that emphasize all these areas. The buzzwords are security and safety. Since the Fourth House of the lunation is involved we may see the building of more prisons and hospitals. There is wide opposition to the Venus of the stock market chart, but not close enough to do more than transient damage to the financial assets placed there. The Eclipse, though across Signs, and therefore less potent, does square the Moon and Nodes of the Mutation chart. Could be bad news for silver, homes, and foodstuffs.

NOVEMBER 1995

7 Full Moon 14 Scorpio Taurus

A Full Moon in Taurus is a high for silver. Economic matters, foreign and domestic trade still dominate. Domestic trade improves, but consumers still have an appetite for foreign goods with the Moon close to the Ninth. While a bit early for Christmas shopping, sales in November could be brisk. People are willing to borrow to spend. Jupiter close to the Fourth gives good numbers on housing and agricultural production despite the closing square with Saturn. Though trading partners put up barriers, we'll be able to make a deal. A number of degrees on the Federal Reserve chart are hit by the major and transient events of this month. Expect a major change in policy or an upheaval in its executive structure. The Fed will lose its autonomy and become just another arm of government. We may be seeing the first overt steps toward this.

The Full Moon falls across the Ascendant of the Mutation chart, putting emphasis on the country and its relationships abroad. However, the building Jupiter Saturn square puts a damper on speculative and entertainment enterprises, and forces the U.S. to deal with expanding cash. We may see the first indications of a shift of the money supply from the speculative to the consumer sector.

10 Pluto enters Sagittarius permanently
11 Jupiter square Saturn 18 Sag/Pisces

Pluto enters Sagittarius just as Jupiter is achieving its square to Saturn. Pessimism dominates as people take account of their situation and realize that, despite the optimism and the often pleasing statistics, they have not come out ahead.

"Fed up" will be the key word of the coming Pluto transit. We will see increasing protest and attack not only on the government in general and the president in particular, but a polarization within the population along religious, ethnic, and racial lines. When the economic pie shrinks, people become less and less tolerant.

The Jupiter Saturn Square is directly antagonistic to the MC of the U.S. chart. The government/president will be hard pressed to solve the economic problems and contraction that this aspect represents. In the United States we must deal with reduced purchasing power, declining consumer buying and higher prices for necessities. While hyper-inflation is not a near threat, we see inflation back in the consumer sector when it has been successfully deflected the past decade and a half.

21 Saturn Direct at 18 Pisces

Bad news for crops and construction. Since this is the Fourth House relative to MC generated cusps, the hardships are a result of government policies and will stimulate new government policies to counteract these hardships. The government uses natural disasters as an excuse to go over budget. The net result of government assistance will be increasing inflation in the real estate market and a subsequent shortage of affordable homes.

22 New Moon in 29 Scorpio

This looks more like an ending than a beginning. It represents a false start in a "repair" or debt venture. The Sun/Mercury conjunction is also an indicator of a selling phase for Mercury, so we have a new direction that emerges out of crisis and trouble. The Lunation emphasizes the Tenth House of the President: more plans that don't quite meet the concerns and needs of the population. Uranus and Neptune in the First indicate an indifferent, confused, and rebellious population concerned about their shrinking purchasing power. Sun and Moon in the Mutation Moon degree is bullish for silver, but only for a day.

23 Sun conjunct Pluto

This conjunction usually equates to a market rise followed by a very sharp drop. Since we do not have a number of cycles reinforcing one another, it may be less than spectacular. However, the entrance of Pluto into Sagittarius now gives us three major planets in Mutable Signs: Jupiter, Saturn and Pluto, followed by Sun, Venus, Mars, and Mercury in the next few days. This is extremely destabilizing and could subject all markets to wild swings. An inflating economy is more likely to swing up; a deflating economy has a serious turn down. If the United States markets experience new highs at this time, despite the Venus bear market and the overall economic downturn that Jupiter square Saturn normally presages, we can take this as a danger signal for excessive, even hyper, inflation. The late seventies were our last such experience, the legacy of ten years of budget deficits that began with the Johnson administration's policy of butter and guns.

DECEMBER 1995

6 Full Moon 14 Gemini/Sagittarius

The year closes rather quietly with a lot of talk and new initiatives that go nowhere. Expect a big runup in the stock market to the eighteenth, and a relatively soft landing beyond.

The full Moon lies across the Fifth/Eleventh Houses. For consumers that means parties and pleasure and lots of money spent on the kids. Go long on toys. Though Congressmen are eager to travel, there could be some heated budget debates, but little of substance. The most profitable Christmas shopping will be done early with a strong mix of domestic and foreign products. This chart looks as if it no longer matters who buys what from whom. The nodes fall across the Fourth/tenth Houses with the North Node on the Fourth. In the great debate, the opposition is winning. Fate is taking charge of our universe.

18 Sun conjunct Jupiter 26 Sagittarius

Both the stock market and the price of gold take a leap up. Given the difficult aspects last month, this could be a recovery rather than a spectacular move.

21 New Moon 29 Sagittarius

The New Moon in the last degree of Sagittarius indicates another fine plan that never gets off the ground. The Nodes across the Third/Ninth give our consumer sector and our exports a boost. By Christmas everybody is back in reality. Before long Jupiter will join the Mutual Reception with Saturn in Pisces. Expect financial manipulation on a grand scale in 1996.

The Capricorn stellium Mercury, Mars, Neptune and Uranus stay in the U.S. Second house, which means lots of activity in the money sectors, and a depletion of assets. In 1996 Jupiter will make its passage through the U.S. Second House, our last year of grace. If we have not cleaned our financial house, if we have not eliminated the deficits, we face hard times. It is unlikely that the president will be reelected in 1996. The mood may be so hostile that we will elect a demagogue or a dictator. When Neptune entered Sagittarius in 1970, the people wanted liberation. When Uranus entered Sagittarius in 1981 they wanted libertarianism. They demanded change. Today we have license. License always leads to a cry for order, a mindless drive to get matters under control. Those who can't take matters into their own hands will elect a leader who will. In retrospect, historians will see 1995 as the start of major changes in the economic and political life of these United States. The foresighted and the wise will prosper.

THE TWELVE HOUSES OF THE ZODIAC

You may run across mention of the houses of the zodiac while reading certain articles in the *Moon Sign Book*. These houses are the 12 divisions of the horoscope wheel. Each house has a specific meaning assigned to it. Below are the descriptions normally attributed to each house.

First House: Self-interest, physical appearance, basic character.

Second House: Personal values, monies earned and spent, movable possessions, self-worth and esteem, resources for fulfilling security needs.

Third House: Neighborhood, communications, siblings, schooling, buying and selling, busy activities, short trips.

Fourth House: Home, family, real estate, parent(s), one's private sector of life, childhood years, old age.

Fifth House: Creative endeavors, hobbies, pleasures, entertainments, children, speculative ventures, loved ones.

Sixth House: Health, working environment, coworkers, small pets, service to others, food, armed forces.

Seventh House: One-on-one encounters, business and personal partners, significant others, legal matters.

Eighth House: Value of others, joint finances, other people's money, death and rebirth, surgery, psychotherapy.

Ninth House: Higher education, religion, long trips, spirituality, languages, publishing.

Tenth House: Social status, reputation, career, public honors, parents, the limelight.

Eleventh House: Friends, social work, community work, causes, surprises, luck, career rewards, circumstances beyond your control.

Twelfth House: Hidden weaknesses and strengths, behind-the-scenes activities, institutions, confinement, psychic attunement, government.

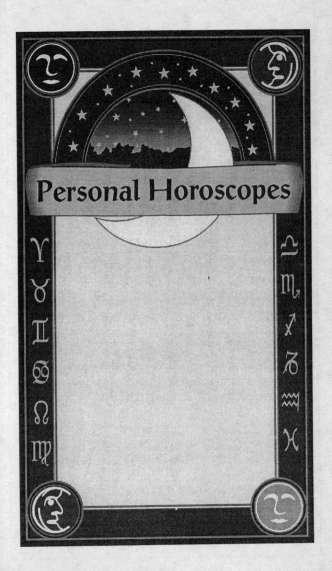

Personal Horoscopes

Sign	Glyph	Dates	Ruler	Element	Quality	Nature
Aries	♈	Mar 21–Apr 20	Mars	Fire	Cardinal	Barren
Taurus	♉	Apr 20–May 21	Venus	Earth	Fixed	Semi-Fruitful
Gemini	♊	May 21–June 22	Mercury	Air	Mutable	Barren
Cancer	♋	June 22–July 23	Moon	Water	Cardinal	Fruitful
Leo	♌	July 23–Aug 23	Sun	Fire	Fixed	Barren
Virgo	♍	Aug 23–Sept 23	Mercury	Earth	Mutable	Barren
Libra	♎	Sept 23–Oct 23	Venus	Air	Cardinal	Semi-Fruitful
Scorpio	♏	Oct 23–Nov 22	Pluto	Water	Fixed	Fruitful
Sagittarius	♐	Nov 22–Dec 22	Jupiter	Fire	Mutable	Barren
Capricorn	♑	Dec 22–Jan 21	Saturn	Earth	Cardinal	Semi-Fruitful
Aquarius	♒	Jan 21–Feb 20	Uranus	Air	Fixed	Barren
Pisces	♓	Feb 20–Mar 21	Neptune	Water	Mutable	Fruitful

ARIES – ♈

MARCH 21 TO APRIL 20

The quality of Aries is fresh and exciting, and promises new beginnings. As the first sign of the zodiac, Aries represents the uncharted path of renewal and growth. With the Sun in Aries, you can express your natural exuberance for life by breaking new ground and seeking adventure. Your eye is always set on what's ahead, and you may show strong courage and assertiveness.

People like your playfulness and enjoy your stimulating energy, but sometimes, in your zeal to keep things moving, you can run roughshod over others' sensitivities. Through your affinity with the energy of your ruling planet, Mars, you can be strongly driven to achieve your aims. You need plenty of opportunities to challenge yourself through your career, and can be well suited for positions which allow you to show leadership abilities.

In relationships, you may relish the pursuit of your intended. Grand gestures kindle your flame, and you thrive on declarations of undying love. You can be an unwavering champion for those you love, and expect equal devotion from your partner. You can be extremely jealous and may not be willing to give someone another chance if they stray from their commitment. Just be sure you don't hold a double standard!

THE YEAR AHEAD

This year promises an expansion of your hopes and dreams and opportunities to develop ever-broadening horizons. Travel, educational pursuits and cultural interests may play a more important role. Jupiter's transit through your Solar 9th House also encourages a connection with your higher mind and the exploration of your ethical values and philosophical attitudes. You can use this energy to progress more consistently toward your goals, and, if you apply yourself, you may achieve advancements which will bring long-term growth.

Additionally, Saturn's cycle through your Solar 12th House emphasizes a year of releasing those things from your past which you no longer need and to become more aware of the workings of your "inner" self. Throughout the year you may feel that you are thrown back into circumstances you thought you had left behind, giving you an opportunity to say good bye to unresolved situations from your past. It's finally time to let go of old crutches you used as support in the past, but which now only get in your way.

Your affirmation for the year:
"I honor the spirit of my inner warrior."

•JANUARY•

Friendships and community activities give you a significant boost, but can also take too much time if you fail to differentiate between productive situations and those which simply exhaust energy. New directions in career and the launching of important projects gain momentum the 1st–15th. You may feel more like devoting some time to your personal interests during the middle part of the month. A new love interest or renewed commitment in an existing relationship adds excitement to your life. You may find that sharing strong philosophical values with your partner adds vitality to your relationship. Mercury's retrograde after the 26th can bring frustrations in getting new projects off the ground, but is an excellent period to follow-up those in progress.

•FEBRUARY•

You're looking for some excitement, and may be feeling especially drawn toward situations which seem to have loosely-drawn boundaries. You need to determine a direction for your career path, or you're likely to veer completely off course this month. Stay honest with yourself, and be clear about your motivations in both career choices and relationships. Your need for freedom of expression can invigorate your love life, although you may have a tendency to be attracted to others who are not quite who they seem to be. If you've felt disappointed in an existing relationship, you may just be seeking an escape to break up the monotony. If you are in a position to seek out a new relationship, give yourself time to learn about the reality of the person before you jump in with both feet!

•MARCH•

You may finally start to see more satisfying rewards for your efforts at work, and can use this time to finalize long-term agreements or contracts, which will assure greater stability. There's a lot going on behind the scenes which can benefit your growth, but if you fail to recognize your part in these situations, you may thwart your progress. Pay attention to your dreams, and give yourself some time to contemplate your future now. Your ability to visualize new directions can help you realize your dreams more quickly now. To satisfy emotional needs, keep a powerful flow of energy between both giving and receiving love and support. One-way ventures rarely provide satisfaction.

•APRIL•

Powerful energy from Mercury, Mars and Jupiter supports your desires to create success in all your ventures this month. Travel can be beneficial to your career through the 16th, but you're also in a good position to create a strong network of support from your peers or mentors. Watch for surprising changes, and stay in touch with your own sense of direction so you can take best advantage of newly created openings. The eclipses of the Moon and Sun are especially significant for you, and may help you get to the core of relationship issues or expose your deepest needs. You have to be willing to do the work to become more aware of what you really want from a love relationship, or you're likely to waste a chance which can turn the tide toward the realization of many long-held dreams.

•MAY•

Let your light shine and take the risk of showcasing your talents and exposing your best ideas to influential people and in advantageous circumstances. Make sure not to investigate new opportunities or something which seems "too good to be true" mid-month, when it's easy to see only what you wish to see instead of looking beneath the surface. Love relationships can flourish now, and make the best progress when you allow for relaxed, natural situations instead of trying to contrive something exceptional out of the ordinary. Venus transiting in Aries through the 16th brings a more positive sense of self worth, but you need to find the best ways to build on your strengths and resources to a strong foundation for yourself.

•JUNE•

Build a positive network of support with others in your field by making a special effort to keep your promises. Complete projects and follow-up on contacts made in the past during Mercury's retrograde through the 17th. This is an excellent time to create enthusiasm from others and to research long-range details of contracts or agreements, but not a good time to sign long-term contracts which have not been investigated. Make a special effort to clarify misunderstandings in intimate relationships and with your family, since most disputes arising now are likely to be the result of poor communication. Strive to resolve conflicts at work, since others are likely to expect your actions to make a difference.

•JULY•

Attention to home and family is necessary, although you cannot ignore your duties and responsibilities at work. Your parents can play an influential role, even if only subconsciously, and you might find acknowledging their needs or requests goes a long way in satisfying your internal conflicts. An open, honest approach to concerns in your love relationship works best, but watch a tendency to be caught off-guard by your partner's anger over past disputes. Your generosity and willingness to share your time and resources works wonders after the 24th. Take a conservative approach in business activities early in the month, and save your futuristic ideas until after the 16th. Know who you're trusting with valuable goods or information to avoid those who would take advantage of your good graces. Watch a temptation to be less than honest yourself, since situations can easily backfire.

•AUGUST•

This month's cycles bring powerful support for creative or artistic expression, and can be the time when you finally realize positive profits for your efforts. Finances, speculative interests, and career advancement show improvements. Social contacts may be just as important as business meetings for your professional upgrading. Your love life gains momentum, and you may feel more confident expressing feelings and needs while Venus transits through your 5th House. However, you may unwittingly hurt another's feelings as a result of your own enthusiastic efforts, which can cause a setback in a close relationship. Avoid underestimating your power and influence in both personal and professional situations.

•SEPTEMBER•

Clarify the reasons for friction or disputes at work, since resolution of difficult situations may be quite simple once you understand the underlying circumstances. This can be a highly competitive period, although taking unnecessary risks from the

1st to the 8th can lead to accidents, or may just create costly disruptions. Research or scientific pursuits bring especially rewarding results if you're willing to do the digging, but inattentive efforts on your part will delay your progress. Mercury's retrograde from the 22nd to the 30th may be accompanied by a period of uncertainty. Giving a situation time to reach its own level might be easier than trying to push for a resolution before its time.

•OCTOBER•

The Lunar Eclipse in Aries can bring a period of increased emotionality on your part, and may result in your tendency to over-dramatize situations. However, your intimate relationships can improve if you take the initiative. Your love life definitely shows promise, with sexual intimacy providing the right ingredients to achieve the solidification of your commitment. At work, changes in the bureaucracy can create confusion during Mercury's retrograde period through the 13th, although you may feel that everything is not out in the open until after the 23rd. By working together with others you can create powerful alliances which will aid your advancement. Horizons seem broader after the 20th, when you may be considering the value of education or travel in advancing your career.

•NOVEMBER•

Others seem to recognize your abilities and efforts more readily than in the past, and you may feel more secure about your future opportunities than you've felt for a long time. Educational opportunities, conferences or workshops can provide just the stimulus you need to keep your program in action. Plan to launch an advertising or public relations campaign to promote your favorite projects. If you're looking for a new source of inspiration, you just may find it by getting involved in special interests or political action. You're in an excellent place to make your position known to others in a way which supports your most cherished ideals.

•DECEMBER•

Travel continues to be a strong influence, or you may be involved in writing, publishing, or just studying something intensely. Achieving goals is paramount, and you may feel that you are unstoppable. The greater the challenge now, the more powerful your energy is likely to be in meeting it. Use your eagerness and enthusiasm in the most appropriate ways, since it's easy to overwhelm others. Impulsiveness can be costly from the 17th to the 21st, so consider the effect of your actions. In romance, be aware of your tendency to be drawn to fantasy rather than reality. This can bring you closer in an existing relationship.

TAURUS – ♉

APRIL 20 TO MAY 21

Taurus qualities include preservation, stability and endurance. With the Sun in Taurus, your ego is driven to make the most of all your resources, and you like to have as many resources available as possible. You're likely to prefer an easy-going pace while developing the secure foundation you need. Approaching life with the attitude of an artist, you have a strong appreciation for things which are both beautiful and utilitarian.

You may be happiest when you've put forth your strongest personal efforts. Before you know it, you can fall into a rut of too much work and too little pleasure. It's important to keep your priority of enjoying those people and things you love while you strive to provide the comfort and stability you've promised to attain. Your earthy nature can provide a firm foundation and consistent nurturing for a satisfying love relationship. You're likely to prefer consistency and commitment over the unstable existence of playing the field.

Since you don't mind hard work, you can be quite successful in career endeavors. Instead of measuring your success in purely material terms, strive to achieve true prosperity in all aspects of your life.

THE YEAR AHEAD

Friends and those who share your special interests and ideals provide a powerful backdrop for a year of inspirational outreach and increased satisfaction. Consistency and responsibility pay off professionally, and you may finally be in a position of influence. However, if you have particular deficiencies which have blocked your success, this is an exceptional time to satisfy those requirements or prerequisites and get on track.

Cooperation and consensus are your best assurances not only of financial growth during the year, but also of increasing intimacy in your personal relationships. With Jupiter transiting through your Solar 8th House, you may also feel more inclined to show your gratitude and appreciation for others who share your life. This energy also stimulates a heightened curiosity about the things which lie beneath the surface, and can help you achieve greater intimacy on many levels with your partner.

Your affirmation for the year:
"I am consciously aware of my inner needs."

•JANUARY•

Outreach, expansion and hope for the future mark your beginning for 1995. By applying your creative imagination to your disciplined efforts you can achieve a high level of success, and may also gain recognition for your achievements. Joint finances can be a source of difficulty, especially if you are not disclosing important details to your partner, or if you feel not forthcoming about his or her own. Sharing your enjoyment of the arts or your special pleasures greatly enhances your love, and you may even have a chance to showcase your talents and impress someone special. Mercury enters its retrograde cycle on the 26th, so try to complete major contracts or agreements before that time. (This is a great time to clean out closets, desks and unfinished family business.)

•FEBRUARY•

Even though you may be more involved with home or family activities, it's unlikely you will be a hermit this month. By making connections with others in your field, especially getting back in touch with those who have been helpful in the past, you can strengthen your position. Venus' transit through your Solar 9th House provides positive indicators for travel, writing or educational pursuits. Although Mercury retrogrades through the 15th, you may also be more communicative, especially at work. Watch out for those power struggles, and step away if they don't involve you personally. Family conflicts can escalate due to misunderstandings early in the month, but your patience and ingenuity offer positive solutions. Instead of concentrating upon your differences, seek common ground.

•MARCH•

An excessively stubborn attitude on your part can bring an escalation of conflicts, especially if you're feeling pressured by authorities or others whose controlling impedes your progress. Before you jump into the fray, be sure the battle is relevant to your situation. Alliances with others who share your views or interests provides a solid basis for fulfilling your personal goals. Time spent with friends can be especially beneficial. Avoid the temptation to become romantically involved with someone at work unless you understand the effect your actions can have upon your career. Love relationships show great promise near the time of the Full Moon on the 16th, when your willingness to explore some intimate secrets adds intensity to the passion you share.

•APRIL•

Greater confidence in yourself shows in the quality of your work. Be alert to any underlying feelings of agitation which may result from some unresolved issues with your family. Deal with your anxieties realistically, in order to quickly resolve your fears or frustrations. With the Solar eclipse in Taurus on the 29th, you are experiencing a period of increasing awareness of your deeper needs on all levels. Change is in the wind, and although you may welcome progress, you may feel reluctant to give up an old security blanket! Patient, consistent effort on your part brings excellent results on the career front, and can even have the same effect in your love life. Be sure you're actually moving forward, since it's easy to become complacent and miss a chance to make some much-needed improvements.

•MAY•

It's easy to let your fantasies overtake your good judgment, although you may enjoy the experience of that imaginary realm tremendously. This is an excellent cycle for sharing your dreams with your partner or trying a new approach to your intimate relationship. However, you may quickly get over your head in a new relationship with someone who could take unnecessary advantage of your good graces. It's definitely a time to look before you leap! Impulsiveness can be costly at all levels, especially in the area of finances. If you run into delays on contracts or agreements after Mercury enters its retrograde cycle on the 24th, research all the possibilities instead of fighting to reach a final decision.

•JUNE•

A tremendous surge of creative energy helps you take a special project into a highly successful arena. This same cycle can also enhance your love life, and may offer exceptional experiences in your relationships with children. By participating in activities which you honestly enjoy, you may also make connections with others who stimulate your imagination, vitality and sense of confidence. Even though some of your expectations may be unreasonably high, you are still in a good position to make long-term decisions after Mercury moves into direct motion on the 17th. Take the time to do necessary research, since you may discover some treasured insights or may even unearth some things of value while clearing out some of those closets. Travel, even short trips close to home, broadens your options later in the month.

•JULY•

Your creativity continues to stimulate easier self-expression, and you're also experiencing a highly productive cycle for career growth. Your spirited show of feelings and needs can help to stabilize a love relationship, or can offer a strong foundation in beginning a new romance. Travel can be especially enjoyable this month, and may stimulate a new surge of creative or imaginative energy. Unusual situations can take you away from the ordinary, or an exceptional individual can open your mind to new ideas and a fresh perspective on your real self. Your tendency to take a conservative approach to change can be an excuse for avoiding letting go, but all indicators are that you're ready for some of those alterations. Go for it!

•AUGUST•

Increasing harmony and understanding at home and within your family relationships becomes a high-level priority. You're eager to translate your internal needs to an environmental level, and might enjoy redecorating, or even moving. However, you're also feeling more driven to get some things accomplished at work which have been dragging along, and may feel that you're being stretched in several directions unless you keep your priorities in order. By letting go of unnecessary details you may be able to free some time and energy to enjoy the results of your hard work with those you love. Finances can be a source of friction with your partner, but you may also need more emotional support and understanding. Take actions which will affirm your stability, security and sense of personal integrity.

•SEPTEMBER•

You may feel more competitive, and are likely to be ready to do battle with anyone or anything which threatens the things you hold dear to your heart. Careful examination of ventures which involve joint resources is necessary before you move forward with a commitment or contract, since you're unwilling to settle for anything less than equitable. However, once you've aired your grievances, you may end up with a situation which is radically improved. A personal relationship runs into trouble if you deny the facts about how you really feel.

If you're fooling yourself, the truth is likely to surface anyway. It's time to look realistically at your life situation instead of just hoping things will change because the "potential" looks promising.

•OCTOBER•

The Moon's Eclipse on the 8th can stimulate a feeling of apprehension, especially if you've been running away from deeper needs. Allow some time for introspection and reflection to reach a sense of inner peace and a resolution to internal conflicts. Mercury's retrograde continues through the 13th, and you may be frustrated with situations at work resulting from poor communication. Watch a tendency to get into a battle of wills with your partner, since some of those deep-seated emotional issues may have little to do with your current situation. Let this be your time to heal guilt, shame or disappointment which has kept you from having the love and the life you deserve. Let go of the feeling that others are somehow more powerful than you.

•NOVEMBER•

Your love life can take off like a rocket this month, especially if you're willing to break down some of those barriers to achieving the ecstasy you desire. Part of your problem may be the issue of commitment, and what you feel you have to "give up" in order to have what you really need. Form a commitment based upon gaining more of you needs instead of losing something. However, if you're in a relationship which needs to end or be altered in a significant way, you may find that letting go gives you more freedom and fulfillment. Finances can be particularly tricky this month if you're spending beyond your limits, so avoid the tendency toward impulsive spending on things which are unnecessary. It's time to get rid of things, attitudes and situations which are stifling your progress and to avoid adding burdens which impede your growth.

•DECEMBER•

Activities which stimulate your mind and provide cultural awareness can be highly invigorating and satisfying. You can more easily attract circumstances which are in greater harmony with your needs and may feel especially drawn to pursuits which have a broader effect upon joining your spiritual needs with the other aspects of your everyday life. Whether you're revitalizing an existing relationship or beginning a new love affair, you'll be more eager to share your ideals, hopes and spirituality with your partner. Others may seek out your expertise, and you may find excellent opportunities to learn from those you have long admired. This is a generous, productive and inventive period for you, a time when you broaden your horizons in such as way as to sense the reality of your true self.

GEMINI – ♊
MAY 21 TO JUNE 22

Diversity, mentality and versatility are Gemini qualities. With your Sun in Gemini, you may show a natural communicative ability and intense curiosity. Others may view you as eternally youthful, since you may always seem to be learning and investigating new ideas, people, places and things.

Attracted to others who show intelligence and wit, you may be most fascinated by a relationship which challenges and stimulates your mind. However, your reluctance to make a commitment to one special partnership may stem from a fear the you might miss something important if you limit yourself. Your intuitive leanings are usually correct, and it's especially important to follow this innate sensibility when making decisions about your personal relationships and career choices instead of always trying to reach every conclusion from a purely logical basis. Your keen ability to blend information with your intuitive insights is one of the the features which sets you apart from the crowd. You will always be learning, changing and on the move, but need to avoid scattering your energy by becoming involved in too many situations at one time.

THE YEAR AHEAD

Although this can be an exciting year of fast-paced growth, you are also challenged to direct your energy and interests in ways which will provide a sense of stability and a firm foundation for your future. Jupiter's transit in opposition to your Sun stimulates a year of reaching toward broader horizons. You may feel drawn to move, expand your living conditions or travel as part of this need for increasing your security base. You're also feeling some restraints while Saturn transits in square aspect to your Sun, and may sense that you cannot have everything at once. Instead, you are likely to have choices which will provide greater responsibility, require increased discipline and lead to greater personal awareness.

Many of the situations which emerge during this year are directly linked to decisions you made about seven years ago, and this can be the year during which you finally satisfy some long-range goals or complete a personal commitment. As you work toward consolidating your energies, you may also feel that you are on the brink of significant breakthroughs.

Your affirmation for the year:
"I am stepping into the light of personal fulfillment."

•JANUARY•

Personal conflicts can rage out of control unless you maintain clarity about your needs and obligations. Even though you may find it easier to allow others to believe what they wish, unrealistic expectations on their part can get you into hot water. Your ideas for progress at work may be well received, but when it comes to putting your plans into action, be prepared to deal with conservative forces whose budget proposals may seem rather skimpy. Patience on your part goes a long way in helping you determine the best way to stimulate stalled projects. Use Mercury's retrograde cycle after the 25th as a good period to get back on track. Be alert to power struggles, since someone else may see your actions as a threat to their security.

•FEBRUARY•

Business travel, educational opportunities, and writing or publishing all provide excellent outlets for your ideas. However, until Mercury finally leaves its retrograde cycle on the 15th, you may continue to experience some delays due to regulations, red tape or other interference. Past transgressions seem to loom unusually large, whether on the personal or professional front, and their effect can be minimized by taking a realistic approach to your current situations instead of getting caught in debris from the past. You can gain from the support and resources of others now, but only if you share the credit (which should be no problem, since you're only too eager to get things moving). A love relationship undergoes deep changes, but can only progress if you're willing to satisfy your honest needs instead of trying to please standards which have very little relevance to your current situation.

•MARCH•

Your quick wit may get you out of a jam early in the month, but you'll also find that your grasp of information and understanding are valuable career assets. Be particularly alert to hidden agendas from your competitors mid-month, when incomplete preparation on your part can bring costly setbacks. After laying adequate groundwork, you're likely to see significant progress in negotiations. Conservative factions still loom large, and you may feel that you're caught in the middle of great ideas which have nowhere to go. Work out the details and set forth a plan within the parameters you've been given, and you may be pleasantly surprised at the results. Any commitments you make now will be taken seriously, so make sure you're ready to take the leap before you make the proposal.

•APRIL•

Significant career advancements may be the result of your strong professional alliances with others who appreciate your strengths. This is a superb

time to get involved in local activities which benefit your community, or to make an effort to connect
with special interest groups. Be alert to the possibility of undermining from those who might have
ulterior motives. Near the time of the Moon's
eclipse on the 15th you may feel an intensification
in a love relationship, and this can be a strong time
to express your desires, needs and intentions to
your beloved. Hesitation is likely to arise from a
mistrust of your deeper needs, so try to release
your anxieties and peer within your inner self for
the true path to the serenity you hope to achieve.

•MAY•

An enticing relationship possibility can distract you
from your current life situation early in the month,
and you may be particularly ready for an escape
from the ordinary. The fireworks can be exceptional, but you might prefer to wait a while before
you make any definite commitments to change your
life. You may simply need a new approach to
expressing your desires, and can also use this
energy to stimulate a relationship. For the next two
months, your ruling planet, Mercury, is transiting in
Gemini. This can be an exceptional time to develop
an understanding of subjects which hold your interest, and can also be a good time to brush up on
skills which could use some polish. Pay particular
attention to details after the 24th, when Mercury
enters its retrograde cycle.

•JUNE•

Even though you may have strong feelings, it might be difficult to feel safe about expressing them. Instead of trying to be sure that your feelings are logical, allow yourself to flow with them and discover where they lead. Your frustration may arise from your mind's attempts to block a deep-seated desire. Family pressures can also develop into a blow-up, particularly if there are too many controls or unrealistic expectations. At work, pay particular attention to those areas in which you are held accountable, and stay on top of legal issues, contracts or important communications. Deal with anger as quickly as possible, and know when to step out of the way when someone else is about to blow.

•JULY•

Control issues can seem oppressive unless you find ways to respond which protect your interests and position. Conservative factions may seem to have the upper hand, but if you have the facts you can still generate enthusiasm and support for your plans or ideas. You may also be experiencing some deep unconscious drives to satisfy family or parents instead of following your own needs. However, rebellion may not be the answer. Instead, You may have greater success embracing those elements in your life which you know to be part of your needs and concentrating on strengthening your sense of self-esteem. Deal with your anger in a straightforward and honest manner, and allow that love which resides deep within you to emerge and flow through yourself to others.

•AUGUST•

Creative vitality permeates your life, and can stimulate a stronger sense of confidence and hope. Get away from your routine and enjoy travel, interaction with others and sharing activities which are simply pleasurable. Differences can provide a source of insight, but you may also experience an inspiration to revitalize your life choices or seek out some new directions. Make adjustments in your finances which allow you to establish a sense of long-term stability early in the month, but be cautious before acting on outside financial advice after the 15th. Romantic fantasies can be highly motivating during the latter part of the month, although you need to be careful about the signals you're sending, since they can easily be misinterpreted unless your intentions are perfectly clear.

•SEPTEMBER•

You're entering a cycle which provides exceptional energy for developing a project or idea over the next ten weeks. During this time, you might also have excellent success in creative activities which involve working in harmony with others. A change of scenery can help you breathe some fresh air into your love life and adds perspective to your inner feelings. Watch for foot-in-the-mouth syndrome through the 7th, when your fascination with someone new can lead you to take actions or make statements which are totally out of character. Your actions and sensibilities are a bit more synchronized after the 17th. You may feel like a hermit for a while, although some intimate time with your sweetie might take you into places you've only known in your dreams.

•OCTOBER•

On the job you may run into some power struggles which are totally illogical, but which can only be resolved by open dialogue. Such political conflicts can have an alienating effect, and you may be tempted to change positions before the negotiations are done. However, if you are called to mediate, it's crucial to stay firm in your own convictions. To strengthen your love relationship now, you may need to release some of your old ideas about the way things should be and make room for the way they are now before you proceed to make creative changes. If you are ending an attachment in a relationship, strive to reach closure with your ex-partner before moving on. There's no need to carry old issues with you.

•NOVEMBER•

Friction with a partner can try your patience, but it may just be time to bring your needs and feelings out into the open. You may crave excitement, but watch the way you go about achieving it, since your tendency toward competitiveness can give you an aggressive edge which alienates those you are trying to impress. Even though your feelings for someone may be strong, you may also resist commitment due to fears based on past experience. Consult with someone you trust before you lock your heart away. Pressures from career can also be at an all-time high, although you are likely to rise to the occasion.

•DECEMBER•

Social obligations related to work can clutter your schedule with events which absorb your free time, but they can be highly significant in aiding your career advancement. Pay special attention to spending, since it's easy to spend beyond your means (keep your credit cards on ice). Although you can benefit from the resources of others now, be sure you understand the obligations before you agree to participate. Avoid getting caught in unnecessary details over contracts or agreements. If you cannot keep it direct and simple, it may not be worth the effort. This is a great time to clear away the things you no longer need and make room for new projects for the year ahead.

CANCER – ♋

JUNE 22 TO JULY 23

Cancer's qualities engage the nurturing, sensitive and growth-oriented experiences of life. With your Sun in Cancer, your ego is strongly involved in support and care-taking, and you may easily create a sense of family wherever you may be. Anyone who knows you well is probably familiar with your "sixth" sense about things, since your intuitive nature can be easily developed. The Moon functions as your ruler, enhancing your sensibility to life's ever-changing cycles.

In career and relationships, you need an opportunity to build a strong foundation that supports your principles and beliefs. Because you may have been strongly influenced by family in your early years, those roots are likely to play a significant part in your conscious and unconscious choices. If you remain locked in old patterns out of fear or instability, you can become overly protective of yourself or others, and may block your ability to receive the support and understanding you need. Once you develop a sense of your own emotional security, you can branch out into areas which allow you to become positively influential in your family and community.

THE YEAR AHEAD

Throughout this year your concentration on increasing your knowledge or expertise, or reaching into broader horizons in your personal and career development, can be especially rewarding. It is important that you become more involved within your community in ways which will be meaningful and rewarding for your own growth. You can also improve your working conditions and make adjustments which will allow a more fulfilling interaction with coworkers or peers.

With Saturn transiting through your Solar 9th House, you may also have opportunities to teach or learn from others. This is an excellent time to study and focus your mind, and can be a positive cycle for professional growth if you're willing to apply the necessary discipline. Jupiter's course through the year emphasizes a need to take care of your physical health and you can create positive changes in your sense of well-being.

Your affirmation for the year:
"My life is guided by Divine Wisdom."

•JANUARY•

Demands from others can seem to envelop much of your time, but you can also take action which will give you more room to exercise your own ideas. By directly networking with others in your field or within your community, you may also be able to create a strong support system, which serves as a positive outlet for sharing your ideas and participation in joint endeavors, but it's also time to take a look at your partnership and to own up to your real needs. Even though you may feel especially vulnerable during the Cancer Full Moon on the 16th, you can restore harmony to your life by acknowledging your true feelings, instead of taking the indirect approach and getting only part of your needs fulfilled. Be cautious with your spending, particularly after Mercury enters its 22nd day retrograde cycle on the 25th.

•FEBRUARY•

Research into the root causes of problems exposes the core of issues, and may lead to positive long-term solutions. Instead of feeling that you're getting the short end of the stick all the time, find ways to give more to yourself. By concentrating on building your sense of self-worth, you can see immediate results in your relationships and from your career. If you ignore this need to bring greater harmony and joy into your life, then you may feel excessively angry and unfulfilled. You have the power to make changes, and some of those alterations may involve releasing burdens which are not yours to carry. By allowing others to take care of their own responsibilities, you can then direct your own energy toward what is yours to manage or uphold.

•MARCH•

Sharing your knowledge and expertise can be highly rewarding and may lead to career advancement or recognition, but you can also use this time to learn more about your work and fine-tune your skills. Take a close look at your finances from the 1st-13th, when expert financial advice can help you make better use of your resources. However, some disputes involving joint finances can be distressing mid-month, even though this is an excellent time to clarify situations. Disagreements over "yours versus mine" can permeate everything from your love life and emotional needs to possessions and career success. You can refocus your energy in relationships by returning to your spiritual center and incorporating greater tolerance instead of feeling victimized.

•APRIL•

The eclipses of the Sun and Moon emphasize a need to examine your personal relationships, and may challenge you to make a determination about family issues or political matters. Instead of just believing something, you need to understand the underlying truth for yourself. If vague communication creates tension in the work place, you may be the one who is called to sort things out, and may wish you could just step out of the way and avoid the situation entirely. You will know if it is important to take a stand, and if you act against your deeper feelings, may regret it later. By taking a creative approach and focusing on future development you can use difficult situations now as a platform for increasing your stability. Friends provide an excellent buffer and support after the 24th.

•MAY•

Love is in the air! You may feel a bit mischievous, and have a tenacious desire to indulge your fantasies. New situations may not be as they appear on the surface, and some investigation of the facts might help you avoid problems. You need a break, and can find a workable way to create it as long as you stay in touch with your real feelings. You may decide to withdraw from an overwhelming commitment which can be disappointing and self-defeating unless your actions affirm what you know. Watch for power plays at work, when you may move into a position of influence after the 16th. However, if the battle does not concern you, avoid being drawn into it, since the real victor may be the one who stays out of the way.

•JUNE•

Even though Mercury is retrograde until the 17th, you may experience significant progress in your career efforts, and can be quite effective by networking with others who can be influential and supportive of your efforts. However, to avoid feeling that you're moving in circles instead of going forward, keep your priorities clearly in order and strive to obtain correct information. Exaggeration of the facts can throw you off track early in the month, when a review can help to clarify the real situation. Keep the record straight about feelings and positions in personal and professional relationships, since allowing others to draw the wrong conclusions about you can lead to misunderstandings if they base their decisions on inaccurate data.

•JULY•

Your sense of self-confidence flows more easily now, and your willingness to express your deeper feelings helps strengthen an emotional bond. Partnerships and commitments are strongly emphasized near the time of the Full Moon on the 12th. A new or existing relationship gains momentum due to your own willingness to release the past and deal with your current situation more completely. However, You may also be ready to let go of an attachment, and bring an unworkable situation to an end. Business travel or conferences may be important, and demand much of your time early in the month. They can bring positive recognition your way from the 16th-22nd. Watch the details from the 21st-26th, when your excitement about new opportunities can lead you to overlook important information.

•AUGUST•

Feelings of impatience and irritability may be the result of family tension or changes at home, and this can distract you from the focus you need in your work. Identify your attachments and emotional involvement before you stubbornly cling to anything, including an idea, since your objectivity may be limited by your emotional intensity. Any situation which feels too confining begins to wear you down this month, but you may have greater choices than you realize about the direction of an agreement or commitment. Take time to do some research and investigate your long-term options before you decide. You are likely to see a way to move into a better circumstance, but it may take some maneuvering before you're in the right position.

•SEPTEMBER•

Your eagerness to move into a more exciting situation may lead to impulsive action, although that may be exactly what you need to get to the right place and time. Trust your creative instincts, since you are in a powerful position to express your talents and special skills. Avoid financial situations involving high risk until after the 6th. A new love interest may appear on the scene, although you're most likely to develop a fascination with someone close to home. By breaking out of a stale routine and into more playful modes, you can revitalize your love life and enliven your relationships with family and friends. In any case, this is an exceptional time to share your talents, and you may even have a chance to emerge as a shining light.

•OCTOBER•

You may be met with a series of confusing situations which distract you from your primary objectives during Mercury's retrograde period through the 14th. However, your concentration continues to focus on creative areas, and you can still enjoy a feeling of easy self-expression. The problem lies with those distractions which seem to come from other people. Maybe you just need a break before you get back to work! Your passion may seem to be at a very high level, and unless you allow time to express those feelings and indulge in some of your fantasies, you may feel exceedingly obsessive about them. Let your creative vitality breathe in everything you do, and give yourself plenty of opportunities to let your hair down. However, do try to show some restraint in financial dealings.

•NOVEMBER•

Higher levels of emotional intensity add impact to your creative expression and can also stimulate greater productivity in your career. Take a look at your attitudes toward your job and your working conditions. This is the time to invigorate your career, make adjustments and repair circumstances which are problematic. Your eagerness may be squelched by more conservative factions mid-month, but if you incorporate their demands or have a way to answer them, then you can reach a powerful level of stability and respectability. Take time for your love life this month, and if you've been keeping a distance from someone you care about, make an effort to reach out and connect with him or her.

•DECEMBER•

Your drive to achieve your aims is growing now, although you may feel an urge to shrink away from the competition. Much of that conflict is likely to arise from a mistrust of yourself or your abilities, and you can definitely do something about that part. Strong emphasis on your Solar 7th House of partnerships may put relationships in the spotlight. Your attitudes about your role in the relationship is changing, and you can take actions which will stimulate renewal or which can be the initiation of a commitment. After all, the promise you make is really a promise to yourself. Strive for a sense of balance whenever possible, but realize that balance is rarely consistent.

LEO – ♌

JULY 23 TO AUGUST 23

Leo represents the qualities of loyalty, magnetism and self-confidence. Because your Sun is in Leo, your sense of your ego self is shaped by these qualities, and you can always radiate a powerful sense of love and warmth which others enjoy. You can be generous and dramatic, and may have a soft spot for family and children. Your sense of honor not only extends to people, but can be a strong ally as you strive to achieve realization of your own dreams.

Although you can be possessive in relationships, you are most interested in developing a love which will give you plenty of room to express yourself and to show the depth of your passion. If you're hurt, you can lash out in ways which can be destructive to anything or anyone in your path. You need room in your career to exercise leadership and power, and can probably handle wielding authority better than most. However, it is crucial that you avoid a tendency to become so self-absorbed that you lose your connection to those who may be under your command. Like your ruler, the Sun, you can shine brightly and can become the guiding light to inspire others to show their greatest strengths.

THE YEAR AHEAD

Your creativity, confidence and feeling of optimism are boosted this year by Jupiter's transit through your Solar 5th House in trine aspect to your Sun. Artistic and creative pursuits can be highly stimulating and may provide a strong basis for advancement in your career or personal recognition. Other planetary influences stimulate a feeling that you are on the brink of important changes, although the exact circumstances of these changes may not manifest themselves right away. By carefully examining your own attitudes, and releasing your attachments to elements from your past which impede healing and transformation, you can play a more active role in engineering these new directions.

Saturn's cycle can also provide challenges within your relationships, and you may have more opportunities to examine your attachments and to develop an understanding of your deeper needs. From a spiritual level, this cycle provides an exceptional backdrop from which to release those attitudes, fears or experiences of guilt which have stood in the way of manifesting your dreams.

Your affirmation for the year:
"I am open to expressing my creativity
in everything I do."

•JANUARY•

Instead of hoping a situation will change, take the bull by the horns and get to the core of financial disputes, tax liabilities or other money issues. Even though a partner may not be as open with information as you might like, you can still extract what you need to rectify a situation. You may also be frustrated by difficulties rooted in the past, and unless you deal with them directly, they may continue to re-emerge like bad dreams. To move forward in a love relationship you must deal with obstacles in your path, even if you once created them as part of your defense against vulnerability. Barriers can break down in the midst of sharing a fanciful or purely enjoyable experience, when you realize that some of your fears have no place in your current situation. You must also honor your sense of personal boundaries and respect your own needs and those of your lover.

•FEBRUARY•

Cooperative effort on your part goes a long way toward resolving difficulties and decreases the level of distraction from your goals. You may still run into problems reaching final agreements until after Mercury moves into direct motion on the 15th. Joint finances can continue to be a source of dispute, although you may be able to reach a workable solution near the end of the month. Give extra attention to your partnership, and increase your consideration of your partner's needs. Use your arguments as a means to expose problems at their core, and realize that gridlock is not the only solution. Talking about your concerns, needs and feelings may be easier during the latter half of the month, but you can still get sidetracked from the real issues. Getting stuck in old fears remains your biggest trap, and can block your success in intimate relationships and career alike.

•MARCH•

Cooperative ventures fare better, although you may still be scurrying to make adjustments and maintain harmony. Use your talents and artistic sensibilities to help you attain your goals. In fact, your business relationships work best when you allow room for each person to use his or her best attributes instead of forcing awkward situations. Barriers to intimacy are also easier to breech this month, particularly following the Full Moon on the 16th. Travel opens doors on all fronts after the 21st, and may provide an opportunity to showcase your special talents, or act as a strong supporter of the talents of others. Those restraints which have blocked your forward progress diminish after the 22nd.

•APRIL•

Stabilize your sense of self-confidence through educational pursuits, travel, teaching, writing and public speaking, which also offer particularly positive benefits to your career advancement. Enlist the support of others whose influence can have a beneficial impact on your project, proposal or ideas, but investigate what will be required from you before you agree to the terms. The energy of the Lunar Eclipse on the 15th stimulates a strong need to connect your heart, mind and spirit with those you love. Participate in activities which are personally inspiring, and find time to get away from the rat race and reconnect with the center of your spiritual self early in the month. Be aware of the expectations and responsibilities associated with your professional position or place in the community, since this can be a time when your influence can reach further than you realize.

•MAY•

Political or ideological affiliations have a strong influence upon your career advancement. Your role in uniting disagreeable factions can place you in an enviable position. However, your own ethics, morals and beliefs may be tested during the process. Attempt to finalize contracts and agreements before the 17th, and if there is a delay, use the period of Mercury's retrograde after the 23rd to research, gather information and confirm alliances. If power struggles arise with family members later in the month, they may simply reflect a difference in your priorities. Strengthen your romantic options through travel, when you can either deepen an existing bond or attract a new love. But be wary of a flirtation from the 12th-18th, when the results of your teasing can disrupt your existing circumstances.

•JUNE•

Extra care with your spending and finances helps you avoid trouble. Important contracts and documents need extra review during Mercury's retrograde through the 17th, although this is an excellent period in which to clean up your act and edit, audit or practice until everything meets your high expectations. Make careful assessments before you spend, and if you're forced to make unexpected expenditures, do your best to know something about the product or property before you buy it. In matters of the heart, you may feel hungry for high levels of attention and affection, but will have a more satisfying experience if you strive to give as much as you receive. Leave time for romance this month, even though your top priority may seem to be making money.

•JULY•

You may feel like spending a bit more time alone through mid-month, and can also experience higher levels of anxiety due to stress at work. Time for introspection near the Full Moon on the 12th helps bring a sense of calm and understanding. If unfinished business from the past stirs up trouble, try to bring the situation to a close instead of stuffing it under the mattress. This is an excellent cycle in which to complete projects, and you may finally see some daylight in long-lasting disputes. Once old issues are settled, you may feel like starting out on a new path. The Leo New Moon on the 27th marks a cycle of increasing confidence and courageous effort. Get away from your normal environment for a few days in order to change your perspective and gain fresh insights.

•AUGUST•

Romance, creativity and self-expression add zest and vitality to your life this month. Joining forces with others helps generate long-lasting impact, and may place you in a position to lead the way for immediate advancement in your status. If you've been waiting for the right time to tell someone how much you care, you're in an exceptional position to communicate your feelings and receive positive feedback. Your partner may also have some needs which have been denied or forgotten, and the Full

Moon on the 10th brings this situation into the light. Pay immediate attention to family demands from the 18th-31st. Consider time for travel or vacationing before the 25th, since disruptions can alter your plans after that time.

•SEPTEMBER•

You may feel like escaping pressures early in the month, but everywhere you turn can seem like a dead end. Find that place within yourself which is your personal retreat—perhaps some extra time spent in artistic pursuits or enjoying your favorite recreation will give you the peace you seek. Your family may require extra attention, and even though you may be trying to work things out to suit them, it's easy to feel overburdened by their expectations. If emotional tension arises in your love life, it could stem from your concern about money, taxes or other concerns which are beyond the scope of your partnership. Instead of allowing these things to form a wedge in your relationship, take time away from your daily routine to reconnect at a deeper level.

•OCTOBER•

Instead of just trusting that things will be done the way you wish, take time to follow through on important communication, documentation or personal contact until after Mercury turns direct on the 14th. This is a strong period for you, even though you may feel more easily agitated and are likely to have little patience when things go awry. Try a diplomatic approach, but avoid misleading tactics or indirect pressures which can backfire against you. Look into any situations which seem to be laced with deception, since you can easily uncover the root of the problem and clarify them before they get out of hand. Legal disputes or power struggles with family or authorities can escalate between the Lunar Eclipse on the 8th and the Solar Eclipse on the 24th. However, your persuasive manner helps you achieve the final results you desire.

•NOVEMBER•

That dry spell is finally ending, with increasing levels of creative, imaginative energy providing ample opportunities for you to showcase your talents. By increasing your productivity you can enhance your professional reputation and may even have some fun in the process. Watch for a tendency to feel unspoken pressures which stem from your own expectations of perfection or fear of failure. Make a realistic assessment of the situation before you proceed into new territory, but trust that your enthusiasm and excitement can stimulate the support you need. Now is the time to go after the things you wish to have and to take the initiative in relationships.

•DECEMBER•

Your efforts are more strongly directed toward work, although you can still enjoy yourself. Instead of feeling that the entire burden has to fall on your shoulders, coordinate your efforts with others. However, if you're unhappy with their performance, you can become overbearing in your demands, so try to keep things in proper perspective before you lose your sense of control. Get rid of unnecessary clutter in your work, environment and your attitudes, and target more streamlined processes. This is an excellent period to begin a program of self-improvement and more conscious attunement to your life experiences. Enjoy the everyday instead of resenting the fact that all your time cannot be spent in the limelight.

VIRGO – ♍

AUGUST 23 TO SEPTEMBER 23

Virgo represents the qualities of perfection, discrimination and efficiency. With your Sun in Virgo, your ego and identity are strongly tied to your sense of practicality and conscientious way of operating in the world. Fine detail may be your trademark, and your analytical mind and keen organizational ability may be highly prized in education, business or other areas. Your quest to know and understand can make learning your lifelong occupation.

In career choices, you may seek to become involved in a field which challenges your mind and offers some diversity. Even though others may observe that you appear to accomplish your tasks with great ease, you know the time, thought, analysis and planning which precedes your actions. In matters of the heart, you are most drawn to a relationship which allows you to experience the healing nature of love and tenderness. You feel most bonded when you know that there is a purpose to your love connection. You feel most alive when you know your thoughts and deeds are enhancing the quality of life.

THE YEAR AHEAD

You can use the cycles in 1995 to help you enhance your stability and further define your personal and professional image, and you may feel a strong urge to expand your base of operations. Jupiter's transit through your Solar 4th House stimulates a desire to reach into areas of increasing influence, security and greater affluence. Establishing a balance between your basic personal needs, the demands you feel from others and the opportunities you experience through your career can be stressful. With your attention to detail, you can arrange an agenda that will allow you to accomplish these things in fine form.

Even though you may feel like breaking away from some old traditions, you are also challenged by Saturn's opposition to your Sun sign to take a realistic view and eliminate only those things which are no longer viable or useful. One of the best ways to work with these cycles is to make sure that you have allowed adequate time, energy and resources to keep your promises, and that some of those promises are to yourself.

Your affirmation for the year:
"I gladly embrace every opportunity
to fulfill my needs."

•JANUARY•

It's easy to burn the candle at both ends, and to feel that your priorities are constantly growing while your time is shrinking. By initiating projects early in the month, you'll see better success and may have time to fulfill the social obligations which are part of the job. If new responsibilities emerge, determine a sense of the long-range picture before you agree to take them. Tension from your partner may arise if you've been ignoring your relationship in favor of other obligations in your life. Make time for romance, and if you still sense some distance between you, try to include your partner in your other activities. Easygoing conversation about your expectations can help alleviate most issues.

•FEBRUARY•

While Mercury retrogrades through the 15th you may run into frustrating delays at work and may have to work harder to keep lines of communication open and clear. With extra attention to research and investigation, you can make this time work for you. However, high levels of creativity abound, and you may also experience tremendous satisfaction through children or your favorite pastimes as a positive balance to your busy schedule. Romantic encounters may be most satisfying after the 20th, and you can add some zest to a stale partnership by indulging in your favorite fantasies after the 23rd.

•MARCH•

Social obligations, partnerships and obligations to others demand most of your time. Keep your boundaries intact by defining what you can and cannot do, since you could end up with all the responsibility and little recognition for your efforts. Instead of feeling pressured by details of contracts or financial agreements, analyze the elements singularly to help clarify the effect upon your life and weigh the options. Trust your abilities and allow your self-confidence to emerge. After all, you know the best ways to proceed for yourself. In personal and professional relationships you may feel that you've become the scapegoat for another's discontent or ineptitude. Reassure yourself, determine your own position, then take action from that level.

•APRIL•

Benefits arise from showing your loyalty to a partner or colleague, and you can strengthen your own stability by allowing others to show their support for your efforts. Take advantage of conferences, meetings or business travel as an opportunity to present your best work. The restraint you feel from others' expectations and demands can be highly stressful now, but your self-assurance can be bolstered by keeping your priorities in tact. You may feel prompted to release an old attachment or eliminate self-defeating attitudes during the Lunar eclipse on the 15th, which will open the way for new growth. By the time of the Solar eclipse on the 29th, that change of scenery will be a most welcome sight. Share it with someone you love.

•MAY•

Academic or educational pursuits and travel have a prominent place in your career advancement, and you may also gain recognition through teaching, writing or publishing. Business travel can be highly profitable, and you may find it easier to connect with others who are in influential positions near the time of the Full Moon on the 14th. Before you bank on another's promise of support, be sure there is substance and commitment to back up his other words, since you can run into difficulty if you lay yourself on the line for another who is not forthcoming with his or her end of the obligation. Your desire to connect to the depths of yourself stimulates a greater sense of mindfulness and spirituality, which can also extend into your relationships.

•JUNE•

High levels of impatience with the status quo can motivate you to make significant changes in many aspects of your life. This is an exceptional time to become more physically active or to take the initiative in advancing your career. However, it's also easy to overextend yourself by underestimating your obligations. Complete long-standing projects or obligations during Mercury's retrograde through the 17th, and be aware that you may also have a chance to initiate new projects during this time. Just watch for a tendency to scatter your energy, or to become distracted and lose focus. Your mental ingenuity can lead to advancement in your position after the 20th. Keep the romance in your life alive by getting away from the rat race, even if only for an afternoon.

•JULY•

Connections to others provide the backdrop for your most significant activities, and may be the key to professional success and personal satisfaction. Political interests or community activities can be especially rewarding, and you may be prompted to take action on issues which are personally important to you. Since you're in no mood to carry along much dead weight right now, you may be cutting your losses and moving on, leaving behind situations, people or attitudes which have been stifling your progress. You've heard the story of the straw that broke the camel's back. . . . Focus your energy instead on creating some fireworks in your love life and opening your heart to receiving the love, support and respect you need and deserve.

•AUGUST•

Watch your budget, since it's easy to spend impulsively or exhaust resources more quickly than you anticipated. You have little patience for people or situations which impede change or growth, and can use your influence to help bring about some much-needed change at work or within your relationships. You may yearn for that perfect partner, dreamy career or lifestyle which seems beyond your grasp, but you are in an exceptional position to get closer to creating your life through determining your true wants and needs. Search your inner feelings, and decide how much of that dream is escape and how much is the path you wish for your life. The New Moon in Virgo on the 25th marks a positive time to create that path and to put your plans for achieving those dreams into action.

•SEPTEMBER•

Special efforts to make personal contact with clients or peers improve your career situation. Income through public speaking, teaching or writing can enhance your financial picture and may help stabilize your professional reputation. Outreach through advertising, public relations or other forms of presentation helps sharpen your image if executed correctly, but avoid alienating others by trying to be someone other than whom you know yourself to be. Encourage those who share your life to express their feelings and needs, and make an effort to rise above suspicions and rely more on the facts of a situation. Suppositions can be costly and misleading, and can escalate into difficulties which try your patience and which may bring costly delays once Mercury enters its retrograde cycle on the 22nd.

•OCTOBER•

Prosperity on all fronts promises a more satisfying life experience, although you might be tempted to count your chickens before they hatch. Unless you have substantial support and adequate research, your plans can fall through, or may seem to evaporate through the 9th, so do your best to clarify and create accurate data. Once you've established the facts and lined up your commitments, more stable progress ensues. Following the Sun's eclipse on the 24th you may feel more motivated to reach into new territory and can see strong success in developing some new material or creating a strong support network within your profession. This is an excellent time to plan a romantic getaway within easy distance, but which offers a change of scenery.

•NOVEMBER•

Activity levels on the home front increase, and you may decide to make some home improvements, move, or become more enterprising around the house. Tension in the family can also escalate, but you are in an excellent position to deal with these issues directly and avoid alienating those who play a significant role in your life. Criticism from others hits close to home, but you can also draw more critical evaluation to yourself by failing to let others know where you stand and how you feel. If you are unhappy in your work situation, you may also decide that it's time to break out of an old pattern and start out fresh. Take advantage of the chance to learn new skills or to improve your skills and abilities through classes, or workshops which can help bolster your sense of self-worth.

•DECEMBER•

With a positive emphasis on creative self-expression, you are likely to enjoy this cycle and experience this time as one of breakthrough into exciting new directions. Love relationships take on an air of excitement and may provide an invigorating inspiration to your artistic sensibilities. It's time to ask for the support from your partner that you need, and to express the depth of your love and affection to others. Allow more hours for play, recreation and spontaneity, but try to stay in familiar territory during the middle part of the month, since jumping into new experiences can have shocking results. Investments and speculative interests show promise early in the month, and again after the 22nd. Your best source of future capital comes from exercising your own creativity and showing your talents to others.

LIBRA – ♎

SEPTEMBER 23 TO OCTOBER 23

Libra's qualities reflect grace, charm and refinement. With your Sun in Libra, you may possess an inner radiance of these qualities and bring a sense of harmony and beauty wherever you go. Your fair-minded objectivity often places you in the position to mediate when others are in dispute, since you can see both sides of an issue. You may have trouble trying to make choices for yourself unless you have plenty of time to weigh all the alternatives. Your sense of logic rarely rests.

Even though you may "understand" a lot about relationships, creating a successful relationship may not be easy for you. Mortal entanglements rarely compare to your ideal partner, but with time, you can develop the right connection as you become more secure within yourself about your own values and needs. You are a true people person, and have a knack for counseling others and public relations. Your refined sensibilities may be highly sought in business, politics or the arts.

THE YEAR AHEAD

A desire to open your mind to new ideas and fill your life with new opportunities can lead you to spend more time in educational pursuits, travel, writing or communication while Jupiter transits through your Solar 3rd House this year. Your confidence and optimism are strong, even though you will be faced with the need to direct and focus your energy and efforts in ways which will increase your effectiveness. The temptation to try everything that comes along can be a problem if you begin to scatter your energy and undermine your overall productivity.

You're in an excellent cycle to study or learn, and may also have the opportunity to teach others (a tremendous learning experience!). Additionally, with Saturn transiting through your Solar 6th House you may have increased responsibilities at work, or could take on a supervisory position which requires more discipline. You can make improvements in your overall health by carefully examining your lifestyle and establishing programs or routines which support and strengthen your vitality. Pushing yourself beyond your physical limits now will be more noticeable — unless you're working to improve your overall stamina and health level.

Your affirmation for the year:
"I am confident about my abilities
to create a bright future."

•JANUARY•

Although the year may begin with a challenge to become more stable and secure, you realize that stability does not necessarily equal inactivity. Watch for political back-stabbing or manipulation from others at work or during business meetings, when your desire to get things moving may not jive with someone else's ideas about maintaining power. Focus on future growth possibilities in order to get out of the quagmire of problems from the past, but realize that you may still have to satisfy some who are more conservative than yourself. Good intentions may not be sufficient to keep the peace, but there is hope after the 21st for more creative and imaginative possibilities.

•FEBRUARY•

Even though Mercury is in retrograde through the 15th, your creativity levels continue to be high, and you may see excellent results from your efforts. However, expect to make some adjustments to proposals or plans early in the month which will satisfy budgetary requirements or time constraints. Think before you speak or sign important documents, since you may find that you've gotten into a situation which is too burdensome if you act impulsively. Support from others gives you the boost you need, and you're definitely in the mood to party and get out of the winter doldrums. Even in the midst of a busy schedule, your inventive approach can make up for the lack of time to share with your sweetie. Watch a tendency to appear to be too detached later in the month, which can alienate the one you wish to draw closer.

•MARCH•

Demands from work can be exhausting, particularly if you've fallen behind schedule, or feel pressured by something you thought was already finished. Your focus may be on more artistic or pleasurable activities than mere duties, but some creative planning on your part allows you to organize your schedule and accomplish your aims more effectively. Take a direct approach when dealing with conflicts at work instead of trying to placate and avoid confrontation. A friend can be the catalyst for a new romance early in the month, although you may may not feel like making a commitment until after the New Moon on the 30th.

•APRIL•

Increasing social activity adds spark to your life, and can stimulate more personable interaction with your peers or coworkers. Your concern for the welfare of others and efforts to make improvements will not go unnoticed. Keeping too much to yourself can have an alienating effect, although you

418 / 1995 MOON SIGN BOOK

may feel a bit too vulnerable to expose your deeper
yearnings to anyone you do not trust near the time
of the Lunar eclipse in Libra on the 15th. Before you
become tempted to make someone else the bad
guy, take a look at your own attitudes and actions
in your personal relationship. Honest interaction
and expression will only lead to improvements,
and if the relationship is really important to you,
the vulnerability may be worthwhile, leading to the
rebirth of a vital love. If a relationship has outlived
its usefulness, your connection is likely to wither
away near the time of the Sun's Eclipse on the 29th.

•MAY•

You're on the move, and may have more opportunities to travel and network with others. Newly
formed contracts and commitments can be more
easily agreed upon prior to the 10th, but long-standing situations may need more time. Your position
can also be boosted by the support of others,
although you may lose a source you thought to be a
sure thing. Mercury's retrograde may bring a
chance to recapture this supporter, but you may discover that you're better off without them. Partnership can undergo changes, and your attentiveness
to your partner's shifting priorities is crucial to
maintaining the integrity of your relationship. Your
wandering eye can get you into trouble mid-month,
but if you're free to pursue the object of your desire
you might be surprised at the end results.

•JUNE•

Educational pursuits, travel and other means of expanding your sense of connection to the world continue to provide inspiration and new direction. However, you also need some time to reflect on changes before you jump into a unknown situation, and will benefit from honoring your intuitive guidance in such matters. You're likely to be thinking a lot about your future, and may need to discuss your options and dreams with your partner before you take action. Even though the sexual chemistry in your love life can be quite enticing early in the month, you may feel reluctant to explore your desires unless the environment is just right. Family ties and home-oriented activities take priority later.

•JULY•

Your public persona may be quite different from the way you feel privately early in the month, and your desire to protect your innermost feelings should be honored. However, if there is strong conflict between the way you feel and what you must do, it is likely to show in the quality of your presentation. Deal first with your inner issues, and then you can keep your personal and private lives in their proper perspective. Cultural, educational or religious activities provide a good outlet for making new contacts, and may stimulate a period of sharing your hopes for the future with your partner. Honor your urge to make contact with your family near the time of the Full Moon on the 12th, even if you keep it brief. Your energy and enthusiasm about your work flow more readily after the 24th, when you may also gain the respect and support from professional allies you've hoped to gain.

•AUGUST•

Advancement or recognition in your career provides the encouragement you need to increase your momentum. Define roles clearly when working in group or cooperative projects, since leaving too many dangling details will open the door for power struggles. Clarify your budget to avoid financial disputes. Love relationships blossom now, and you may feel more wiling to allow another person to move closer to you. Try a different approach in asking for your emotional needs, and be open to the needs of others. Even though it may feel more natural to give than to receive, you have to allow a balance of both in your intimate relationship in order to nourish its growth. Develop a sense of love which has no limitations or conditions, but start with yourself first.

•SEPTEMBER•

Your easy articulate sensibilities can be highly influential in personal and professional situations. You may be called on to mediate conflicts between others, or can feel drawn into disputes which you feel are not your own. Try to maintain your impartiality and know when to step out of the way. Your ideas carry more weight and your ability to communicate your position is strengthened now, although you may feel that you're not quite ready to get your favorite project off the ground yet. Mercury transits in Libra for the next two months, which can support a good period of networking or other interactive activities. Your patience with others can wear thin, however, and you may lose your tolerance for someone who shows poor taste or bad judgment.

•OCTOBER•

You're eager to experience some new energy in your love life, and may be strongly attracted to someone, even though you know nothing about him or her. Try to be clear about your unconscious motivations, since you may just need an escape from the everyday and could be interested in the challenge of something that just breaks up the monotony. This can certainly be a time of self-discovery if you stay tuned-in to your inner needs, and you may finally be able to express your true feelings about a partnership during the Lunar eclipse on the 8th. However, the real key to having your needs met involves supporting your own self-worth and taking action which will bolster your ability to respect and appreciate yourself more fully. Make an effort to stabilize your finances after the Solar Eclipse on the 23rd.

•NOVEMBER•

Take advantage of conferences, meetings or business travel as a means to inspire your creativity and for the chance to meet some new people. You can make progress in your career by letting others know you're out there. Careful attention to financial planning now can also have a stabilizing effect on your emotions, but worry over details which are never clarified can undermine your confidence. Nourish a love relationship through consistent effort toward improving communication instead of just spending time together in mindless activities. If you have the opportunity, you'll also be able to incite some romantic sparks by getting away from it all.

•DECEMBER•

Although many of your efforts may be targeted toward family or home, you can also make progress in your career by staying in touch with your professional allies through various forms of communication. Business meetings or presentations show special promise from the 1st-11th and again after the 26th. However, your family may need more of your time, and your need to connect to them may also be greater than usual for this time of year. Mend fences with siblings early in the month, and know when to stay out of battles. Don't forget to stay open with your partner, since his or her support now can be more meaningful.

SCORPIO – ♏

OCTOBER 23 TO NOVEMBER 23

The qualities of Scorpio represent intensity, passion and transformation. With your Sun in Scorpio, you project an air of intrigue and mystery and can develop a strong sense of the subtle levels of perceiving a situation. You can become a tremendous catalyst for change, and can be an effective healer through your words and actions. However, it may take time for you to learn how to avoid becoming personally involved in such experiences and allow the energy to work through you.

In relationships with others, you may always keep some part of yourself hidden, even after you develop trust. But you can be completely involved in loving and prefer a passionate lover who will allow you to share your deepest desires. Even though you may not think of yourself as overwhelming, you can be, and this can thwart some career opportunities or relationship possibilities unless you find ways to channel your intensity.

THE YEAR AHEAD

Your creative and self-expressive focus is positively supported this year, and you may feel more confident about your abilities. An undercurrent of restlessness may mark your deeper feelings, as though you are primed for some significant alterations in your life, although you may not be entirely clear about the end result of the changes you're sensing. While Jupiter transits through your Solar 2nd House throughout the year you are also likely to feel more optimistic about your financial situation and may have greater resources available to you as a result of your efforts.

You are also likely to feel more willing to take on a committed love relationship, and may become more involved with children than in the past while Saturn transits through your Solar 5th House this year. This is an especially important period in which to fine-tune your talents or abilities, and can mark a cycle of significant discipline and focus in any artistic or creative pursuits. The Solar eclipses complete their last cycle in the Taurus-Scorpio axis for this century, and can have a strong influence on your feelings about yourself and your deeper needs. If you've been waiting for the right time to release old resentment or to heal wounds from the past, it has arrived.

Your affirmation for the year:
"I am filled with love and joy!"

•JANUARY•

Community activities and interaction with others who share your political views or special interests can provide an excellent backdrop for more stable realization of your hopes and dreams. Launch a new project or make an important presentation from the 1st-6th, when your persuasive abilities are exceptional. Be especially careful with your finances midmonth, when you may be too busy with details about other things and can easily miss an important obligation or costs which you hadn't anticipated. If the pressures from work mount, your best way to gain perspective can be a short vacation near the time of the Full Moon on the 16th. This is also a good time to drop some barriers in your intimate relationship and experience the joys of loving each other. Home and family draw your focus after the 21st, although career continues to demand much of your energy.

•FEBRUARY•

You may feel more driven in your desire to attain your ambitions, and may run into some challenges from the status quo in the process. By remaining aware of a system, the rules, or the expectations of a superior and incorporating them into your plans, you will see greater success and encounter fewer obstacles. Meetings, conferences or business travel provide support and encouragement and a good forum to show your skills. Be aware of the possibility of delay or a slowdown in progress during Mercury's retrograde through the 15th, and deal with issues immediately or they may surface again later. More pleasurable pursuits draw your attention after the 20th, when romance and intrigue are like the icing on the cake.

•MARCH•

Artistic or creative projects fare nicely, and you may feel more stimulated by pursuing these areas instead of just taking care of your duties. There's no reason you cannot incorporate enjoyment into your everyday schedule now, but be sure you're paying attention to the needs of your family and your career or you may end up sitting in those box seats by yourself. Make the best use of your resources by joining forces with others in cooperative efforts instead of trying to carry the burden alone. Watch your expectations of others, particularly children and lovers, since you can be disappointed if you place unnecessary demands upon them. Instead, get involved and share your needs, concerns and desires with one another in a more supportive manner.

•APRIL•

Those empty promises about career advancement are not worth your efforts, so focus your energy on situations which offer a better platform for professional growth. Your applied efforts now go a long way toward attracting positive recognition and can bring excellent results. You may still experience some hostility from superiors or antagonism from authorities unless you are staying within the confines they dictate, but you have the ability to turn the tide by watching for signals which indicate defensiveness on the part of others. In all matters, including emotional commitments, you may be asking yourself, "Is it really worth it?" Gauge your value on your deeper feelings instead of focusing on the externals. After all, you have to live with your choices.

•MAY•

You may feel more vulnerable now, especially near the time of the Full Moon in Scorpio on the 14th. However, this is a powerful time to eliminate attitudes which stand in the way of your personal fulfillment. Tension with your partner may be the result of secretive or deceptive actions, and you may lose your sense of trust unless you maintain honesty with yourself. Conflicts about career can filter into your relationship, and you may even feel some pressure from family or their expectations which make it difficult to reach a decision based purely on your own needs. While sorting through the debris, stay connected to the knowledge that you deserve to have your needs met.

•JUNE•

Clarify details about your finances now, and use Mercury's retrograde period through the 16th to uncover details or finish reports which outline your financial picture. Joint resources can be a source of tension, especially if you had plans and your partner stands in the way. Instead of holding back, try to be forthcoming with your partner about your hopes and dreams, since any undermining on your part could damage your relationship. Their lack of support (or your lack of support of their efforts) could simply be a matter of not understanding the whole picture. The larger perspective is easier to grasp after the 21st, so perhaps a little patience would be helpful in reaching a resolution.

•JULY•

Positive alliances with others bolster your career and encourage you to become more fully involved in community activities or political action. Travel and educational pursuits are also highlighted, and may lead the way to professional advancement and recognition. You may also become intrigued by some interesting reading, and can use this time to probe your own consciousness about your ethical and moral ideals. Rough waters in personal relationships calm now, and you may feel more confident about your love life. Excitement from unanticipated connections with others can be highly invigorating and may spark the beginning of a new love or the revitalization of a relationship which had lost its energy.

•AUGUST•

Even though your career may be moving along nicely, it's easy to be overconfident and ignore the expectations from others which can cause problems if they are not met. Differences with authorities over your financial ideas or proposed budget for a project could be distressing, but you can present a plan which satisfies them later in the month. Your enthusiasm can burn out more easily now, so if you begin to feel overwhelmed or disinterested, take time to recharge. Spend time working behind the scenes whenever possible, but realize that you will probably be pulled into the spotlight before you're ready to deal with it. Friends can provide the encouragement and support you crave, although you may differ on political issues.

•SEPTEMBER•

Professional connections work to your benefit, although trusting someone who is jealous of your position with important information early in the month can work against you. Pay attention to the details of contracts and make sure to follow-through on significant communication to avoid the delays caused by having to repeat the same thing later. Friends continue to play a significant role, and your relationship may unexpectedly change directions and become more romantic if the situation is right for both of you. Any love relationship benefits from more direct action on your part, and you may feel especially willing to ignite a situation which has been dormant for too long.

•OCTOBER•

Even though you may run into problems due to deceptive communication or incomplete information through the 13th, the situation may be purely unintentional. You still need to take responsibility to clarify any problems which arise, or you can unwittingly undermine your position. This is an excellent time to get rid of things from your past which are no longer part of your life, but burning all your bridges is probably not the best idea. Your passion to create life on your own terms can extend into every aspect of your life, but is especially important in the personal arena of love relationships. This is the time to create room for love and self-acceptance instead of feeling that love is something which should come from someone else. Search your inner self during the Solar eclipse in Scorpio on the 24th and allow the masks you've worn to hide from your own needs to drop away.

•NOVEMBER•

You're eager to fill your life, but can easily overspend or exhaust your resources if your motivation comes from a fear of loss. Now is the time to build your reserves and find the best ways to increase your material worth, professional support and emotional stability. Impulsiveness can be too costly, so avoid the temptation to use that plastic money unless you have adequate reserves to cover your spending. You may feel somewhat awkward in an emotionally vulnerable circumstance mid-month, but may feel more confident if you are in familiar territory. Finally, your hard work pays off, and applied efforts on your part can make the difference in every aspect of your life. Just stay alert to that small voice within yourself that whispers encouragement or caution.

•DECEMBER•

Interaction with others in your professional field can answer some of the questions you've had about your goals. This is a good time to attend workshops or seminars which help you sharpen your skills, and can also be an excellent period to build professional friendships. During the Full Moon on the 6th, make a careful evaluation of your finances. You may feel satisfied that you can take a reasonable speculative risk, or you might be ready to consider purchasing property. Your attitudes and values are shifting, and can also reflect changes in your relationship. Unexpected news or contact may lead to a breakthrough in a close relationship, but can also be the key to success in your artistic pursuits.

SAGITTARIUS – ♐

NOVEMBER 23 TO DECEMBER 22

Sagittarius represents the qualities of expansion, optimism and generosity. With your Sun in Sagittarius, you may project these qualities and can show levels of confidence and warmth which inspire others. Your direct manner and independent approach to life give you the image of one who is footloose and fancy free, but you are serious about your desires to fulfill your dreams. Honesty is high on your priority list, and you appreciate the value of an open mind. However, your interests can vary widely, and you can confuse others who may think you've settled into a niche when you suddenly pack your bags and head off on a new adventure.

Rather than destroying things in order to change the world, it is your hope that through uplifting the minds of humanity you can create trust and understanding. You need a partner who can allow you plenty of room to follow these ideals, and will flourish in a career which gives you the freedom to be yourself. With your ability to inspire others to believe in themselves, you can use your influence to help shape the philosophy of a company, city, state or nation.

THE YEAR AHEAD

You may feel uplifted throughout the entire year while Jupiter, your ruling planet, transits in Sagittarius. This period is closely linked to the year 1983, and may allow you to take steps to fulfill some of the promises which opened to you during that time. However, instead of feeling a need to drastically alter everything in your life, you may crave some real stability and are challenged to balance your responsibilities with your needs to reach toward broader horizons. Many of the connections you make this year will continue to have an influence in your life for the next decade.

If you are involved in writing, publishing or other communicative career activities, this can be your chance to advance your career and expand your influence. You are also experiencing positive energies for the pursuit of education through formal programs and may find travel to be a positive life-altering experience. Because Saturn is transiting in conflicting square to the Jupiter cycle, your outreach may be more confined, but you will also be able to focus your energy more readily.

Your affirmation for the year:
"I have abundance enough to share."

•JANUARY•

Your self-esteem improves with Venus and Jupiter transiting in your sign, but you can undermine that feeling by allowing pressures from others, guilt or uncertainty to dampen your enthusiasm. Alter your expectations in a way which will allow you to rely more upon yourself and less upon others when making important choices. Although this can be a powerful time for career, you may also decide that you can no longer deal with a situation which thwarts your progress and break away from unrealistic restraints. Consider your ambitions and long-range plans carefully before you take action which could drastically alter the course of your life.

•FEBRUARY•

Travel and education set the trend, and can help you further your professional reputation. Mercury's retrograde cycle through the 15th can be an exceptional time for learning, and may also offer a chance to reconnect with someone who has been helpful in the past. Be sure to complete projects which have been dangling, and make a special effort to follow through on lagging communication. Take advantage of every opportunity to make presentations, attend conferences or participate in political action which supports your ideals. Plan a romantic interlude away from your daily routine near the time of the Full Moon on the 15th. But after the 20th you might prefer a cozy fire and time to cuddle up with your sweetheart (or a good book!).

•MARCH•

Excellent reception for your ideas inspires you to pursue your plan of action. Presentations, business travel or other connection with those in your field provide a chance for you to let your light shine. It can be hard for others to resist your enthusiasm in either business or personal circumstances. Through your attempts to create better communication, all your relationships can improve, even though you may still feel some strong resistance from your family about some of your plans or actions. Your honest disclosures help to clarify the situation mid-month. However, you can blemish your bright image through impulsive action or incomplete preparation, so know what you're talking about before you open your mouth. Design your spending plans carefully to avoid blowing your budget.

•APRIL•

Imaginative ideas keep the momentum going and influence your career path in a positive manner. Although conservative factions are still at work, you may be able to satisfy them by showing the direction new plans can take. Watch a tendency to include unnecessary information or to confuse your hopes with the facts, which can be misleading and may generate skepticism on the part of your detractors. Your primary interest revolves around your love life, and you will want to make room for the full expression of your most passionate desires. Share your hopes and plans for the future with your loved ones near the time of the Lunar eclipse on the 15th, but know that it is your vision which is likely to guide you along the path. Whether you're initiating a new relationship or involved in an existing commitment, your charm is difficult to resist.

•MAY•

Demands from others can pull you away from self-involved situations and may even influence a successful outcome. As long as you maintain your high ethical standards and can reach a satisfactory agreement, this can be an excellent time to participate in joint ventures. Investments may also show good rewards early in the month, although you might have more satisfactory results if you can allow the situation to ripen more fully before harvesting your profits. Communication can be problematic due to delays or regulatory red tape from the 21st-31st, a situation intensified by Mercury's retrograde on the 24th. If your plans stall, don't panic. Focus on clearing up the difficulties and realize that when things are moving again (and they will), you'll be in good form.

•JUNE•

Interactions with others draw your primary focus through cooperative ventures, social activities and partnerships. With Mars transiting through your Solar 10th House, a competitive spirit arises which can spur you to achieve more than you thought possible in your career. You are likely to get in over your head from the 11th–18th, when it's difficult to say no to some of the opportunities knocking at your door. If you feel short-tempered, it may be because you have little resilience remaining due to the demands of your schedule. Release tension by staying physically active and keep your focus on your priorities, since straying too far from your obligations now can be extremely burdensome later.

•JULY•

Finances and situations involving shared resources or partnerships can be in a tangle. These situations or legal disputes can take some time to resolve, particularly if you're dealing with a stubborn attitude. New financial dealings require you to be alert to the fine print, since you may act impulsively instead of researching a situation. Emotionally, you may crave more time to feel close to those you love. Resisting the need to drop some of your barriers which have blocked intimacy can weaken your bond with your partner, especially if career pressures or family problems have created a wall

between you. It may be easier to take a break after
the New Moon on the 27th, but that can seem too
far away early in the month. Make an effort to find
time for intimate sharing or quiet reflection.

•AUGUST•

By sharing your spiritual needs and hopes for the
future with your partner, you strengthen your
commitment to one another. Friends can also be a
powerful source of reinforcement, and may encourage you to follow that path which allows you to
finally see the realization of your dreams. Your
enthusiasm sparkles and generates new backing
from those who can bolster your career. In fact, you
may achieve the recognition which you had hoped
to reach. High levels of inspiration lift your spirits
and help boost your confidence about expressing
your ideas and desires. Take advantage of opportunities to write, travel, speak or attend conferences
which will allow you to interact with others who
understand and further your aims.

•SEPTEMBER•

A positive attitude on your part goes a long way
toward shaping your success, advancement and
recognition from authorities or others who can
advance your career. Special interest groups or
political action can also have a strong influence on

your path. By showing appreciation for those people, situations and things you value, you strengthen the momentum of your efforts. It is also important that you value yourself and your efforts, allowing your own satisfaction with a job well done to shine through in a healthy way. Familial ties can require extra attention near the time of the Full Moon on the 8th, when you may experience a striking contrast in your perception of your parents and finally release some pent-up emotions from the past. An emerging sense of freedom bolsters your self-expression on the 24th.

•OCTOBER•

Even though you may have several opportunities presented to you, careful investigation is important prior to your decision to participate. By reading the fine print, you can avoid becoming tangled in loopholes which escape your attention unless you're looking for them. The Lunar Eclipse on the 8th stimulates an acceleration in realizing some of your hopes, and can mark a time when your self-expression leads you to invite others to share your dreams. This is an excellent time to allow your spontaneity to work to your advantage in romance, in relationship to your children or through your creative self-expression. However, after the solar eclipse on the 24th, you may feel less impulsive and might prefer extra time for quiet reflection.

•NOVEMBER•

You are feeling highly energized and need good outlets for your restless energy. Romance can flourish, whether you're seeking a new love or deeply involved in an existing one. This is your time to forge a path and create life on your own terms, although you may still feel some hesitation due to self-doubt. Examine the origins of this feeling, since it may be a result of early influences which are no longer valid. Your urge to break away from these restraints can be frustrated by circumstances which impede progress—you know, one of those "tests" so prominent in life experience. You'll see significant progress following the New Moon on the 22nd.

•DECEMBER•

Stabilize your finances by making shrewd moves and using your best judgment in investment situations. It's time to expand, but you also need to avoid the tendency to stretch yourself beyond reasonable limitations. Basically, your judgment should be sound, and your actions may stir up changes which gain attention. Your lead can be the model for others, but that doesn't mean you're responsible for their actions. Be alert to the possibilities of deception or faulty judgment based on impulsive decision-making from the 15th-22nd. Plan to get away from the rat race for a while after the 22nd, in a romantic interlude.

CAPRICORN – ♑

DECEMBER 22 TO JANUARY 21

Capricorn represents the qualities of structure, responsibility and practicality. With the Sun in Capricorn, your ego is strongly shaped by a need to be in control of life. Your ambitions can be high, and if you are focused on a particular goal, your determination can be unwavering. By showing reliability and taking responsible action, you can easily gain the respect and admiration of others.

Even though you might prefer the simple beauty of nature, your drive to reach the peak can lead you into demanding professional situations. You may have difficulty allowing yourself to become emotionally involved with others unless you have achieved the level of success in the outside world which satisfies your goals. Keeping your heart on ice is not easy, since you are a sensitive individual who needs support and love. You can bring a sense of stability into a relationship, but you also enjoy the sensual pleasures of life. To repress or deny these needs will ultimately work against your satisfaction with yourself and your life experience.

THE YEAR AHEAD

Even though you may still be in the midst of shifting some of your priorities, you are experiencing greater stability and order in your life this year, and may feel more confident about your choices and life direction. Saturn, your planetary ruler, is transiting through your Solar 3rd House in a supportive relationships to your Sun, and brings a positive sense of structure and self-confirmation. You may be involved in educational pursuits, or just taking more time to improve your skills, understanding or abilities.

Although the cycle of Jupiter during 1995 can bring a period of stronger connection to your inner self, you may have some difficulty allowing sufficient time in your life to listen more carefully to that inner voice. By acknowledging this aspect of yourself, you can become more confident that your decisions and actions are in harmony with your spiritual and emotional needs. In many ways, this cycle encourages a feeling of acceptance of the natural order of things, which in itself can create a feeling of inner peace as you release the past with love and open to new possibilities. This is your time to discover new dreams or awaken dreams which have been slumbering for decades.

Your affirmation for the year:
"I have faith in myself."

•JANUARY•

The year begins with imagination and hope, with a strong sense of confidence in your ability to create a more positive future. Significant business negotiations or meetings can launch you into an exceptional position through the 20th. Mercury enters a retrograde cycle on the 26th, when some alliances may drop away, leaving you in the precarious position of carrying the ball without a complete team. By developing a more comprehensive support system or adequate back-up mechanisms, this interruption should not cause difficult setbacks. Romance also plays a powerful role this month, and you may feel more willing to take risks meeting someone new or sharing deeper feelings in an existing relationship. Just be careful to project a realistic image of yourself, since it's easy to try to adapt yourself to what you think someone else desires.

•FEBRUARY•

Clarification of financial dealings during Mercury's retrograde through the 15th helps you avoid pitfalls which could lead to disputes. You may also secure the support of others, although investors or partners need to define their role or involvement before you agree to their participation. Otherwise, you may run into power struggles which undermine the effectiveness of your undertaking. In personal relationships, you may face issues of intimacy and vulnerability. Even if you've been with your partner for a while, you may discover some hidden secrets which have been a barrier for some time. Search within yourself for your own fears, and determine whether or not you're in a safe position to expose your deeper needs to your partner. A more freely expressive sharing emerges after the 21st, with time to indulge some of your fantasies.

•MARCH•

Your concentration on networking, communication and data-gathering leads to clarification of the facts which allows you to feel more confident in proceeding with a project or idea. However, you may still feel some resistance from highly conservative factions if you're moving into experimental areas. Your understanding of their concerns and your honest evaluation of your own doubts will help you strengthen your position and assure greater success. If you feel defensive, take a careful look at the reasons for your vulnerability. You may have good cause to protect yourself, but if there is none, then it's time to drop some of those barriers and banish doubts. Pay attention to demands from family after the 24th, when careful consideration of your feelings is necessary before you speak your mind.

•APRIL•

A feeling of rebellion against the controls others try to place on your life may stem from unresolved frustrations with your parents. During the Lunar eclipse on the 15th, you can more easily reach into those closets of emotion and get rid of some garbage which undermines your sense of confidence in yourself. It's crucial to be aware of the hidden agendas (including your own) operating in the work place, since this may be the key to understanding the resistance you've been experiencing. After the 21st your creative and industrious efforts overcome the resistance and forge a path which is more enjoyable and pleasing to you. Find ways to express yourself and allow your spontaneity to emerge during the Solar eclipse on the 29th.

•MAY•

Higher levels of creative energy and applied imagination help you gain favor with others and make the improvements you've been considering. This can help offset some of the pressures in your relationship which arise from repressed or unresolved issues from the past. If you're sharing more enjoyable experiences, you are likely to feel more free about expressing your feelings. If you're involved in a relationship which is deteriorating and you are unable to revitalize it, you may reach an end to your involvement. A situation which has room for growth can blossom now if you're willing to open your heart. Finances can be a source of concern, particularly in regard to tax liability or indebtedness, so be realistic before you take any risks.

•JUNE•

Much of the tension which has been keeping you on edge seems to resolve now in favor of a more relaxed and confident attitude. Take advantage of educational opportunities and situations which allow you to strengthen your kills or knowledgability. Everyone may seem overly concerned with their own circumstances, to such a great extent that they cannot hear or understand your opinions or ideas until Mercury leaves its retrograde cycle on the 17th. Use this period to address the concerns voiced by others, or to improve your product or idea, since you may have greater success launching it after the 28th anyway. Watch a tendency to isolate yourself unnecessarily, and get out into the world and socialize a bit more.

•JULY•

It's easy to become bogged down comparing yourself with other people or their situations. Even though partnerships are a strong focal point, you may feel uncooperative if you sense that your partner is gaining greater recognition than you. You may feel unnecessarily competitive, but still need to honor that urge by channeling your energy into healthy challenges, such as sports or games, instead of playing psychological games which undermine the strength of your relationships. Differences in ethical or moral viewpoints can lead to a breakup of an association, and may test your own stance. Pay attention to your feelings and positions during the Full Moon in Capricorn on the 12th, and know that others may be more capable of understanding your needs and demands during this time.

•AUGUST•

Everything seems to be work related or carry some type of baggage that seems heavy or exhausting. Clarify your motivations, since you may be trying to accomplish aims which are counterproductive to your real needs or desires. Financial control dilemmas arise again this month, and may be particularly trying when dealing with joint ventures. Even though you may be tempted to take your marbles and go home, it's crucial to work out the difficulties so you don't drag them into other areas or new situations. Unforeseen expenses can stall progress on a project, but you should be back on track by the 26th. Just don't jump into anything without knowing the risks and options, and define the chain of command before you take on new responsibilities.

•SEPTEMBER•

Although a flexible attitude stimulates faster progress early in the month, you still may have to take a firm stand on your position in business dealings. Draw support by presenting a plan that brings traditional values in line with innovative ideas, instead of scrapping one for the other. Your patience with family is limited, particularly if you feel that your parents or their priorities are taking control over a situation you want to manage. Pure rebellion may not be your style, but to avoid alienating support from those you care about, create a structure or plan that acknowledges needs beyond your own, but which allows you to feel that you are breaking out of unnecessary restraints toward fulfilling your needs. Reconsider your options after Mercury retrogrades on the 22nd.

•OCTOBER•

Unexpected changes early in the month can throw you off balance, but may also get you out of a rut! Before you decide to alter your life, weigh the alternatives and give the situation some time to develop. If you have limited options presented and a situation seems out of your control, determine your best response before jumping into the action. Your deeper feelings and needs for stability can guide you during the Lunar Eclipse on the 8th, although you may still be unable to attain the predictability your life had prior to these shifts. Get involved with your community; connect with friends and others who share your interests and take on leadership roles. Even though you may doubt yourself, chances are that you are the right person for the job.

•NOVEMBER•

You may need time to rejuvenate or rest, and can benefit by taking time out of your busy schedule to restore energy. However, you still need to stay in contact with friends or allies. Relationships which demand too much of your attention now can feel like unwanted burdens, and it's critical that you find ways to limit your participation which will allow you to stay connected while still maintaining your own autonomy. Many career opportunities may be on a slower track, but remain committed to your objective or goals. Do your homework this month and get everything in order, since you'll have little time to regroup later.

•DECEMBER•

You have a stronger foothold now and can take definite steps to create the right situations in developing your aims and objectives. If you've been waiting for the right time to make a romantic overture, the right time may be now. Your confidence level may be higher if you've first developed a line of communication. In business dealings, you have the advantage, although you may be tempted to reach out to someone who has little substance. Investigate the situation before signing contracts or agreements, and walk away if your suspicions are confirmed. However, some risks are worth taking. Your magic has returned!

AQUARIUS – ♒

JANUARY 21 TO FEBRUARY 19

Aquarius qualities project the unconventional, futuristic and universal. With your Sun in Aquarius, your ego is connected to the need to express the unique qualities of yourself in ways which will set you apart from the crowd. You have a high regard for the quality which sets human beings aside from other living creatures—cognitive thought. You may spend much of your own life developing your mind and awareness. You may seem to march to a different drummer, and resist restraints upon your freedom of expression.

You need plenty of space and opportunity to express your originality through your career, and can be successful in many fields of endeavor. However, you might prefer areas which are a mental challenge. Friendship is important, along with the unconditional love which friends express to one another. When seeking a special relationship, you will be most comfortable if you know you are friends above all else. Your loyalty and devotion in a relationship can be endless and timeless once you've made a commitment.

THE YEAR AHEAD

During 1995, Uranus, your planetary ruler, moves into Aquarius, marking the beginning of a long cycle (about eight years) of personal realization and new direction. The intensity and timing of these changes will depend upon your exact birth date. By releasing the vestiges of the past which are no longer relevant to your life and moving into a freer form of self-expression, you can experience some exceptional shifts in your life circumstances which seem much like taking flight.

Throughout this year, the transit of Jupiter in your Solar 11th House signifies a time when your goals and life can be redirected in such as way that will open new horizons through your career. Your vision of the future may be more positive and can be confirmed by greater satisfaction with your work. To make the most of this cycle, you will also be challenged to use your energy and resources at an optimum level and avoid wasting what is truly valuable. Saturn's transit through your Solar 2nd House tests your values, and can expose those areas of your self-worth which are unstable.

Your affirmation for the year:
"I trust my intuitive guidance."

•JANUARY•

By becoming more active in pursuit of your special interests or political aims, you may meet influential individuals who can open doors to greater success. You may also have a strong influence on the success of others. It's easy to become overly committed, so review your schedule and be honest with yourself about your time and resources prior to your agreement to participate. Unexpected expenditures or time constraints may emerge which disrupt your plans. Financial squabbles can dampen a relationship, but before you argue over money with your partner, determine if that is the real issue. You may be reacting to situations which have their roots in the past instead of responding to your current circumstances.

•FEBRUARY•

Make careful choices regarding your professional or personal alliances, since associating with individuals or causes which are not in your best interests can be costly. Mercury's cycle in Aquarius continues all month, but during the retrograde through the 16th you may feel that you're making a series of adjustments concerning things you began in January. Relationships can be filled with turmoil, particularly if your partner is feeling a lack of support from you. You may become so embroiled in the battle that you lose track of what you were arguing about, so try to take some time away from the conflict to get clear about your real feelings. If there is no hope for repair, it may be time to end the relationship. Before you jump into something new, take a deep breath. That new love may exist only in your fantasies!

•MARCH•

Progressive change is best achieved by linking an innovative plan with an existing situation, since you still have some conservative opposition to a totally new concept. Your creative imagination works to your benefit, and some of those projects you pulled off the shelf last month are looking pretty good right now. Watch for some competition or challenge to your position, and be ready to put forth your best efforts by mid-month. Finances need some extra attention, and it's probably best to review your budget more than once to be sure you're staying on track. In matters of the heart, try giving more of yourself, knowing that loving is a process of giving and receiving. This is an excellent time for adventurous romance and sharing your fantasies.

•APRIL•

Keeping lines of communication open and following through on important informational projects can be exciting and leads to career success. However, you may run into some misleading data, or can even uncover deception in the ranks, so be alert to the details of contracts and negotiations, and watch for signs of jealousy or undermining near the time of the Lunar eclipse on the 15th. You may be on the go a lot this month, and can run into some unexpected disruptions in your plans, so try to be flexible. If you're open to change, shifting circumstances can give you an opportunity to take the lead. However, demands from home or family can put a damper on your plans later in the month.

•MAY•

Disagreement over contracts or family resources can create problems, but you can find a solution through imaginative options. Stay in touch, and avoid the tendency to try to wish something away. Mercury transits through your Solar 5th House for the next two months, stimulating powerful mental creativity and drawing situations into your life requiring you to express your feelings, thoughts and needs. If you are dissatisfied with a relationship, talk about your concerns. Arguments or conflicts, when handled with compassion, can lead to better understanding of mutual needs. Ignoring anger now will only lead to distorted feelings about the relationship. If you're beginning a new relationship, let go of old fears arising from past experiences and trust your intuitive guidance.

•JUNE•

Your creative energy continues to be strong, although you may have some internal conflicts between what you want to be doing and your obligations to others. Clarify these concerns within yourself to avoid undermining your own efforts. If you experience problems dealing with joint finances or investments, seek out compromises which work to your mutual benefit. Just be careful to avoid getting caught holding the bag while your partner gets away with little responsibility or effort. During the Full Moon on the 12th you have a chance to break out of your past and deal with a situation from its current position. You may also feel more free from attachments which inhibit your growth on personal or professional levels. The most crucial issues involve your ability to allow yourself to go more deeply into your emotional needs without letting your mind get in the way.

•JULY•

You may feel that all you are doing is working, no matter what the circumstances. Your attention to those duties and responsibilities to which you have obligated yourself can place you in a position of strength. If you experience some delays in returns from your speculative investments or creative efforts, keep the faith. You may simply need to clarify some of the details before things get moving again. If you're single now, you might prefer to stay unattached for a while, since getting caught up in another's issues will not seem to be at all appealing. If you are involved in a commitment, then you are likely to hunger for more spark and less predictability. Search within yourself for ways to change your own approach or attitudes and determine what you are willing to do to make changes.

•AUGUST•

Cooperative associations can be critical to your success, and you'll experience better results by offering your support and admiration for the efforts of others. Even though you may feel positive confirmation in regard to partnerships or joint ventures, you may still need to renegotiate your position to get the most from your association. Social obligations can have a beneficial effect on your career, and you may even enjoy the social aspect of business gatherings more than in the past. Take advantage of these times to show your talents and diversity. Financial matters require extra attention later in the month, when it's also best to avoid speculation in favor of taking time to research your options. Take advantage of business travel, conferences and meetings to present your ideas.

•SEPTEMBER•

Your feelings about a financial situation can alter your perception of the facts from the 1st through the time of the Full Moon on the 8th, although it is probably important to consider both. Make an effort to keep business separate from emotional ties whenever possible. You may have a change of heart about your position on an issue which can alter your plans early in the month, although you may sense that situations at work are somewhat unstable and may require even further alterations.

Interactions with others on the professional front are paramount, and even though you may not like somebody, you're likely to have consistent dealings with them in order to accomplish the job at hand. Your involvement in pursuits which stimulate your mind and expand your awareness can draw you toward better circumstances for intimate relationships after the 24th.

•OCTOBER•

Mercury's retrograde through the 13th can work to your benefit in uncovering the real facts of a situation and stabilizing supportive alliances which assure a stronger position in negotiations, legal disputes or business presentations. However, it's probably best to wait until later in the month to sign final contracts, since your plans may be changing and iron-clad agreements could limit your options. Improve your love relationship by getting away from routine. Returning to a scene which was once meaningful in your relationship can ignite a flame which has been faltering. Watch your own tendency to feel aloof or withdrawn during the Lunar eclipse on the 8th, when you may really want to say something important but fear getting locked into a commitment that limits your freedom. Look carefully at your fears, and be aware of your tendency to overly romanticize a situation without considering the reality before you take a definitive stance.

•NOVEMBER•

Your confidence and optimism are exceptionally high, and you may feel more comfortable in community involvement or association with special interests. These circumstances can boost your standing and may lead to improving your reputation, but be sure you can afford the time before you declare your commitment. You may run into tempting career opportunities, but without investigating the details you could become drawn into a circumstance which has greater responsibilities than you were lead to believe. Once these are clarified, you can decide. Streamline for efficiency and eliminate activities which drain your energy.

•DECEMBER•

Finances improve now, and you may feel some relief from obligations which once drained your resources. Some time for creative reflection and preparation for the future is highly beneficial to your psyche, and may also give you the insight which will allow you to improve your life. A romantic relationship can blossom into a significant commitment, and you may find your feelings deepening. Share your favorite pleasures and give yourself time to enjoy your fantasies. However, be alert to the situations brewing behind the scenes midmonth to make sure your position is still stable. Then, sit back and enjoy the fruits of your labors.

PISCES – ♓

FEBRUARY 19 TO MARCH 21

The qualities represented by Pisces are associated with the aspects of life that rise above the ordinary into the world of imagination, poetry and compassion. With your Sun in Pisces, your ego is filtered through a visionary quality. Others may not realize your strengths, since your sensitivity may be more apparent. But much of your strength arises from those sensibilities which allow you to touch the spiritual, artistic, beautiful and imaginative elements that shape the deeper aspects of the human psyche. You may prefer a career which allows you to be involved with uplifting the human spirit and need to be allowed to grow at your own pace.

Romance may have been invented by Pisces, and you can become completely involved in the dance of love. You may seek a partner who feels like a soul mate, but you can also be easily deceived in affairs of the heart. By staying aware of the difference between your needs and the needs of others, you can keep your emotional boundaries more clearly intact and enjoy more fulfilling relationships.

THE YEAR AHEAD

You may feel the stimulus to break through barriers which have prevented you from realizing your dreams in your career, relationships and spiritual quest. This is a year of inspiration and focus and a time during which many opportunities to improve your life situation are presented to you while Jupiter transits through your Solar 10th House. But your awareness of the realities and responsibilities required of you is also strong, with Saturn transiting in Pisces. To make the most of this time, it is crucial that you put forth your best efforts and avoid a tendency to take blocks in your path as a sign of defeat. Those blocks may serve the purpose of punctuating the need to look at elements of your life which need to be dealt with realistically or eliminated entirely.

Educational opportunities, travel or networking with others in your field of interest help you expand your proficiency this year. You may also feel drawn to explore different cultures or beliefs and can experience this as a year of more comprehensive awareness of yourself, your life and of the totality of the world in which you live.

Your affirmation for the year:
I am aware of the truth of myself.

•JANUARY•

Determining your goals for the future is crucial, and you may feel more confident about moving toward achieving them if you have the support of friends or others who believe in you. Use your creative imagination and ability to visualize to help you create a real feeling of moving toward these goals. Competitive situations can arise, and you may feel caught between the demands of different factions at work. Establish your loyalties before you become drawn into a situation which is uncomfortable. A partnership can be tested to the limit with turmoil escalating out of control if either of you fails to stay in touch with your real needs. Counsel from a friend or trusted advisor helps alleviate the situation. Loving relationships are more delightful during the Full Moon on the 16th.

•FEBRUARY•

Strong alliances from friends and professional associates keep the light shining in your life. Community activities or special interest groups offer enjoyable experiences, and you may discover a new love through sharing your favorite interests. An existing relationship is strengthened through sharing your dreams, and you may find that your image of the future is positively altered by allowing someone else to be part of your plans. During Mercury's retrograde through the 15th you may feel progress slowing and may have difficulty getting the information you need to get something moving. Concentrate on going back to the source of previous situations, or upon completing projects already underway. And don't let turmoil at work distract you from your responsibilities.

•MARCH•

Persistent focus allows you to stay on course, even though disputes over job responsibilities can be a problem. Clarify what is expected of you or get details about legal or tax situations before you proceed. And be aware of the influence of your emotional attachments when making important decisions. Contracts or agreements are best after the 14th, even though you may be on opposite sides of the fence prior to that time. Even though competitive or disagreeable aspects of a relationship seem to be the order of the day, you can reach an understanding and move into more free-flowing interaction. But you may also decide that you no longer wish to continue your involvement and break away if a resolution cannot be reached near the time of the Full Moon on the 17th.

•APRIL•

Greater concerns about your financial obligations can be worrisome through the time of the Lunar Eclipse on the 15th, although you can strengthen your position during this time by attention to budget and elimination of unnecessary expenditures. Business conferences or meetings can bring positive results after the 18th. You may be more focused on long-term than immediate situations, and even in matters of the heart you may be considering more long-term options. Your emotional sensitivity increases, and you can allow fears based on past losses to dampen your enthusiasm in a romantic situation or to undermine you own feelings of self esteem. Open your heart to forgiveness and release the past, making room to listen to your inner voice during the Solar Eclipse on the 29th.

•MAY•

Diffuse misunderstandings before they have a chance to escalate by staying in contact with authorities or family members. Selfish attitudes have a detrimental effect on any relationship at this time, and you may decide to walk away from a circumstance which is one-sided. A long-term project at work can seem like it's gone on forever, but you're heading down the home stretch and can meet your deadline through consistent effort. If conservative factions or legal details get in the way

of your progress, clarify who's in charge and strive
to reach consensus. Once Mercury enters its retrograde cycle on the 24th you may run into silly arguments which seem to have little relevance. But if
they block resolution, the do have relevance, so try
to get the facts straight and keep things moving.

•JUNE•

Some situations this month may seem like a repeat
of the battles of January, although now you can see
the whole picture more clearly and can perform
better. Your personal aims can be altered by pressure from others or even by disruptions due to the
influence of others. You may have to work harder
to stay in touch with your own priorities, but by
doing so, you'll see the wheels of progress rolling
again. Use Mercury's retrograde through the 17th
as a time to put the finishing touches on agreements and to satisfy long-standing obligations. But
be cautions of those you trust with valuable information or property early in the month, since you
could be mislead by someone whose motives are
unscrupulous. Allow extra time for family matters
or home improvements later in the month, and get
ready for more enjoyable pleasures after the New
Moon on the 27th.

•JULY•

Creative and artistic pursuits are highly favored now, and by taking advantage of this time to showcase your talents or abilities you may gain the recognition that will allow you to further your pursuits. Enchantment is in the air, and you can bring this sense into your everyday life as well as using your imagination in relationships with lovers, children or friends. You can become the essence of love and compassion, but only if you allow your feelings to flow freely without judging your worth in a negative sense. You have discipline and imagination working to your benefit now, but can be distracted by competition or others who seem to need more of your talents and energy than you can comfortably give to them. Keep your priorities in order.

•AUGUST•

Review your financial records and take time to look into joint ventures to determine their validity in your life. Taxes, insurance or debt issues can be a source of frustration, particularly if you try to sweep them under the carpet. Your partnership needs reevaluation, and you will benefit by determining the types of roles you can play. Old wounds may surface in close relationships, or if you've lost trust in your partner it can affect your sexual intimacy. Contemplation of your deeper feelings is crucial to the outcome of this situation, since trying to satisfy surface problems will only add to the conflict. At work, watch for hidden agendas, and be alert to the possibilities of undermining of your efforts by another who is jealous of your position.

•SEPTEMBER•

Getting more involved in social activities can strengthen your position at work or may lead to career opportunities. But your greatest possibility for growth is likely to come from direct involvement in educational pursuits or travel which broaden your knowledge and understanding. You may also have a chance to guide or teach others, and by sharing your skills or understanding can confirm your own abilities. During the Full Moon in Pisces on the 8th you may feel more connected to your need to be part of a harmonious partnership. But you also must air your concerns and needs in order to strengthen your bond. Honesty with yourself and your partner about your emotional attachments helps you overcome barriers to intimacy after the 24th.

•OCTOBER•

It may be impossible to move forward in relationships until you deal with unfinished business, some of which may have nothing to do with your current situation. Watch your dreams, since they can be a clue to your own internal conflicts. By delving into your psyche now you can eliminate some old ghosts which keep interfering with your growth. At work, this is an excellent time to research details or clarify budget disputes, especially during Mercury's retrograde through the 13th. Avoid becoming mislead by an associate whose selfish aims may not be immediately apparent. By the time of the Solar Eclipse on the 23rd you may have a broader view of the picture. Trust your creative impulses, and stay involved with situations that fill your soul.

•NOVEMBER•

Although you may not always feel exceptionally driven to achieve your ambitions, gaining some recognition would certainly feel great right now. Opportunities arise through travel, study, writing or publishing which can improve your career and may also strengthen your faith in yourself. It is quite likely that you will rise into apparently sudden prominence, and your manner of dealing with your increased influence can determine the difference between success and failure. You are perfectly willing to put forth the effort, but can be intimidated by someone else who seems to be stronger. Your allies may be hoping for your success instead of cheering for the old champion. In all relationships determine your limitations, and take on responsibilities which belong to you instead of trying to carry the burden for everyone else.

•DECEMBER•

Your leadership or support in political affairs or community activities can inspire the types of change which bring greater peace and understanding of a difficult situation. You are challenged to allow more love and support to enter your life, and this can be hard, since it probably feels easier for you to give than it is to receive. A new experience of love arises after the 14th, when you can enjoy realizing some of your dreams. You are more capable of joining your imaginative fantasies with the reality of a situation in your career, as well, and can be the guiding light when others are uncertain of their faith. Share time with friend, and widen that circle to include those who may only be waiting for your invitation.

Resource Guide

★ Products and Services

Now <u>You</u> Can Own
The Ultimate Talking Board Set!

Enjoy the "Cadillac" of Talking Boards at an affordable price! This board is designed like no other to enhance the enjoyment and ease of your sessions. Use the board to access information about yourself, your life, and your personal growth from the "realms of non-form." Ask about (or even talk to) deceased loved ones. Inquire about your past lives. Obtain answers to questions on virtually any subject! The redesigned version of this ancient device comes with a complete booklet of instructions and a <u>30-day unconditional money-back guarantee.</u> Order today and you too will see why thousands feel that they would trade this board for no other!

Constructed from 1/8 inch reinforced oak plywood beautifully silk-screened and varnished; the round 18" board and 4" indicator make use uniquely effortless.

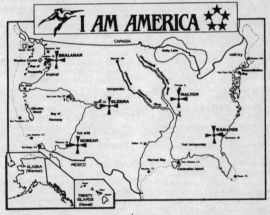

Abbe Bassett
Personal Astrology Services

♉ ♑

Vocational Guidance: Explores your birthchart to reveal your potential. Very effective for those beginning work, making career changes, or stuck in dead end jobs. Describe what you enjoy, your talents, training, and job experience. $50

♈ ♒

Complete Natal Report: Discusses your birth chart in response to your specific concerns and provides insights to their resolution. Defines your transits and progressions and solar arc directions for one year and introduces spiritual lessons contained in them. $85

Compatibility: This is a useful tool for discovering the relationship dynamics between you and a lover, partner, friend, or enemy. Send birth data for both people. $65

Child Guidance: Provides a useful tool in discovering the emerging personality of your child. Shows how your child relates to you, his or her environment, school, and friends. Illuminates interests and talents. $65

Solar Return: Gives a clear picture of what to expect in the coming birthday year. Deals with trends and influences for the year as well as personal dynamics and what the year will bring. $65

♌ ♊

Horary: Cast for the moment of an inquiry, reveals issues related to the question and trends pertaining to the matters involved. Deals with influences concerned with the resolution of the question. $65.

Detailed Natal: Deals with a specific set of questions in view of transiting influences, solar arc directions and progressions for the year. Provides answers which are specific in nature. $65.

Speculation Reading: Provides lucky numbers and dates based on your horoscope and name. (Please give full name!) Discusses lucky trends, influences and investments in your life. Gives an outline of luck in your life. $65

♋ ♎

Send a detailed letter with your birth data: month, day, year, time of day, city, state, country where you were born, with check to:

Abbe Bassett
Personal Astrology Services
P.O. Box 17, Essex Junction VT 05453-3030

Please allow 3-5 weeks for your order to be completed.

THE PRAYER SYSTEM THAT NEVER FAILS

Almost all of us at some time or another have prayed to God when in need – only to later feel disappointed that our prayers were unanswered. Either God isn't there or He is simply too busy to attend to our needs – this is the impression we are left with. Only desperation drives us to prayer: when all else has failed and we are at the end of our tether – only then do most of us turn to prayer: and then we pray with that sinking feeling that our supplication will not be heard.

Also at the back of our minds is the lingering impression that prayers were only answered in Jesus' time, a time when miracles were commonplace. All the great miraculous events recorded in the Bible happened so long ago – in a time when man seemed closer to God, life was far simpler, and God's prophets walked amongst us.

BUT THE REAL REASON WHY OUR PRAYERS ARE NOT ANSWERED IS THAT WE DO NOT KNOW HO TO PRAY. THE PLAIN FACT IS THAT OUR PRAYERS NEVER REACHED GOD IN THE FIRST PLACE.

What you should know is that THE SAME GOD WHO MADE MIRACLES HAPPEN 2000 YEARS AGO CAN – AND DOES – MAKE MIRACLES HAPPEN TODAY: BUT ONLY IN RESPONSE TO THOSE WHO KNOW HOW TO CONTACT HIM

Now – for the very first time, in absolutely simple and plain English – the mysteries of the Gospels have been unveiled to reveal JESUS' OWN SYSTEM OF ANSWERED PRAYER.

THE PLAIN FACT IS THAT ONCE YOU KNOW THE RIGHT WAY OF PRAYING YOU WILL ALWAYS RECEIVE A GUARANTEED ANSWER FROM GOD.

All this is revealed in the new book 'THE PRAYER SYSTEM THAT NEVER FAILS' – a book which itself is the result of prayer! Having discovered the hidden secrets of Successful Prayer, the author Dr. D.J. Lightfoot prayed to be directed to a publisher who would publish his findings. We are happy he was guided to us because we were struck by the power and simplicity of what he wrote, and feel privileged to be the ones to make it public.

THIS IS NO ORDINARY BOOK ABOUT PRAYER. Unlike other books it shows how to acquire that rarest quality which most of us lack: FAITH – the faith to know that our prayers will be answered.

This remarkable book reveals how the PUREST and DEEPEST FAITH can be yours – effortlessly! – as a gift form God!

Lack of faith is the greatest single stumbling block to the answering of prayer – this book provides you with the immediate removal of that obstacle. You will feel blessed and renewed as you read this book – not because of any air of heavenliness about it, but BECAUSE OF THE SHEER COMPELLING LOGIC OF THE AUTHOR'S REVELATIONS.

YOU WILL FEEL DEEP IN YOUR HEART ONCE YOU READ THIS BOOK THAT FOR THE FIRST TIME IN YOUR LIFE YOU _KNOW_ THAT YOUR PRAYERS WILL BE HEARD AND ANSWERED!

This book is called 'THE PRAYER SYSTEM THAT NEVER FAILS' precisely because it contains that. WITHIN ITS PAGES ARE THE SECRETS OF A LIFE FILLED WITH BLESSEDNESS AND GOOD FORTUNE ... A LIFE FREE OF SORROW AND SUFFERING!

Nor is this a book of rituals or impossible-to-follow instructions. It shows how to pray anywhere and any time: and most importantly of all: HOW YOU CAN BE TOTALLY ASSURED OF AN ANSWER TO YOUR PRAYERS.

This book can be used by persons of all faiths. The principles in it are universal and apply just as readily to Muslims, Hindus and Jews as they do to Christians.

And neither is it necessary to be a church-goer or a religious person in order to get your prayers answered. ANYONE CAN RECEIVE AN ANSWER TO THEIR PRAYERS ONCE THEY APPLY THE SECRETS IN THIS BOOK.

But why should anyone turn to prayer at all, especially if they are not religious? It is important to distinguish between the prayer of the religious and the prayer of the average person who seeks the solution to a pressing problem. It is ironic that the religious person can pray all his life and never receive an answer to his prayers. The fact is that he is praying the wrong way, that is the 'usual' way. But the person who hasn't seen the inside of a church or mosque for ten years will obtain a definite, positive result if he prays in the manner described in this book.

And what can one pray for? WHATEVER YOUR NEED YOU CAN PRAY FOR IT – AND WITH THIS BOOK'S SYSTEM YOU CAN FEEL ABSOLUTELY CERTAIN OF A POSITIVE ANSWER FORM GOD! Because God responds to only one kind of prayer – as Dr. Lightfoot demonstrates from the Bible and his own and the personal experiences of others – and THAT KIND OF PRAYER HE ALWAYS ANSWERS!

God wants you to be financially secure and happy – and will give abundantly ONCE YOU KNOW THE GUARANTEED FORMULA FOR REACHING HIS HEART!

He can give you true love and friendship ... and will give abundantly. ONCE YOU KNOW THE GUARANTEED FORMULA FOR REACHING HIS HEART!

He can give you true love and friendship ... an adoring mate ... a successful marriage ... an end to bitterness between yourself and another. If your partner has deserted you for another God can reconcile you– once you know the right way to pray!

God can help you in a difficult legal situation – THE SAME MIRACLES THAT GOD MADE HAPPEN 2000 YEARS AGO CAN BE MADE TO HAPPEN (FOR YOU) AGAIN RIGHT NOW!

God can protect you from physical danger. He can immobilize your enemies and tormentors. He can make those of evil intent towards you soften their hearts.

If you are in financial difficulty turn to God with a prayer, follow this book's simple formula, and you will experience not only immediate peace but RECEIVE DIVINE HELP in solving your problems!

But the most miraculous of all are the modern duplications of what Jesus made happen 2000 years ago: the walking of the lame, sight restored to the blind, etc.

THERE IS VIRTUALLY NO ILLNESS OR DISABILITY THAT CAN NOT RESPOND TO THE SCIENTIFIC PRAYER SYSTEM OF JESUS. In some cases where there is no hope only prayer can effect relief ... and sometimes a TOTAL CURE. Advertising restrictions prevent us from describing prayer's efficacy in this way,, but the book explains all. NOBODY WITH A SERIOUS HEALTH PROBLEM SHOULD IN OUR VIEW, OVERLOOK THE POSSIBILITIES OFFERED BY PRAYER, as revealed in this book.

So we urge you to reconsider the value of prayer – in the light of this book's revelations. Prayer, as originally revealed in the Bible, DOES work, but only for those who understand the mystery behind Jesus' parables. The mystery is de-mystified in plain, direct English in this book. The secrets disguised by Jesus' sayings are revealed to unfold the greatest spiritual and material potential for every man, woman and child. NOTHING IS UNATTAINABLE THROUGH THE MIGHTY POWER OF THIS PRAYER SYSTEM.

This book explains step by step the vital ingredients required for successful prayer, showing when and how to pray: how to receive faith: and the ways in which God will answer you. The book's instructions culminate in one page of Nine Master Secrets which reveal at a glance everything you need to know in order to always get your prayers answered. But there is more: In addition to 'THE PRAYER SYSTEM THAT NEVER FAILS' this book also contains the entire text of Dr. Lightfoot's first work "THE POWER STRUGGLE' which is a striking account of the age-old conflict between good and evil, and how this cosmic struggle is manifesting itself on planet Earth today.

The dream of most people is to have God on their side. Now at last this can be so for you. To order your copy of this important book send just $14.95.

Send money order or personal check made payable to Finbarr for $14.95 to: **Finbarr International, 16 Turketel Rd., Folkestone CT20 2PA, England.** Price includes express air mail: delivery guaranteed within 14 days. We have been shipping books worldwide since 1946: for our complete catalogue of books add $1. Readers in England send £6.

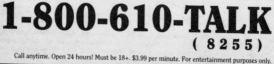

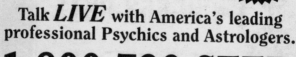

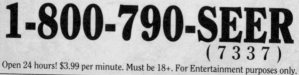

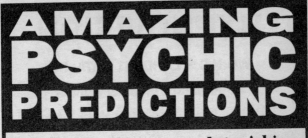

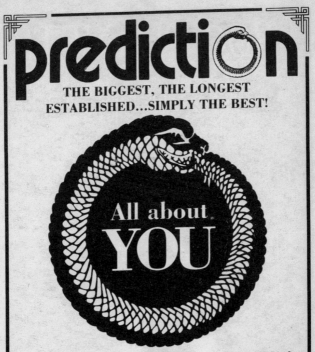

Sensual Products

**How to order them without embarrassment.
How to use them without disappointment.**

Today, people are interested in improving the quality of their lives and exploring their own sensuality with options from the **Xandria Collection**.

What is The Xandria Collection?

It is a very special collection of sensual products. It includes the finest and most effective products available from around the world. Products that can open new doors to pleasure (perhaps many you never knew existed)!

Our products range from the simple to the delightfully complex. They are designed for the timid, the bold or for anyone who has ever wished there could be something more to their sensual pleasures.

The Xandria Collection has had the same unique three-way guarantee for nearly 20 years.

First, we guarantee your privacy. Everything we ship is plainly packaged and securely wrapped, with no clue to its contents from the outside. All transactions are strictly confidential and we <u>never</u> sell, rent or trade any customer's name.

Second, we guarantee your satisfaction. If a product seems unsatisfactory, simply return it for a replacement or refund.

Third, we guarantee the quality of our products for one year. If it malfunctions, simply return it to us for a replacement.

Send for the **Xandria Gold Edition Catalogue**. It's price of $4.00 is applied, in full, to your first order.

Write today. You have absolutely nothing to lose, and an entirely new world of enjoyment to gain.

Gifted
Psychics

Unlock Life's Mysteries
--
Love - Money - Health
Career - Relationships
The Future

1-800-908-LIFE
(908-5433)

En Español   1-900-745-1192
NO CREDIT CARD NEEDED TO CALL
$3.99/Minute - APE San Rafael CA - 18+Years

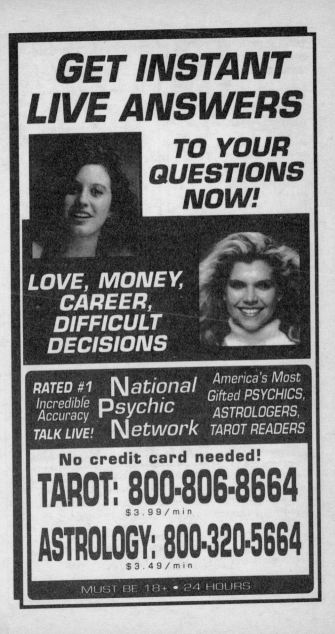

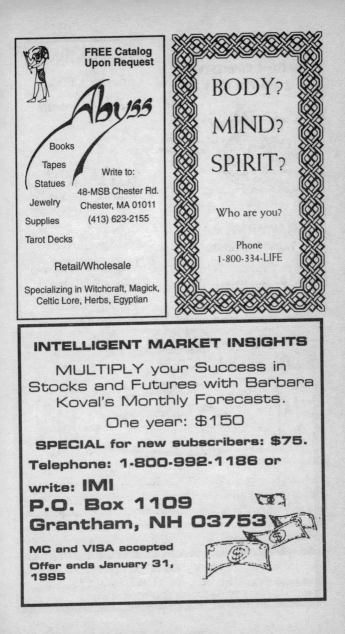

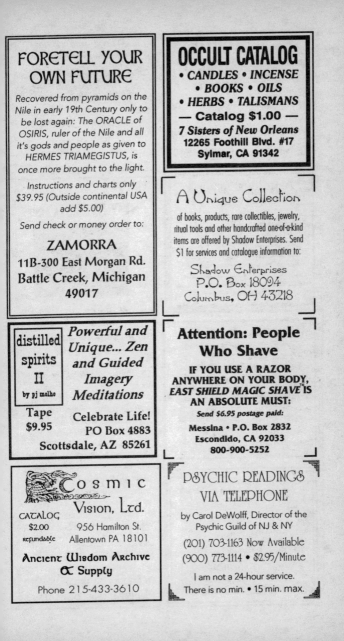

Classifieds

Ancient Teachings

FREE REVEALING REPORT. How to get almost everything you ever wished for. Amazing, ancient secrets, magickal spells, rituals. WizeWorld-LA, P.O. Box 1337, Huntington Beach CA 92647

Astrology

JAN MOODY, CERTIFIED astrologer. Horoscope readings. No wild predictions. Calm, problem solving approach. MC/Visa. 207-363-1238

NO BULL! THE real astrological influences daily for real people by a real astrologer! Janice Scott-Reeder's Cosmic Corner℠ 1-900-680-7779. Touch tone needed! $1.79/ min. 18+. Catalogue $2. Box 499-MS, Deerfield FL 33443

Audio Video

I'M A FREE person, Are you? Non religious material, 120 min. tape $10. Action, c/o P.O. Box 1568, Overgaard Arizona 85933

Books

LIFE AFTER DEATH. An alternate view. Write for transition. $2. (mailing and materials). Hastings, 874 N. Park Ave., Pomona CA 91768

HOW TO BECOME a son, or daughter, of God. 60-page booklet includes Biblical verification. Send $5. to: Mr. B.E. Stewart, 771 Belland Ave., St. Paul MN 55127

Business Opportunities

LET THE GOVERNMENT finance your small business. Grants/loans to $500,000.00. Free recorded message: 707-448-0270 (GC7)

Catalogs

MORE ENERGY! LESS stress! Better sleep! Highest quality, wholesale! Catalog, $1. cash, SASE: Adams, Box 3332, West Palm Beach FL 33402

Crystals

CRYSTALS, FREE GIFTS! $1 refundable for details and price list. Ariels' Crystals, Box 387L, Marcy NY 13403

Health & Healing

HERBAL HEALER ACADEMY offers you alternatives to chemical drugs! Medicinal Herbology correspondence courses /natural medicine supply catalog/ newsletter - $4. - HC32 97-B, Mountainview, AR 72560

PERSONALIZED MUSICAL HEALING tapes for your mind, body & soul. $15. Harmony Ministries, Box 1568, Overgaard Arizona 85933

FACELIFT NATURALLY! "Youth-Skin Secrets /Image Games Revealed." Infopak $1. AAP, P.O. Box 14189, Coral Gables, FL 33114

Instruction

THE MOST COMPLETE & advanced metaphysical, magical & psychic power development correspondence course ever offered. Ancient secrets finally revealed by 5000-year-old magical order. Our simple to understand, and easy to apply methods can make your dreams into reality. Free brochure. Very reasonable rates. Priesthood, 2301 Artesia Blvd., 12-188A Redondo Beach CA 90278 310-397-1310

Magick

MAGICAL GOODS, FREE catalog, mystical oils and incense, Isle of Avalon 800-700-ISLE. In California: 714-646-4213

Personals

FREE PERSONALITY TEST. Your personality determines your happiness. Know why? Call 1-800-334-LIFE.

Products

UNIQUE DESIGNS "BORN Again Pagan" or "Howl at the Moon" - button $1.50, bumper sticker $2., 8" diameter iron-on transfer $5. Catalog $1., free w/order. KLW Enterprises, 3790 El Camino Real, #270M, Palo Alto CA 94306-3314

Publications

FELLOWSHIP OF ISIS and Wiccan Correspondence Courses. Crystal Moon International Metaphysical Digest: quarterly, 70+ pages. Sample/information US $6.50. Astrology/Occult Catalog US $3. refundable. Box 802-LM, Matteson IL 60443-0802

Readings

EXTRAORDINARY PSYCHIC COUNSELOR, Randal Clayton Bradford, will tell you the best possible future in any situation, and how to make it happen. "Cuts straight to the truth"...accurate, detailed and specific." Established worldwide clientele by telephone. AMEX/MC/Visa 310-823-8893 or 213-REALITY.

CLARIFY YOUR LIFE! Anna Victor Hale—Psychic-Astro-Intuitive counseling. $1.99 per min. MC/VISA /M.O., 1-800-438-1266

LIVE READINGS! 90% ACCURATE psychic astrological answers. Walk through other's minds! $2.40 per minute. Checks by phone, Mastercard/VISA 800-488-3786

JOIN OUR PSYCHIC Calling Card™ family for the reading of your lifetime. Live! 24 hours. 1-800-549-7337 or 1-900-773-7374 ext. 5772. $3.99/min. 18+. Neat Stuff Catalogue $2. The Psychic Network® Box 499-MS, Deerfield FL 33443

ACCURATE TELEPHONE READINGS by experienced clairvoyant counselor. By appointment. Susan 301-645-1226

KNOW THYSELF. SIMULACRA of your soul. For free information write to: P.O. Box 776, Mesilla Park NM 88047

$10 - 3 QUESTIONS. BIRTHDATE, hair color, SASE. Additional questions $3 each. Barrett, 3049 Lydius St., Schenectady NY 12303

Reincarnation

THE TWO CRUCIFIXIONS Poster-size illustration of the star figures and configuration of the heavens which was the first Bible and the common ancestor of almost all religion. Included is a booklet of explanation. $15. 675 Fairview Drive, #246, Carson City NV 89701

Reap the Benefits of Earth-Aware Gardening

This growing season, be kind to the earth while reaping your most bountiful harvest ever! The *1995 Organic Gardening Almanac* presents over 30 articles from farming, gardening and land-scaping experts to give you leading-edge organic techniques.

Whether you own a 500-acre farm or a four-by-six foot plot, your crops, gardens and flower beds will be larger, healthier and of superior quality with these successful methods.

By combining the best of modern tech-niques with ancient lunar timing methods, you can enjoy superior crops and a more beautiful earth!

- **Consult the Moon tables for growing healthier, more abundant and tastier crops**

- **Condition your soil for better produce**

- **Fertilize with bat guano, compost and other natural plant foods**

Llewellyn's 1995 Organic Gardening Almanac
256 pp. ✦ softbound ✦ 5 ¼ x 8 ✦ Order # K-904 ✦ $5.95
Please use order form on last page.

Enrich Your Life With Magic And Nature!

*L*lewellyn's Magical Almanac presents an amazing array of information on herbs, recipes, aromatherapy and healing elixirs; amulets, talismans, charms and spells; seasonal rituals and holidays; and an abundance of mystic wisdom culled from Earth religions around the world.

This magical but practical almanac contains a calendar section that provides a daily reference to the phases and signs of the Moon and the Moon's energy, as well as color and incense correspondences.

Invite nature and the magical realm into your home or office by ordering this beautiful guide today!

- Bring the "old ways" into your everyday life

- Enrich your life with natural recipes, homespun wisdom and magical practice

- Explore Tibetan, Voodoo and Native American spiritualities and much more!

Llewellyn's 1995 Magical Almanac

312 pp. ✦ softbound ✦ 5 ¼ x 8 ✦ Order # K-906 ✦ $6.95

Please use order form on last page.

Llewellyn's Computerized Astrological Services

Llewellyn has been a leading authority in astrological chart readings for over thirty years. Our professional experience and continued dedication assures complete satisfaction in all areas of our astrological services.

Llewellyn features a wide variety of readings with the intent to satisfy the needs of any astrological enthusiast. Our goal is to give you the best possible service so that you can achieve your goals and live your life successfully.

When requesting a computerized service be sure to give accurate and complete birth data including: exact time (a.m. or p.m.), date, year, city, county and country of birth. (Check your birth certificate for this information.) *Accuracy of birth data is very important.* Llewellyn will not be responsible for mistakes made by you. An order form follows for your convenience.

Computerized Charts

Simple Natal Chart
Before you do anything else, order the Simple Natal Chart! This chart print-out is programmed and designed by Matrix. Learn the locations of your midpoints and aspects, elements, and more. Discover your planets and house cusps, retrogrades and other valuable data necessary to make a complete interpretation.
APS03-119 . . . . $5.00

Personality Profile
This is our most popular reading! It makes the perfect gift! This ten-part reading gives you a complete look at your "natal imprint" and how the planets mark your destiny. Examine your emotional needs and inner feelings. Explore your imagination and read about your general characteristics and life patterns. Very reasonable price!
APS03-503 . . . . $20.00

Life Progression

Discover what the future has in store for you! This incredible reading covers a year's time and is designed to complement the Personality Profile Reading. Progressions are a special system with which astrologers map how the "natal you" develops through specified periods of your present and future life. We are all born into an already existing world and an already existing fabric of personal interaction, and with this report you can discover the "now you!"

APS03-507 . . . . **$20.00**

Transit Report

Know the trends of your life—in advance! Keep abreast of positive trends and challenging periods for a specified period of time in your life. Transits are the relationships between the planets today and their positions at the moment of your birth. They are an invaluable aid for timing your actions and making decisions. This report devotes a paragraph to each of your transit aspects and gives effective dates for those transits. The report will begin with the first day of the month. Be sure to specify present residence for all people getting this report!

APS03-500 – 3-month report **$12.00**
APS03-501 – 6-month report **$20.00**
APS03-502 – 1-year report **$30.00**

Biorhythm Report

Ever have one of those days when you have unlimited energy and everything is going your way? Then the next day you are feeling sluggish and awkward? These cycles are called biorhythms. This individual report will accurately map your daily biorhythms. It can be your personal guide to the cycles of your daily life. Each important day is thoroughly discussed. With this valuable information, you can schedule important events with great success. This report is an invaluable source of information to help you plan your days to the fullest. Order today!

APS03-515 – 3-month report **$12.00**
APS03-516 – 6-month report **$18.00**
APS03-517 – 1-year report **$25.00**

Compatibility Profile

Find out if you really are compatible with your lover, spouse, friend or business partner! Do you have the same goals? How well do you deal with arguments? Do you have the same values? This service includes planetary placements for both individuals, so send birth data for both. Succeed in all of your relationships!

APS03-504 . . . . **$30.00**

Personal Relationship Interpretation

If you've just called it quits on one relationship and know you need to understand more about yourself before you test the waters again, then this is the report for you! This reading will tell you how you approach relationships in general, what kind of people you look for and what kind of people might rub you the wrong way. Important for anyone!

APS03-506 . . . . **$20.00**

Tarot Reading

Find out what the cards have in store for you! This reading features the graphics of the traditional Rider-Waite card deck in a detailed 10-card spread, and as a bonus, there are three pages explaining what each Tarot card means for you. This report is also custom made to answer any question you might have. Order this exciting tarot reading today!

APS03-120 . . . . **$10.00**

Lucky Lotto Report
(State Lottery Report)

Do you play the state lotteries? This report will determine your luckiest sequence of numbers for each day based on specific planets, degrees and other indicators in your own chart. Provide your full birth data and middle name, and specify the parameters of your state's lottery: i.e., how many numbers you need in sequence (up to 10 numbers) as well as the highest possible numeral (up to #999). Indicate the month you want to start.

APS03-512 – 3-month report **$10.00**
APS03-513 – 6-month report **$15.00**
APS03-514 – 1-year report **$25.00**

Numerology Report

Find out which numbers are right for you with this insightful report. This report uses an ancient form of numerology invented by Pythagoras to determine the significant numbers in your life. Using both your given birth name and date of birth, this report will accurately calculate those numbers which stand out as yours. With these numbers, the report can determine certain trends in your life and tell you when the important periods of your life will occur.

APS03-508 – 3-month report $12.00
APS03-509 – 6-month report $18.00
APS03-510 – 1-year report $25.00

Ultimate Astro-Profile

This report has it all! Receive over 40 pages of fascinating, insightful and uncanny descriptions of your innermost qualities and talents. Read about your burn rate (thirst for change). Explore your personal patterns (inside and outside). The Astro-Profile doesn't repeat what you've already learned from other personality profiles, but considers often the neglected natal influence of the lunar nodes plus much more.

APS03-505 . . . . $40.00

SPECIAL COMBO OFFER

Buy both and save!
APS03-214 . . $40.00

Personality Profile & Compatibility Profile
Learn about the real you and discover what the
future holds with that special someone!

Astrological Services Order Form

Include all birth data plus your full name for all reports.

Service name and number _____

Full name (1st person) _____

Birthtime _____ ❏ a.m. ❏ p.m. Date _____ Year _____

Birthplace (city, county, state, country) _____

_____

Full name (2nd person) _____

Birthtime _____ ❏ a.m. ❏ p.m. Date _____ Year _____

Birthplace (city, county, state, country) _____

_____

Include letter with questions on separate sheet of paper.

Name _____

Address _____

City _____ State _____ Zip _____

Make check or money order payable to Llewellyn Publications, or charge it!

❏ VISA   ❏ MasterCard   ❏ American Express

Account Number _____

Exp. Date _____ Daytime Phone _____

Signature of Cardholder _____

❏ **Yes!** Send me my **FREE** copy of **New Worlds!**

Mail this form and payment to:

Llewellyn's Personal Services, P.O. Box 64383-K903, St. Paul, MN 55164-0383. Allow 4-6 weeks for delivery.

"I just feel more confident about the future...."

How do you feel about *your* future?

Although we can never know <u>exactly</u> what the future will bring, we can uncover some of the significant influences that will be shaping our lives. The Life Progression Reading is a detailed report that examines the significant astrological events influencing your life today. These planetary aspects—that were not present at your birth—profoundly affect the way you'll deal with life. By understanding how these motivational forces influence your attitudes, emotions, desires and feelings, you can make choices about what to expect in life, and how you are going to react to it. Such awareness empowers you to make intelligent decisions about the people and situations in your life—making the difference in whether or not you are happy.

The Life Progression Reading also reveals the potential negative and positive experiences that you'll soon be facing, along with your best opportunities for growth and change, and the possibilities involving your health, career, finances, relationships and family.

The valuable insights you gain from this chart will help you understand yourself and your life situation so you can successfully negotiate the challenges the future brings.

The Life Progression Reading
For Your Journey Into The Future
APS03-507 $20.00

To order, use the "Astrological Services Order Form" in the back of this book.

SUPER DISCOUNTS ON LLEWELLYN DATEBOOKS AND CALENDARS!

Llewellyn offers several ways to save money. With a four-year subscription you receive your books as soon as they are published. The price remains the same for four years even if there is a price increase! We pay postage and handling as well. *Buy any 2 subscriptions and take $2 off! Buy 3 and take $3 off! Buy 4 and take an additional $5 off!*

Subscriptions (4 years, 1996-1999)

- ☐ Astrological Calendar ·· $40.00
- ☐ Sun Sign Book ·· $19.96
- ☐ Moon Sign Book ·· $19.96
- ☐ Daily Planetary Guide ·· $31.80
- ☐ Organic Gardening Almanac ··· $23.80

Order *by the dozen* and save 40%! Sell them to your friends or give as gifts. Llewellyn pays postage and handling on quantity orders.

Quantity Orders: 40% OFF
1995 1996

☐	☐	Astrological Calendar	12/$72.00
☐	☐	Sun Sign Book	12/$35.93
☐	☐	Moon Sign Book	12/$35.93
☐	☐	Daily Planetary Guide	12/$57.24
☐	☐	Magical Almanac	12/$50.04
☐	☐	Organic Gardening Almanac	12/$42.84
☐	☐	Myth & Magic Calendar	12/$72.00

On single copy orders, include $3 p/h for orders under $10 and $4 for orders over $10. We pay postage for all orders over $50.

Single copies of Llewellyn's Almanacs and Calendars
1995 1996

☐	☐	Astrological Calendar	$10.00
☐	☐	Sun Sign Book	$4.99
☐	☐	Moon Sign Book	$4.99
☐	☐	Daily Planetary Guide	$7.95
☐	☐	Magical Almanac	$6.95
☐	☐	Organic Gardening Almanac	$5.95
☐	☐	Myth and Magic Calendar	$10.00

Please use order form on last page.

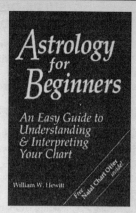

LLEWELLYN ORDER FORM

Llewellyn Publications
P.O. Box 64383-K903, St. Paul, MN 55164-0383

You may use this form to order any of the Llewellyn books listed in this publication.

Give Title, Author, Order Number and Price.

_____

_____

_____

_____

_____

_____

Shipping and Handling: We ship UPS when possible. Include $3 for orders $10 & under; $4 for orders over $10. Llewellyn pays postage for all orders over $50. Please give street address (UPS cannot deliver to P.O. Boxes). Next Day Air cost—$16.00/one book; add $2.00 for each additional book. Second Day Air cost—$7.00/one book; add $1.00 for each additional book.

Credit Card Orders: In the U.S. and Canada call 1-800-THE-MOON. In Minnesota call 612-291-1970. Or, send credit card order by mail. Any questions can be directed to customer service 612-291-1970.

❑ Yes! Send me your free catalog!

❑ VISA ❑ MasterCard ❑ American Express

Account No. _____

Exp. Date _____ Phone _____

Signature _____

Name _____

Address _____

City _____ State _____ Zip _____

Thank you for your order!